Hall and Papell's
Macroeconomics

STUDY GUIDE

Hall and Papell's
Macroeconomics

David H. Papell
UNIVERSITY OF HOUSTON

Sarah E. Culver
UNIVERSITY OF ALABAMA AT BIRMINGHAM

 W • W • NORTON & COMPANY • NEW YORK • LONDON

In writing this study guide, I benefited greatly from the editorial comments and suggestions of Drake McFeely. For the Fifth Edition, I was fortunate to work with Ed Parsons. I am grateful to Michael Brandl and Natalie Hegwood for their careful reviews of the Fifth Edition, and to Levent Akdeniz, Amy Aukstikalnis, Cheryl Holsey, Stephen Kerman, and Tina Phillips for their work on previous editions. The feedback that I have received on the first four editions from students at the University of Houston was very helpful in preparing the Fifth Edition. Last, but not least, I am grateful to my wife, Bonnie, and to my daughter, Darci, whose efforts made writing the Fifth Edition easier, and harder, respectively.

—D. H. P.

My greatest debt goes to my teacher, adviser, and mentor since my undergraduate economics days, David Papell. I am grateful to Matt Arnold and Karl Bakeman for their editorial support and patience. Stephen, Sam, and Alec make all the hard work worthwhile.

—S. E. C.

Printed in the United States of America.
Composition and layout by Cathy Lombardi.

ISBN 0-393-92630-3 (pbk.)

W. W. Norton & Company, Inc., 500 Fifth Avenue, New York, NY 10110
   www.wwnorton.com

W. W. Norton & Company Ltd., Castle House, 75/76 Wells Street, London W1T 3QT

1 2 3 4 5 6 7 8 9 0

CONTENTS

Part V   Macroeconomic Policy

PREFACE

The purpose of this study guide is to help you learn the material in Taylor and Papell's *Macroeconomics*. It isolates the major learning objectives, reviews the major terms and concepts, and provides self-tests and problem sets for every chapter in the text. A word of caution before you continue, however: The study guide will help you learn the material more easily, but it is not a substitute for reading the textbook.

Each chapter in the study guide opens with a section called *Main Objectives*, which highlights the basic topics covered in the text chapter. This is followed by a section called *Key Terms and Concepts*, which reviews and explains the chapter's most important concepts. Next comes the *Self-Test*. Here, there are three types of questions: fill in the blank, true-false, and review. You will find answers to the *Self-Test* at the back of each chapter. Finally, each chapter includes a *Problem Set*, where *Worked Problems* that include step-by-step solutions precede *Review Problems* and *Graph It* exercises that you work yourself. Answers to the *Review Problems* and *Graph It* exercises are also found at the back of each chapter.

These exercises may seem too difficult initially, but we encourage you to stay with it. Working through all the problems will develop your understanding of macroeconomic modeling and its applications. With practice, you will become more confident with the concepts and the mechanics.

While every student studies differently, you might use the study guide in the following way. First, read the chapter in the textbook without worrying too much about understanding everything. Second, read the *Main Objectives* and *Key Terms and Concepts* sections in the study guide. If you come across a concept that you do not understand, go back to the text. Third, take the *Self-Test* as if you were taking an exam. Write down your answers and be sure to provide an explanation for the true-false questions. Refer back to the text or to the study guide to make sure you understand the questions you missed. Fourth, work through the *Problem Set* and *Graph It* exercises, using the *Worked Problems* to learn how to solve the different types of numerical problems. Finally, reread the chapter in the text to make sure you understand it completely. You should now be well prepared to answer the questions and problems in the back of each text chapter.

Part I

Introduction

CHAPTER 1	# Economic Growth and Fluctuations

MAIN OBJECTIVES

An economy grows, evolves, and fluctuates. Over the past 30 years, the average growth of the United States economy, measured as the total production of goods and services, has been about 3.2 percent. However, this growth has been anything but steady. Short-run fluctuations in economic activity occur in every country and at all times throughout history. Further, they are irregular and hard to predict with much accuracy.

The 1970s and early 1980s were a turbulent economic time, when fluctuations in real gross domestic product, employment, inflation, and interest rates were larger and more erratic than at any time since the Great Depression of the 1930s. More recently, the United States experienced two of the longest peacetime expansions on record, from November 1982 to July 1990 and from March 1991 to March 2001.

To explain both how the economy grows and why it fluctuates over time, macroeconomists construct models. These models do not exist in a vacuum. Policy makers utilize macroeconomics in their attempts to improve economic welfare. The macroeconomic models that we will study are used by policy makers to evaluate proposals to increase long-term economic growth, help mitigate recessions, and keep inflation low and stable. Chapter 1 introduces the basic properties and terminology of macroeconomic models.

KEY TERMS AND CONCEPTS

Macroeconomics is the study of economic growth and fluctuations. While the long-run growth of the economy is largely determined by factors such as population growth and technological progress, this growth is irregular. The economy

3

undergoes both **recessions**, periods of contracting economic activity, and **recoveries**, periods of above-average economic growth following a recession. The top of a recovery is a **peak** and the bottom of a recession is a **trough**.

Real gross domestic product (GDP) is the most comprehensive measure of total product in the United States. It adjusts the dollar value of goods produced for changes in prices. The **rate of inflation** is the percentage change in the average price of all goods in the economy form one year to the next.

The **employment rate** is the ratio of employed workers to the working-age population. The **unemployment rate** is the percentage of workers who are looking for work and have not yet found it. The **rate of interest** is the amount charged by lenders per dollar per year, expressed as a percent. The **real interest rate** is the rate of interest minus the expected rate of inflation. The **money supply** consists of currency and deposits at banks. The money supply divided by the price level is called **real money**.

Potential GDP (or **potential output**) is the amount of output that would have been produced had the economy been in neither boom nor recession. Over time, real GDP fluctuates from its long-run, or potential, growth path. Employment is highly correlated with GDP, and therefore falls during recessions. Inflation tends to be higher when the economy is near its peak and lower when it is in a trough. Interest rates are procyclical; they move together with output, rising during recoveries and falling during recessions.

Describing macroeconomic behavior in complete detail would prove unwieldy—too much is going on. So economists construct **macroeconomic models**, simplified descriptions of how consumers and firms behave and interact, to explain fluctuations. In this way, they can test their theories against observation, or note how different theories interact, without extraneous detail. We pay a great deal of attention in this course to macroeconomic models with **flexible** and **sticky prices**. Models with flexible prices assume that wages and prices adjust rapidly according to traditional supply-and-demand analysis. In this way, workers and machines are kept fully employed, so that the economy always operates at its long-run potential output. Models with sticky prices postulate that this adjustment takes time and explain fluctuations by bottlenecks in the adjustment process.

The **long-run growth model** explains the general upward path of the economy over time. The three sources of growth are rising employment; increases in the stock of plant, equipment, and other capital; and improvements in technology. Because the economic growth model abstracts from short-run fluctuations, it explains the level of potential GDP that the economy will produce.

The **economic fluctuations model** explains temporary movements, booms and recessions, around the long-run growth path of the economy. In other words, it explains movements of actual GDP around potential GDP. The three sources of economic fluctuations are shocks, or sudden changes, in spending by families and businesses, policy by Congress and the Federal Reserve, and world markets. Slow price and wage adjustment plays an important role in determining the extent of the effects of the shocks.

The long-run growth and economic fluctuations models are illustrated in Figure 1–1. The long-run growth model explains the steady upward path of potential GDP, while the economic fluctuations model explains booms and recessions. While the figure is a stylized depiction of a fictional country, the actual figure for the United States shows a similar pattern of growth and fluctuations.

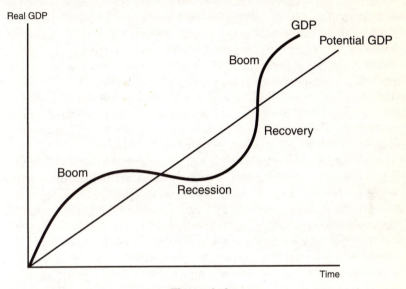

Figure 1–1

Neither the long-run growth model nor the economic fluctuations model provides a complete description of the economy. The economic fluctuations model can explain booms and recessions but cannot explain the growth of potential GDP. The long-run growth model can account for potential GDP but cannot explain short-run fluctuations.

Gradual price adjustment bridges the gap between the economic fluctuations model and the long-run growth model. In its simplest form, the idea of price adjustment is that, when output is less than potential GDP, there is pressure on prices to adjust downward. When output exceeds potential GDP, there is pressure on prices to adjust upward. Sticky prices, fixed in the short run but flexible in the long run, are explained by the process of price adjustment.

The **complete model**, the macroeconomic model developed in the remainder of the book, incorporates these concepts. The model assumes sticky prices—fixed in the short run to explain fluctuations in output and employment and flexible in the long run. Price adjustment explains the transition from the short-run to long-run potential GDP.

Despite many controversies within macroeconomics, most macroeconomists agree on five core principles. The first involves the observation that the long-run growth rate of the economy (or the growth rate of potential GDP) can be decomposed into the sum of the growth rate of labor productivity and the growth rate of the labor force. Therefore, factors that influence labor productivity, such as the growth of capital per hour of work and the growth rate of technology, and factors that influence the labor force participation rate have an impact on potential GDP growth.

Second and third, although there is no long-term trade-off between the rate of inflation and the rate of unemployment, we observe a trade-off in the short run. This implies that central bankers should adhere to a long-run target rate of inflation while keeping the growth of aggregate demand stable.

Fourth, when we examine the behavior of individual firms and consumers, we discover that expectations of the future play an important role. The theory of rational expectations is that firms and consumers, in forming their expectations, use whatever information is available to them in the most effective manner. While this seems innocuous, it has far-reaching implications for the study of consumption, investment, and price adjustment.

From these four principles comes the final one: Policy makers should make changes gradually by following clear rules. A **monetary policy rule** describes how central bankers change an instrument of monetary policy according to developments in the economy. Since the mid-1980s, the Federal Reserve has followed a **Taylor rule**, whereby the overnight interest rate is increased when inflation rises above the **inflation target** and when GDP exceeds potential GDP. This monetary policy is largely responsible for the relatively stable growth over the last 20 years. Key to its success is the **Taylor principle**, which stresses the importance of changing the *real* interest rate when inflation and GDP deviate from their optimal rates.

SELF-TEST

Fill in the Blank

1. The economy is in a _____ if production and employment are falling.

2. When production and employment are increasing rapidly, the economy is in a _____.

3. During the 1970s and early 1980s, fluctuations in the United States economy were larger and more erratic than at any time since _____.

4. The _____ is the percentage change in the price level from one year to the next.

5. _____ is the most comprehensive measure of total production in the United States.

6. The nominal interest rate minus the expected rate of inflation is the
   _____.

7. If prices were _____, workers and machines would be fully
   employed.

8. The _____ explains the general upward path of the economy over
   time.

9. The _____ explains booms and recessions.

10. If firms and consumers make the most of the information available to
    them, they are said to form their expectations _____.

11. _____ output is the amount of output that would be produced if
    the economy is in neither boom nor recession.

12. _____ GDP adjusts the dollar value of goods produced for
    changes in prices.

13. The money supply divided by the price level is called _____ money.

True-False

14. A peak is the bottom of a recession.

15. Interest rates are procyclical.

16. The economy is in a recovery if production and employment are increasing
    rapidly.

17. Economic fluctuations have increased since World War II.

18. Fluctuations in employment follow closely the fluctuations in real GDP.

19. With sticky prices, output always equals potential GDP.

20. Declines in inflation usually occur during recessions.

21. The recession in the early 1980s was the largest in the last 80 years.

22. The employment rate is the ratio of employed workers to unemployed
    workers.

23. The U.S. economy experienced a recession in 2001.

24. The model of long-run growth explains the temporary or transitory
    movements of GDP away from potential GDP.

25. All macroeconomists agree that changes in the money supply have little
    effect on employment and output in the long run.

26. Monetary policy rules accurately describe the Federal Reserve's monetary
    policy behavior of the 1970s.

Review Questions

27. What is the long-term pattern of economic fluctuations in the United States?

28. Explain why macroeconomists are concerned about economic fluctuations.

29. What other economic variables fluctuate along with GDP?

30. What determines potential output?

31. What is a simple expression of the idea of price adjustment?

32. What is meant by rational expectations?

33. What is assumed about prices in the complete model?

34. When did the U.S. economy last experience a recession?

35. What are the three sources of economic growth?

36. What are the three sources of economic fluctuations?

37. Why does neither the long-run growth model nor the economic fluctuations model provide a complete description of the economy?

38. What is the Taylor principle?

MATH REVIEW

Competence in basic mathematical concepts is fundamental to understanding the economic models presented in the text. Complete the following exercises to assess your basic mathematical skill level prior to further chapter review.

Percentage Change

Calculating the percentage change in a variable helps us determine economic statistics such as the inflation rate and the growth rate of the economy. The equation for calculating the percentage change in a variable Y from Y_0 to Y_1 is given by

$$(Y_1 - Y_0)/Y_0 \quad \text{(percentage change in variable } Y\text{)}$$

1. Calculate the percentage change in Y if $Y_0 = 100$ and $Y_1 = 117.5$.

2. Calculate the percentage change in P if $P_0 = 105$ and $P_1 = 110$.

3. Calculate the percentage change in Q if $Q_0 = 85$ and $Q_1 = 80$.

Graphing

Graphing algebraic equations is a skill that helps you visually understand what the equations signify.

4. a. In the table that follows, list the values of Y according to the equation

$$Y = 8 + 2X$$

X	Y
1	$Y = 8 + 2(1) = 10$
2	$Y =$ _____
3	$Y =$ _____
4	$Y =$ _____
5	$Y =$ _____

Plot the coordinates from the preceding equation on the graph provided and connect them.

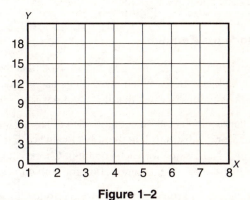

Figure 1–2

The slope of a curve is measured as the "rise over run" or change in Y divided by the change in X. Calculate the numerical slope of the equation from 4a. Note that this equation could easily signify an upward-sloping supply curve or an upward-sloping savings curve.

b. As in 4a, calculate the values of Y according to the following equation and plot the solved coordinates in the graph provided.

$$Y = 20 - 2X$$

X	Y
1	$Y = 20 - 2(1) = 18$
2	$Y =$ _____
3	$Y =$ _____
4	$Y =$ _____
5	$Y =$ _____

Calculate the slope for the equation in 4b. What is different about this slope compared to the slope of the equation in 4a? Note that this equation could signify a downward-sloping demand curve or a downward-sloping loanable fund demand curve.

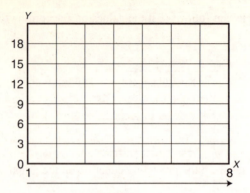

Figure 1–3

Solving Simultaneous Equations

Go back to the previous two equations in 4a and 4b. Note that there is one common coordinate to both equations. When there exists one unique pair of X and Y that satisfies both equations, we say that the equations solve simultaneously.

4. c. Set the equations in 4a and 4b equal to each other and solve for X. To check your work, substitute Y in the solved value of X to determine if the value of Y is the same for each equation. Check your graphs to determine that the pair is the intersection for both curves.

5. Unlike the equations in Problems 4a and 4b, the following equation does not have a constant slope. Plotting the solved coordinates should reveal a curve similar to an aggregate demand curve. In the table that follows, list the values of Y according to the equation

$$Y = 5,000 + 3,000/P$$

P	Y
.5	$Y = 5,0000 + 3,000/.5 = 5,000 + 6,000 = 11,000$
1	$Y = $ _____
1.5	$Y = $ _____
2	$Y = $ _____
2.5	$Y = $ _____
3	$Y = $ _____

PROBLEM SET

Worked Problems

1. Suppose the demand for output (GDP) is given by the expression $Y = 4,000 + 2,000/P$, where Y is output and P is the price level. Potential output is $Y^* = \$5,000$ billion.

a. Draw potential output and the output demand curve on a diagram with the price level P on the vertical axis and output Y on the horizontal axis.

b. What is the price level P if prices are flexible?

c. Suppose that prices are fixed and $P = 1$. What is the level of actual output? Is actual output Y above or below potential output Y^*? Is there pressure on the price level to move upward or downward?

d. Suppose that prices are fixed and $P = 3$. What is the level of output now? Is it above or below potential output? What pressure is there on prices?

a. *Potential output is a vertical line where output = potential output = $5,000 billion. The output demand curve is downward sloping because output demanded is lower if prices are higher. This is depicted in Figure 1–4. Numerical solutions to b, c, and d are plotted on Figure 1–4.*

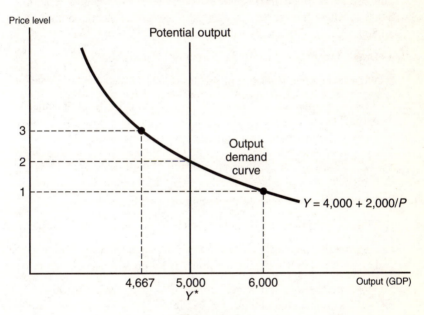

Figure 1–4

b. *If prices are flexible, output equals potential output. Thus 4,000 + 2,000/P = $5,000 billion, which can only hold if P = 2.*

c. *If prices are fixed and P = 1, actual output Y = 4,000 + 2,000/1 = $6,000 billion. Since potential output Y* = $5,000 billion, actual output is above potential, putting pressure on the price level to move upward.*

d. *If prices are fixed and P = 3, actual output Y = 4,000 + 2,000/1 = $6,000 billion. Since potential output Y* = $5,000 billion, actual output is below potential, putting pressure on prices to fall.*

2. Suppose that the price level is 100 in the year 2002, 110 in 2003, and 115.5 in 2004. What would the rates of inflation be for 2003 and 2004? If people expect the rate of inflation to be the average rate of inflation in the previous two years, what would be the expected rate of inflation for 2005? If the nominal interest rate in 2005 is 10 percent, what is the real interest rate?

The rate of inflation would be 10 percent in 2003 and 5 percent in 2004. The expected rate of inflation for 2005 is 7.5 percent, the average of the inflation rates for 2003 and 2004. The real interest rate in 2005 is 2.5 percent, which equals the nominal interest rate, 10 percent, minus the expected rate of inflation, 7.5 percent.

Review Problems

3. Suppose the output demand curve is given by the expression $Y = 5,000 + 3,000/P$, where Y is output and P is the price level. Potential output $Y^* = \$6,500$.

   a. Draw potential output and the output demand curve.

   b. What is the price level P if prices are flexible?

   c. Suppose that prices are fixed and $P = 3$. What is the level of actual output? Is actual output Y above or below potential output Y^*? Is there pressure on the price level to move upward or downward?

4. Suppose the output demand curve is still given by $Y = 5,000 + 3,000/P$, but potential output $Y^* = \$8,000$.

   a. Draw potential output and the output demand curve.

   b. What is P if prices are flexible? Compare your answer with Problem 3b.

   c. Suppose that prices are fixed and $P = 3$. What is the level of output now? Is it above or below potential output? What pressure is there on prices?

5. Suppose that the output demand curve is now given by $Y = 6,500 + 3,000/P$, with potential output $Y^* = \$8,000$.

   a. Draw potential output and the output demand and supply curves.

   b. What is P now if prices are flexible? Compare your answer with Problem 4b.

   c. Suppose that prices are fixed and $P = 2$. What is the level of output now? Is it above or below potential output? What pressure is there on prices?

6. The price level was 65.2 in 1978, 72.6 in 1979, and 82.4 in 1980. What were the rates of inflation for 1979 and 1980? If people expect the rate of inflation to be the average rate of inflation for the previous two years, what was the expected rate of inflation for 1981? The nominal interest rate in 1981 was 14.0 percent. What was the real interest rate?

7. The price level was 118.3 in 1988, 124.0 in 1989, and 130.7 in 1990. What were the rates of inflation for 1989 and 1990? If people expect the rate of inflation to be the average rate of inflation for the previous two years, what was the expected rate of inflation for 1991? The nominal interest rate in 1991 was 5.4 percent. What was the real interest rate?

8. The price level was 172.2 in 2000, 177.1 in 2001, and 179.9 in 2002. What were the rates of inflation for 2001 and 2002? If people expect the rate of inflation to be the average rate of inflation for the previous two years, what was the expected rate of inflation for 2003? The nominal interest rate in 2003 was 1.0 percent. What was the real interest rate?

GRAPH IT

1. Plot the answers to Problem 1, Parts b–d on the graph you drew in Part a (reprinted here).

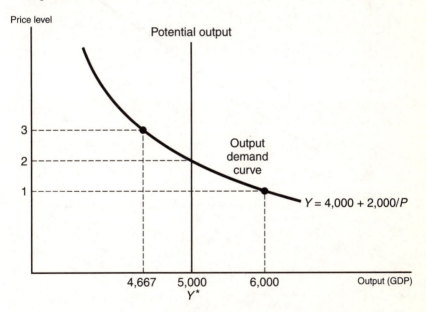

Figure 1–4

2. Plot the answers to Problems 3 and 4 on the same graph. What shifted, AD or potential output? What happened to the price level if prices are flexible?

3. Plot the AD curve from Problem 3 and the AD curve from Problem 5 on the same graph. Compare the two functions. If potential output is $8,000 billion (as in Problem 4), what happens to the price level as AD increases?

ANSWERS TO MATH REVIEW

1. $(117.5 - 100)/100 = .175$ (or 17.5 percent)
2. $(115 - 110)/110 = .045$ (or 4.5 percent)
3. $(80 - 85)/85 = -.059$ (or negative 5.9 percent)
4. a.

X	Y
1	$Y = 8 + 2(1) = 10$
2	$Y = 8 + 2(2) = 12$
3	$Y = 8 + 2(3) = 14$
4	$Y = 8 + 2(4) = 16$
5	$Y = 8 + 2(5) = 18$

Slope = change in Y/change in $X = 2/1 = 2$.

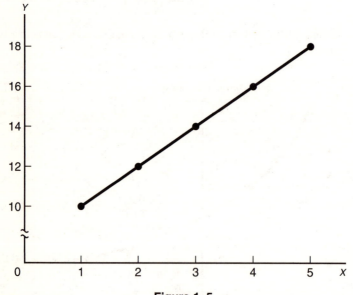

Figure 1–5

b.

X	Y
1	$Y = 20 - 2(1) = 18$
2	$Y = 20 - 2(2) = 16$
3	$Y = 20 - 2(3) = 14$
4	$Y = 20 - 2(4) = 12$
5	$Y = 20 - 2(5) = 10$

Slope = change in Y/change in $X = 2/-1 = -2$.
The slope is a negative number, which implies a downward-sloping curve.

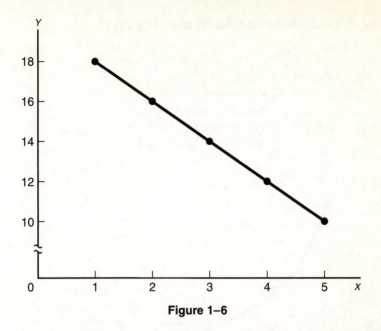

Figure 1–6

c. 4a = 4b; $8 + 2X = 20 - 2X$; collect terms to get $4X = 12$; solve for $X = 3$. Plugging $X = 3$ into 4a solves for $Y = 14$. Plugging $X = 3$ into 4b solves for $Y = 14$ also. Therefore, the two equations intersect where $X = 3$ and $Y = 14$.

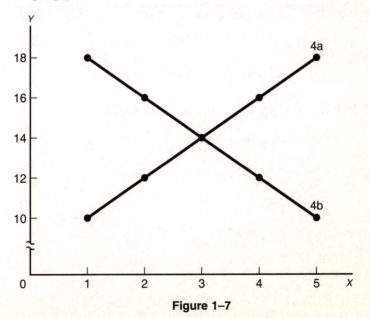

Figure 1–7

5. The table that follows is plotted on the next figure.

P	Y
.5	$Y = 5,0000 + 3,000/.5 = 11,000$
1	$Y = 5,0000 + 3,000/1 = 8,000$
1.5	$Y = 5,0000 + 3,000/1.5 = 7,000$
2	$Y = 5,0000 + 3,000/2 = 6,500$
2.5	$Y = 5,0000 + 3,000/2.5 = 6,200$
3	$Y = 5,0000 + 3,000/3 = 6,000$

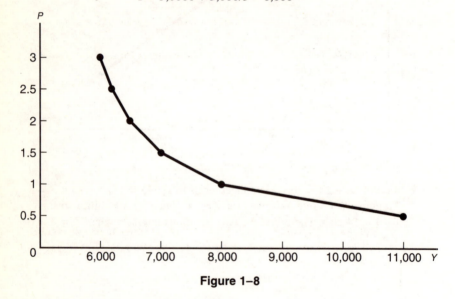

Figure 1–8

ANSWERS TO THE SELF-TEST

1. Recession
2. Recovery
3. The Great Depression of the 1930s
4. Inflation rate
5. Real gross domestic product
6. Real interest rate
7. Flexible
8. Long-run growth model
9. Economic fluctuations model
10. Rationally
11. Potential
12. Real
13. Real
14. False.   A peak is the top of a recovery.
15. True.   They fall during recessions and rise during recoveries.

16. True. That is the definition of a recovery.
17. False. They have decreased in magnitude.
18. True. Employment falls during recessions and rises during recoveries.
19. False. With sticky prices, output can diverge from potential GDP.
20. True. In the past 25 years, almost all of the significant declines in the rate of inflation occurred during recession periods.
21. False. The Great Depression was much larger.
22. False. The employment rate is the ratio of employed workers to the working-age population.
23. True. The last recession lasted from the peak of March 2001 to the trough of November 2001.
24. False. The model of long-run growth explains the general upward path of the economy over time.
25. True. There is no controversy over the long-run effects of monetary policy.
26. False. The Federal Reserve adopted monetary policy rules beginning in the mid-1980s.
27. Economic fluctuations were very large during the 1920s and 1930s, decreased during the 1950s and 1960s, and increased, although not back to their pre–World War II levels, during the 1970s and 1980s. Recent macroeconomic performance exhibited even less volatile fluctuations, with relatively mild and short-lived recessions.
28. Macroeconomists are concerned about fluctuations because people can be adversely affected, an example being unemployment and layoffs during recessions.
29. Employment, inflation, interest rates, and exchange rates also undergo fluctuations.
30. Potential output is determined by the productive capacity of the economy, which in turn is determined by the volume of productive factors—labor, capital, and technology.
31. When output is less than potential GDP, there is pressure on prices to adjust downward. When output exceeds potential GDP, there is pressure on prices to adjust upward.
32. Rational expectations means that consumers and firms, when forming their expectations about the future make the most of the information available to them.
33. Prices are assumed to be sticky or fixed in the short run but flexible in the long run.
34. As of 2004, the U.S. economy last experienced a recession during 2001.
35. The three sources of growth are rising employment; increases in the stock of plant, equipment, and other capital; and improvements in technology.
36. The three sources of fluctuations are shocks in spending by families and businesses, policy by Congress and the Federal Reserve, and world markets.

37. The economic fluctuations model cannot explain the growth of potential GDP, while the long-run growth model cannot explain booms and recessions.
38. The Taylor principle stresses the importance of raising the real interest rate when inflation rises in the conduct of monetary policy.

SOLUTIONS TO REVIEW PROBLEMS

3. a. Potential output is a vertical line where $Y^* = \$6,500$. The output demand curve is downward sloping.
    b. If prices are flexible, output equals potential output. Therefore, $5,000 + 3,000/P = \$6,500$, and $P = 2$.
    c. If prices are fixed and $P = 3$, actual output $Y = 5,000 + 3,000/3 = \$6,000$. Since potential output $Y^* = \$6,500$, actual output is below potential, putting downward pressure on the price level.
4. a. Potential output is a vertical line with $Y^* = \$8,000$. The output demand curve is unchanged.
    b. If prices are flexible, $5,000 + 3,000/P = \$8,000$, so $P = 1$. The price level is lower than in Problem 3b. This shows that, if prices are flexible, an increase in potential output with unchanged aggregate demand will lower prices.
    c. $Y = 5,000 + 3,000/3 = \$6,000$. Since $Y^* = \$8,000$, output is till below potential, and there is still downward pressure on prices.
5. a. The output demand curve has a higher intercept but the same slope as before. The potential output line is the same as in Problem 4.
    b. If prices are flexible, $6,500 + 3,000/P = \$8,000$, so $P = 2$. The price level is higher than in Problem 4b. This shows that, if prices are flexible, an increase in aggregate demand with unchanged potential output will raise prices.
    c. If prices are fixed and $P = 2$, $Y = 6,500 + 3,000/P = \$8,000$, which is also equal to potential output. There is no pressure on prices to either rise or fall.
6. The rate of inflation was 11.3 percent in 1979 and 13.5 percent in 1980. The expected rate of inflation for 1981 was 12.4 percent. The real interest rate in 1981 was 1.6 percent.
7. The rate of inflation was 4.8 percent in 1989 and 5.4 percent in 1990. the expected rate of inflation for 1991 was 5.1 percent. The real interest rate in 1991 was .3 percent.

8. The rate of inflation was 2.8 percent in 2001 and 1.6 percent in 2002. The expected rate of inflation for 2003 was 2.2 percent. The real interest rate in 2003 was −.6 percent.

ANSWERS TO GRAPH IT

1. To construct an AD curve, first solve the equation using different values of P, as in the following table:

P	Y
.5	$4,000 + 2,000/.5 = 8,000$
1	$4,000 + 2,000/1 = 6,000$
1.5	$4,000 + 2,000/1.5 = 5,333$
2	$4,000 + 2,000/2 = 5,000$
2.5	$4,000 + 2,000/2.5 = 4,800$
3	$4,000 + 2,000/3 = 4,667$

Second, plot the combinations of P and Y that solve the AD function:

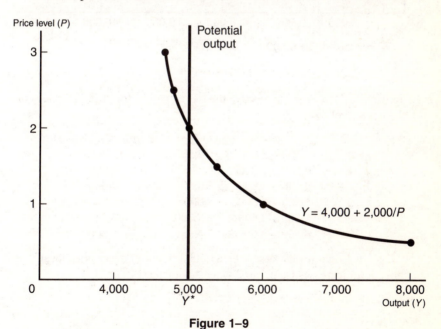

Figure 1–9

2. The AD curve is plotted in the math review section's Problem 5; see Figure 1–10. Potential output increased from $6,500 billion in Problem 3 to $8,000 billion in Problem 4. The price level dropped from 2 to 1.

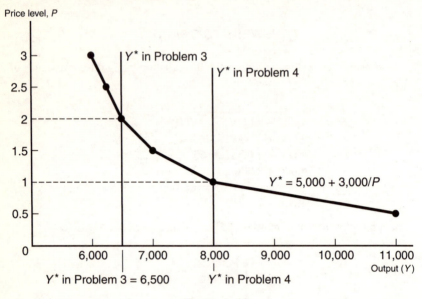

Figure 1–10

3. To derive AD in Problem 5, solve the AD equations for different values of the price level.

P	Y (from Problem 5)	Y (from Problem 3)
.5	6,500 + 3,000/.5 = 12,500	11,000
1	6,500 + 3,000/1 = 9,500	8,000
1.5	6,500 + 3,000/1.5 = 8,500	7,000
2	6,500 + 3,000/2 = 8,000	6,500
2.5	6,500 + 3,000/2.5 = 7,700	6,200
3	6,500 + 3,000/3 = 7,500	6,000

AD shifted right (or increased) by $1,500 billion for every price level. The price level increases from 1 to 2 when AD increases.

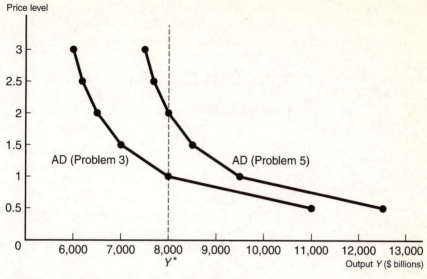

Figure 1–11

CHAPTER 2

Measuring Economic Performance

MAIN OBJECTIVES

In Chapter 1 we introduced the important concepts of real gross domestic product (GDP), employment, and inflation. In this chapter we see how these variables are defined and measured. Three different ways to measure GDP as spending, production, and income, are discussed and we see how each adds up to the same thing. You should also become familiar with the concepts of saving and investment and understand how transactions with the rest of the world are measured.

KEY TERMS AND CONCEPTS

Gross domestic product (GDP) can be measured in terms of production, income, or spending. **Production** is the dollar value of the goods and services produced during a period of time. **Income** is wages and interest paid by firms, plus profits earned by owners of firms. **Spending** is the amount of goods and services bought by consumers, other firms, and the government, plus **inventories** (goods produced but not yet sold). Through two accounting rules—including inventories in spending and computing profits as sales minus expenses—production, income, and spending are always the same. This is an identity—simply a matter of definition.

It will most often prove useful to define GDP in terms of spending. **Consumption** is spending by households. It includes purchases of durable goods such as automobiles nondurable goods such as food, and services such as medical care. **Investment** is the sum of spending by firms on plant, equipment, and inventories and spending by households on housing. **Nonresidential fixed investment** is spending on structures such as office buildings and on equipment for use in business, such as computers. **Residential fixed investment** is spending on construction of new houses and apartment buildings. Note that spending on new houses is included in investment, not in consumption. **Inventory investment** is the value of goods that are produced, but not sold, during a given period. If more goods are sold than produced, inventory investment is negative for the period. **Government purchases** is that portion of total government outlays for spending on goods and services by state, local, and federal governments.

For a country with a closed economy, one that does not trade with other countries, this would exhaust our categories of spending. Goods produced could be either consumed (except for new houses) if sold to households, invested or added to inventories if sold to firms, or counted as government purchases if sold to the government, so that spending would equal production. We could then say that GDP is equal to consumption plus investment plus government purchases.

Since countries trade with other countries, these categories are incomplete. Some of the goods we produce are purchased by foreigners. These are our **exports** and are included in our GDP. On the other hand, part of our consumption, investment, and government purchases are of goods produced by foreigners. These are our **imports** and should not be counted as part of our GDP. Exports minus imports is called **net exports**. For an open economy, GDP is equal to consumption plus investment plus government purchases plus net exports. When net exports are positive, there is a **trade surplus**. When net exports are negative, there is a **trade deficit**.

The **capital stock** is the total amount of productive capital—factories, equipment, and houses—in the economy. **Investment** is the flow of new capital that is added during the year to the stock of capital. Since part of the capital stock is always wearing out, or **depreciating**, part of investment goes to maintain the existing level of capital stock. New investment is equal to investment minus depreciation. GDP includes gross investment.

GDP can increase either if the physical amount of goods and services produced increases or if prices rise. GDP adjusted for changing prices, called **real GDP**, measures the physical amount of production. To clarify the distinction between real GDP and GDP, sometimes the term **nominal GDP** is used for the dollar value of goods and services produced. Nominal GDP is synonymous with GDP.

In order for gross domestic product to measure the value of production, it is necessary to avoid double counting. Thus only new purchases are counted in spending. Purchases of old houses and used cars are not included because they contributed to GDP when new. Furthermore, only goods purchased at the end of the production line, as final goods, are counted in spending. If General Motors purchases steel to produce an automobile, the steel is an **intermediate good** and is not counted. When the car is sold, the value of the steel is included as part of the automobile, which is the final good.

The concept of **value added** is used to prevent double counting when GDP is computed by production. The value added by a firm is the difference between the revenue a firm earns by selling its products and the amount it pays for intermediate goods produced by other firms. If Goodyear buys rubber and steel to produce steel-belted radial tires, the value added is the difference between what it earns from the tires and what it pays for the rubber and steel. GDP is the sum of the value added by all firms in the economy.

Gross national product (GNP) is GDP plus net factor payments, which in turn is defined as factor income from the rest of the world (what Americans earn by working and investing capital abroad) minus factor income to the rest of the world (what foreigners earn by working and investing capital in the United States). The difference between the two concepts is that GDP measures the value of goods and services produced in the United States, while GNP measures the value of goods and services produced by Americans.

GDP can also be computed as the sum of all incomes in the economy. In the actual statistical accounts there is no measure of income that is exactly comparable to GDP. The closest is **national income**, which is approximately equal to net national product minus sales and excise taxes. **Personal income** equals national income plus government and business **transfer payments** (social security and other benefits) plus interest on the government debt and from other nonbusiness sources minus social security taxes minus corporate retained earnings. **Disposable personal income**, often just called **disposable income**, is personal income minus income taxes. Disposable income is equal to GDP plus government transfers plus interest on the government debt plus net factor income and transfer payments from abroad, minus taxes.

Saving is income minus consumption. We can use this definition to analyze saving for various sectors of the economy. **Private saving** is disposable income minus consumption. **Government saving** equals the income received by the government (tax receipts minus government transfers minus interest on the government debt) minus government spending on goods and services. A positive value for government saving is also called a **government budget surplus**. A negative value is a **government budget deficit**. **Rest of world saving** is payments received from the United States minus payments made to the United States. It equals the negative of the sum of net exports plus **net factor income payments** plus **net transfer payments from abroad**.

The **balance of payments** is divided into current account, capital account, and financial account transactions. The **current account** equals net exports plus interest payments between the United States and the rest of the world. The **capital account** measures net international transfers such as government grants, debt forgiveness, and remittances. The **financial account** measures international borrowing and lending. When an American borrows from a foreigner, either by taking out a loan or by selling a bond, it is a financial account surplus. An American lending to a foreigner falls into the category of financial account deficit. When the United States imports more than it exports, it runs a current account deficit unless it is receiving international transfers. In order to finance the deficit, it has to borrow from the rest of the world, creating a financial account surplus. Thus the negative current account is matched by the positive financial account. Put another way, the sum of the current and capital-financial accounts is equal to zero.

The **exchange rate** is the price of dollars in terms of foreign currency and measures how much foreign currency, say 150 Japanese yen, one can buy with 1 dollar. When the exchange rate rises, say to 200 yen, foreign goods become cheaper compared to home goods. The euro is the common currency that 12 European countries have adopted since its introduction in 2002.

The **rate of inflation** is the percentage rate of change in the general price level form one period to the next. There are two ways to measure inflation. The first, **price indexes**, is calculated directly from data on the prices of thousands of goods and services. The best-known price index, the **consumer price index (CPI)**, measures the cost of living for a typical urban family. The weights on the individual prices in the CPI are based on a survey of consumer buying habits. Another widely used index is the **producer price index (PPI)**, which measures the prices charged by producers at various stages in the production process.

Workers who wish to protect themselves against inflation can negotiate **cost-of-living adjustments (COLAs)** to have their payment rise in proportion to the increase in the CPI. The purpose of this is to fix one's real, instead of nominal, wage. Social security payments and many collective-bargaining agreements now incorporate COLAs.

The second way to measure inflation is to deflate nominal values by dividing them by the real values they represent. For instance, the ratio of nominal to real GDP is called the **GDP implicit price deflator**. There are deflators for each component of GDP. The **consumption deflator**, for example, is the ratio of nominal to real consumption.

People are classified as employed if they are working. **Employment** in the United States is measured by two surveys, one of households and one of establishments where people work. In the long run employment grows with potential GDP to create more output firms require more workers. Employment falls with output during recessions and rises during recoveries. Employment is not a complete measure of the input of labor in production because the average number of hours worked each week also falls during recessions and rises during recoveries. **Total hours of work**, employment multiplied by average hours worked, is a better measure.

SELF-TEST

Fill in the Blank

1. Gross domestic product can be computed by measuring _____, _____, or _____.

2. When GDP is adjusted for _____, the result is real GDP.

3. Consumption is spending by _____.

4. The two types of fixed investment are _____ and _____.

5. Net investment is gross investment minus _____.

6. _____ investment consists of goods produced but not yet sold.

7. Net exports equal _____ minus _____.

8. To avoid double counting, we include only purchases of _____ goods when computing GDP.

9. Personal income minus income taxes is _____ personal income.

10. If government saving is negative, there is a government budget _____.

11. An important principle of the balance of payments accounts is that the _____, _____, and _____ should sum to zero.

12. The index that measures the cost of living for a typical urban family is the _____.

13. The _____ measures prices charged by producers at various stages of the production process.

14. The ratio of nominal GDP to real GDP is the _____.

True-False

15. We know that measuring GDP by either production, spending, or income each adds up to the same thing because of long experience with macroeconomic theories.

16. Spending on new houses is the only type of household spending that is not included in consumption.

17. The capital stock increases by the total amount of investment spending.

18. GDP is both the dollar value of all final goods and services produced in this country during a given period of time and the sum of all the value added by firms during the same period.

19. Both nominal and real GDP measure the dollar volume of production.

20. GDP increases if you buy either a new or a used car.

21. If Ford sells more automobiles, GDP will increase whether they are purchased by Americans or foreigners.

22. If you buy 100 shares of IBM stock, it is investment and adds to GDP.

23. If a firm replaces an old computer with a new one, it does not add to GDP because the total number of computers remains unchanged.

24. If General Motors produces more cars than its sells, this causes a smaller increase in GDP than if it sold all the cars it produced.

25. When the exchange rate rises, foreign goods become cheaper compared with home goods.

26. If the rate of inflation falls, prices decrease.

27. The consumer price index and the consumption deflator are not exactly identical.

28. The producer price index measures the prices actually paid by consumers.

Review Questions

29. How is GDP computed when measured through spending?

30. What are the components of consumption?

31. What are the components of investment?

32. What is the relationship between the stock of capital and investment?

33. What is the relation between the nominal and real GDP?

34. How is the concept of value added used?

35. What is disposable income?

36. Why does the sum of the current and capital accounts equal zero?

37. What does it mean when the dollar rises?

38. What is the rate of inflation?

39. What are the two ways that the general price level can be measured?

40. Why might you expect cost-of-living adjustments (COLAs) to have become less popular in the last 20 years than in the 1970s?

41. How is employment measured in the United States?

42. Explain why total hours of work is a better measure of labor input to the economy than employment.

PROBLEM SET

Worked Problems

1. Consider a closed economy with expenditure totals given by

   C = $1,200 billion   (Consumption)
   I =   400   (Investment)
   G =   300   (Government spending)
   F =   200   (Government transfers)
   N =   100   (Interest on the government debt)
   T =   400   (Taxes)

   a. What is gross domestic product (GDP)?

   b. What is private saving?

   c. What is government saving?

   d. What is total saving? Show that it equals investment.

   a. *GDP = Consumption + Investment + Government spending.*
      $$Y = C + I + G$$
      $$= 1,200 + 400 + 300 = \$1,900 \text{ billion.}$$

   b. *Private saving = Disposable income – Consumption.*
      Disposable income = GDP + Government transfers + Interest on the government debt – Taxes.
      Using S_p to denote private saving,
      $$S_p = (Y + F + N - T) - C$$
      $$= (1,900 + 200 + 100 - 400) - 1,2000 = \$600 \text{ billion.}$$

   c. *Government saving = Taxes – Government transfers – Interest on the government debt – Government spending.*
      Using $S_g = T - F - N - G$
      $$= 400 - 200 - 100 - 300 = -\$200 \text{ billion.}$$

   d. *Total saving = Private saving + Government saving.*
      $$S = S_p + S_g$$
      $$= 600 - 200 = \$400 \text{ billion, which equals investment.}$$

2. Consider an open economy with expenditure totals given by

   C = $1,200 billion   (Consumption)
   I =   400   (Investment)
   G =   300   (Government spending)
   X =   –100   (Net exports)
   V =   30   (Net factor income and transfer payments from abroad)
   F =   200   (Government transfers)
   N =   100   (Interest on the government debt)
   T =   400   (Taxes)

a. What is GDP?

b. What is private saving?

c. What is government saving?

d. What is rest of world saving?

e. What is total saving? Show that it equals investment.

a. *GDP = Consumption + Investment + Government spending + Net exports.*
$$Y = C + I + G + X$$
$$= 1,200 + 400 + 300 = \$1,900 \text{ billion.}$$

b. *Private saving = Disposable income – Consumption.*
Disposable income = GDP + Net factor income and transfer payments from abroad + Government transfers + Interest on the government debt – Taxes.
$$S_p = (Y + V + F + N - T) - C$$
$$= (1,800 + 30 + 200 + 100 - 400) - 1,2000 = \$530 \text{ billion.}$$

c. *Government saving = Taxes – Government transfers – Interest on the government debt – Government spending.*
$$S_g = T - F - N - G$$
$$= 400 - 200 - 100 - 300 = -\$200 \text{ billion.}$$

d. *Rest of world saving = –(Net exports + Net factor income and transfer payments from abroad).*
$$S_r = -(X + V)$$
$$= \$70 \text{ billion.}$$

e. *Total saving = Private saving + Government saving + Rest of world saving.*
$$S = S_p + S_g + S_r$$
$$= 530 - 200 + 70 = \$400 \text{ billion, which equals investment.}$$

3. Looking into our crystal ball, we see the following data from the early 2000s:

Year	CPI
2011	400
2012	440
2013	462
2014	462

a. Calculate the rate of inflation for 2012, 2013, and 2014.

b. Suppose that the increase in the wage rate for a group of workers that sign an employment contract for the two-year period starting in 2013 is $\Delta W/W = .1$. What happens to the real wage measured in terms of CPI?

c. Suppose instead that the wage rate is partially indexed to the CPI according to the formula

$$\Delta W/W = .05 + .5\, \Delta CPI/CPI.$$

What now happens to the real wage?

d. Finally, suppose that the wage rate is completely indexed to the CPI according to

$$\Delta W/W = \Delta CPI/CPI.$$

What happens to the real wage?

e. If, when these contracts were negotiated, workers and employers believed that inflation for 2013 and 2014 would be the same as it was in 2012, was there any reason for either to prefer one formula over the others? Did these preferences change over time once inflation became known?

a.

Year	Inflation
2012	*10 percent (use as .10 in calculations that follow)*
2013	*5 percent (use as .05 in calculations that follow)*
2014	*0 percent (use as 0 in calculations that follow)*

b. Wages increase by 10 percent each year. Prices increase by 5 percent in 2013 and stay the same in 2014. Real wages increase, since nominal wage increases of 10 percent more than outpace inflation.

c. Wages increase by 7.5 percent in 2013 and 5 percent in 2014. Real wages still increase, although by less than in Part b. See the table.

Year	Inflation	Nominal W adjustment = $\Delta W/W$	Real Wages
2012	*.10*	*.05 + .5(.10) = .10*	*kept pace with inflation*
2013	*.05*	*.05 + .5(.05) = .075*	*outpaced inflation*
2014	*0*	*.05 + .5(0) = .05*	*outpaced inflation*

d. The real wage is constant when the nominal wage, W, is completely indexed to the CPI.

e. If inflation had remained at 10 percent in 2013 and 2014, real wages would have been constant with any of the three formulas, so there was no reason for either workers or employers to prefer one over the others. Since the inflation rate declined, workers ended up better off with less indexation (b) while employers would have been better off with more (d).

Review Problems

4. Consider an economy with expenditure totals given by

C = $1,500 billion   (Consumption)
I =   600   (Investment)
G =   500   (Government spending)
F =   300   (Government transfers)
N =   100   (Interest on the government debt)
T =   1,000   (Taxes)

   a. What is GDP?

   b. What is private saving?

   c. What is government saving?

   d. What is total saving? Show that it equals investment.

5. Consider an open economy with the same expenditure totals as in Problem 6, except for

X = $100   (Net exports)
V =   −20   (Net factor income and transfer payments from abroad)

   a. What is GDP?

   b. What is private saving?

   c. What is government saving?

   d. What is rest of world saving?

   e. What is total saving? Show that it equals investment.

6. Consider an economy with expenditure totals given by

C = $2,300 billion   (Consumption)
I =   700   (Investment)
G =   800   (Government spending)
F =   100   (Government transfers)
N =   100   (Interest on the government debt)
T =   800   (Taxes)

   a. What is GDP?

   b. What is private saving?

   c. What is government saving?

    d. What is total saving? Show that it equals investment.

    e. What is the government budget deficit?

7. Consider an open economy with the same expenditure totals as in Problem 8, except for

$$X = -\$200 \qquad \text{(Net exports)}$$
$$V = 50 \qquad \text{(Net factor income and transfer payments from abroad)}$$

    a. What is GDP?

    b. What is private saving?

    c. What is government saving?

    d. What is rest of world saving?

    e. What is total saving? Show that it equals investment.

8. The following data on the price level (CPI) are from the early 1960s.

Year	CPI
1960	29.6
1961	29.9
1962	30.2
1963	30.6

    a. Calculate the rate of inflation for 1961, 1962, and 1963.

    b. Suppose that the increase in the wage rate for a group of workers that sign an employment contract for the two-year period starting in 1962 is $\Delta W/W = .01$. What happens to the real wage measured in terms of the CPI?

    c. Suppose instead that the wage rate is partially indexed to the CPI according to the formula

$$\Delta W/W = .005 + .5 \, \Delta CPI/CPI.$$

What happens to the real wage?

    d. Finally, suppose that the wage rate is completely indexed to the CPI according to

$$\Delta W/W = \Delta CPI/CPI.$$

What happens to the real wage?

    e. If, when these contracts were negotiated, workers and employers believed that inflation for 1962 and 1963 would be the same as it was in 1961, was there any reason for either to prefer one formula over the others? Did these preferences change over time once inflation became known?

9. The following data are from the late 1970s:

Year	CPI
1976	56.9
1977	60.6
1978	65.2
1979	72.6

a. Calculate the rate of inflation for 1977, 1978, and 1979.

b. Suppose that the increase in the wage rate for a group of workers that sign an employment contract for the two-year period starting in 1978 is $\Delta W/W = .065$. What happens to the real wage measured in terms of the CPI?

c. Suppose instead that the wage rate is partially indexed to the CPI according to the formula

$$\Delta W/W = .032 + .5 \, \Delta CPI/CPI.$$

What happens to the real wage?

d. Finally, suppose that the wage rate is completely indexed to the CPI according to

$$\Delta W/W = \Delta CPI/CPI.$$

What happens to the real wage?

e. If, when these contracts were negotiated, workers and employers believed that inflation for 1978 and 1979 would be the same as it was in 1977, was there any reason for either to prefer one formula over the others? Did these preferences change over time once inflation became known?

10. We now consider the 1980s.

Year	CPI
1982	96.5
1983	99.6
1984	103.9
1985	107.6

a. Calculate the rate of inflation for 1983, 1984, and 1985.

b. Suppose that the increase in the wage rate for a group of workers that sign an employment contract for the three-year period starting in 1983 is $\Delta W/W = .10$. Looking back to the inflation figures from Problem 9, does this seem like a reasonable contract? What happens to the real wage measured in terms of the CPI?

c. Suppose instead that the wage rate is partially indexed to the CPI according to the formula

$$\Delta W/W = .05 + .5 \ \Delta CPI/CPI.$$

What happens to the real wage?

d. Finally, suppose that the wage rate is completely indexed to the CPI according to

$$\Delta W/W = \Delta CPI/CPI.$$

What happens to the real wage?

e. If, when these contracts were negotiated, workers and employers believed that inflation for 1983 through 1985 would be the same as the average for 1980 through 1982, 10.0 percent, was there any reason for either to prefer one formula over the others? Did these preferences change over time once inflation became known?

11. Finally, we examine the late 1990 and early 2000s.

Year	CPI
1999	166.6
2000	172.2
2001	177.1
2002	179.9

a. Calculate the rate of inflation for 2000, 2001, and 2001.

b. Suppose that the increase in the wage rate for a group of workers that sign an employment contract for the two-year period starting in 2001 is $\Delta W/W = .03$. What happens to the real wage measured in terms of the CPI?

c. Suppose instead that the wage rate is partially indexed to the CPI according to the formula

$$\Delta W/W = .015 + .5 \ \Delta CPI/CPI.$$

What happens to the real wage?

d. Finally, suppose that the wage rate is completely indexed to the CPI according to

$$\Delta W/W = \Delta CPI/CPI.$$

What happens to the real wage?

e. If, when these contracts were negotiated, workers and employers believed that inflation for 2001 and 2002 would be the same as it was in 2000, was there any reason for either to prefer one formula over the others? Did these preferences change over time once inflation became known?

ANSWERS TO THE SELF-TEST

1. Spending, production, or income
2. Inflation
3. Households
4. Nonresidential and residential
5. Depreciation
6. Inventory
7. Exports minus imports
8. Final
9. Disposable
10. Deficit
11. Current account, capital account, and financial account
12. Consumer price index
13. Producer price index
14. GDP implicit price deflator
15. False. We know they are the same simply because of an accounting identity.
16. True. IT is included in residential investment.
17. False. It increases by net, not gross, investment. Net Investment = Gross investment − Depreciation.
18. True. The two ways of calculating GDP are equivalent.
19. False. Real GDP measures the physical volume of production and nominal GDP measures the current dollar volume.
20. False. It is unchanged if you buy a used car.
21. True. Both domestic consumption and exports add to GDP.
22. False. Investment is spending that adds to or maintains the capital stock. Buying shares of stock is not investment in the sense used by macroeconomists, and does not add to GDP.
23. False. Purchases of new equipment by firms are investment whether they add to or maintain their capital stock.
24. False. The unsold cars constitute inventory investment, which adds to GDP just like consumption.
25. True. When the exchange rate rises, 1 dollar can buy more foreign currency, making foreign goods cheaper.

26. False. The rate of inflation is the percentage change of the price level. If inflation falls form 10 to 5 percent, prices are still rising, but at a slower rate.
27. True. They are measured differently.
28. False. The producer price index measures the prices charged by producers at various stages in the production process.
29. When measured through spending, GDP is equal to consumption plus investment plus government purchases plus net exports.
30. The components of consumption are durable goods, nondurable goods, and services.
31. The components of investment are nonresidential fixed investment, residential fixed investment, and inventory investment.
32. Investment is the flow of new capital during the year that is added to the existing stock of capital.
33. Real GDP is nominal GDP adjusted for changing prices.
34. The concept of value added is used to prevent double counting when GDP is measured by production.
35. Disposable income is personal income minus income taxes.
36. When there is a current account deficit, it must be financed by borrowing from the rest of the world, resulting in a matching financial account surplus, if no international transfers are received. The three sum to zero.
37. When the dollar rises, foreign goods become cheaper compared to American goods. This causes Americans to buy more goods abroad and foreigners to buy fewer goods in the United States.
38. The rate of inflation is the percentage rate of change in the general price level from one period to the next.
39. The general price level can be measured either by constructing price indexes or by calculating deflators.
40. COLAs protect workers against inflation. With the slowdown of inflation in the 1980s and 1990s, there was less need for protection.
41. Employment in the United States is measured by two surveys, one of households and one of establishments.
42. Total hours of work is employment multiplied by the hours of work of the average worker. It is a better measure of labor input than employment because it incorporates how many hours people work.

SOLUTIONS TO REVIEW PROBLEMS

4. a. $Y = C + I + G$
    $= 1,500 + 600 + 500 = \$2,600.$
   b. $S_p = (Y + F + N + T) - C$
    $= (2,600 + 300 + 100 - 1,000) - 1,500 = \$500.$
   c. $S_g = T - F - N - G$
    $= 1,000 - 300 - 100 - 500 = \$100.$

d. $S = S_p + S_g$
    $= 500 + 100 = \$600 = I.$

5. a. $Y = C + I + G + X$
      $= 1,500 + 600 + 500 + 100 = \$2,700.$
   b. $S_p = (Y + V + F + N - T) - C$
      $= (2,700 - 20 + 300 + 100 - 1,000) - 1,500 = \$580.$
   c. $S_g = T - F - N - G$
      $= 1,000 - 300 - 100 - 500 = \$100.$
   d. $S_r = -(X + V) = -\$80.$
   e. $S = S_p + S_g + S_r$
      $= 580 + 100 - 80 = \$600 = I.$

6. a. $Y = C + I + G$
      $= 2,300 + 700 + 800 = \$3,800.$
   b. $S_p = (Y + F + N - T) - C$
      $= (3,800 + 100 + 100 - 800) - 2,300 = \$900.$
   c. $S_g = T - F - B - G$
      $= 800 - 100 - 100 - 800 = -\$200.$
   d. $S = S_p + S_g$
      $= 900 - 200 = \$700 = I.$
   e. The government budget deficit is $-S_g$, which equals \$200.

7. a. $Y = C + I + G + X$
      $= 2,300 + 700 + 800 - 200 = \$3,600.$
   b. $S_p = (Y + V + F + N - T) - C$
      $= (3,600 + 50 + 100 + 100 - 800) - 2,300 = \$750.$
   c. $S_g = T - F - N - G$
      $= 800 - 100 - 100 - 800 = -\$200.$
   d. $S_r = -(X + V) = \$150.$
   e. $S = S_p + S_g + S_r$
      $= 750 - 200 + 150 = \$700 = I.$

8. a. The rate of inflation was

1961	.011 (1.1 percent)
1962	.010 (1.0 percent)
1963	.013 (1.3 percent)

   b. Wages increase by 1 percent each year. Prices increase by 1.0 percent in 1962 and 1.3 percent in 1963, so real wages fall very slightly.
   c. Wages increase by 1.0 percent in 1962 and 1.15 percent in 1963. Real wages are constant in 1962 and fall very slightly in 1963.
   d. The real wage is constant when the nominal wage is completely indexed to the CPI.
   e. If inflation had remained at 1.0 percent in 1962 and 1963, real wages would have been constant with any of the three formulas, so there was no reason for either workers or employers to prefer one over the others. Since the inflation rate was so close to 1.0 percent, the choice of one formula over another would not have made much difference.

9. a. The rate of inflation was

    1977   .065 (6.5 percent)
    1978   .076 (7.6 percent)
    1979   .113 (11.3 percent)

    b. Wages increase by 6.5 percent each year. Prices increase by 7.6 percent in 1978 and 11.3 percent in 1979, so real wages fall.
    c. Wages increase by 7.0 percent in 1978 and 8.9 percent in 1979. Real wages fall, but by less than in Part b.
    d. The real wage is constant when the nominal wage is completely indexed to the CPI.
    e. If inflation had remained at 6.5 percent in 1978 and 1979, real wages would have been constant with any of the three formulas, so there was no reason for either workers or employers to prefer one over the others. Since the inflation rate increased, workers ended up better off with more indexation (d) while employers would have been better off with less (b).

10. a. The rate of inflation was

    1983   .032 (3.2 percent)
    1984   .043 (4.3 percent)
    1985   .036 (3.6 percent)

    b. Given that inflation was 11.3 percent in 1979, a 10 percent nominal wage increase seems like a reasonable negotiated agreement. Prices increase by an average of 3.7 percent, so real wages increase.
    c. Real wages increase, but by less than in Part b.
    d. Real wages are constant.
    e. With expected inflation equal to 10 percent, there was no reason for either workers or employers to prefer one over the others. Since inflation was actually below 10 percent, workers ended up better off with less indexation (b) while employers would have been better off with more (d).

11. a. The rate of inflation was

    2000   .0336 (3.4 percent)
    2001   .028 (2.8 percent)
    2002   .028 (2.8 percent)

    b. Wages increase by 3 percent each year. Prices increase by 2.8 percent in 2001 and 2002, so real wages rise.
    c. Wages increase 2.9 percent in both years. Since prices increased by 2.8 percent, real wages rose by a smaller amount than in Part b.
    d. Real wages are constant.
    e. With expected inflation equal to 3.4 percent, workers would have preferred full indexation. Since inflation was actually equal to 2.8 percent, real wages would have been highest under Part a, with a guaranteed 3 percent raise. Workers would have preferred this most, whereas employers would have preferred full indexation.

CHAPTER 3	# Unemployment, Job Creation, and Job Destruction

MAIN OBJECTIVES

Unemployment is one of the most visible symbols of an economy's performance. In the United States, 5 to 6 percent of the labor force is unemployed in normal times. During recessions, such as in the early 1980s, unemployment rates can rise above 10 percent. During booms, the unemployment rate can be as low as 3 to 4 percent. For most European countries, normal unemployment rates are even higher. This chapter looks at the causes of unemployment. You will learn how unemployment is measured, how to think about movements into and out of unemployment, unemployment during normal times, and unemployment in recessions and booms.

KEY TERMS AND CONCEPTS

People are classified as **unemployed** if they are not working and are looking for work. The **labor force** is defined as the number of persons 16 years of age or over who either are working or are unemployed. The **unemployment rate** is the percentage of the labor force that is unemployed. Many people who are not working are not counted as unemployed, including students, parents at home taking care of their own children, and those who are retired, sick, or not looking for work for other reasons. They are **out of the labor force**. The **labor force participation rate** is the percentage of the working-age population that is in the labor force. Unemployment is measured by a national survey of households, called the Current Population Survey.

When thinking about unemployment, it is useful to first think about unemployment in normal times, then consider the additional unemployment during recessions. The unemployment rate is never equal to zero. People are always entering the labor force, in between jobs, or chronically unemployed. The rate

39

of unemployment that prevails during normal times is called the **natural unemployment rate**. Currently it is between 5 and 6 percent for the United States.

Movements, or **flows**, into and out of unemployment are very large. Every month, almost 3 percent of the labor force becomes newly unemployed and about the same number leave unemployment. For most people, the duration, or spell, of a period of unemployment is a few weeks, although some people remain unemployed for many months.

We can use the concepts of flows into and out of unemployment to understand the size of the unemployment rate. We define l as the **job-losing rate**, the ratio of the number of people who become unemployed to the labor force; f as the **job-finding rate**, the fraction of unemployed who leave unemployment; and u as the unemployment rate, the fraction of the labor force that is unemployed, all measured over the same month. The inflow into unemployment is the amount l and the outflow out of unemployment is the amount of uf. The flow is the inflow minus the outflow, or $l - uf$.

In normal times, when unemployment does not change from one month to the next, the inflow must equal the outflow, $l = uf$. Solving for the unemployment rate,

$$u = l/f \qquad\qquad (3–1)$$

Over a period of time, the natural rate of unemployment equals the average job-losing rate divided by the average job-finding rate.

Flows into unemployment can be divided into three categories. **Job destruction** occurs when an employer terminates a position, such as when a plant closes. **Job loss without destruction** occurs when a worker loses a job but the employer does not reduce total employment, such as when a worker gets fired and is replaced by another worker. **Personal transitions** occur when people start looking for jobs for other reasons, such as quitting a job, leaving school, or being involved in home activities.

Flows out of unemployment are divided into two categories. Two-thirds of the outflow is the result of successful job search, unemployed workers finding jobs. One-third is caused by unemployed workers leaving the labor force, such as by returning to school or retiring, or by being so discouraged that they stop looking for jobs.

Search theory portrays the activities of job seekers as economically rational. Job seekers do not take the first job that comes along; they balance the benefit of starting an available job right away against the benefit of continuing to look and (possibly) finding a better job later, adjusted by the cost of waiting. Rational job searchers, especially at higher income levels, may wait quite a while before accepting a job.

The natural unemployment rate equals the job-losing rate divided by the job-finding rate. Economies with high rates of job creation, job destruction, and personal transitions will have high job-losing rates (the numerator of the unemployment rate) and thus high natural unemployment rates. Economies with low job-finding rates (the denominator of the unemployment rate) will also have high natural unemployment rates.

Several factors contribute to low job-finding rates. **Efficiency wage theory** says that firms want to make their jobs valuable in order to keep their workers from searching for other jobs. These firms bid up their wages, reducing the number of available jobs, increasing the number of people looking for these jobs, and lowering job-finding rates.

Union wage premiums, unions successfully raising wages, cause wages to be bid up, and job-finding rates to decrease, in the same manner as efficiency wages. If **minimum wages** substantially raise the wages for low-wage workers, these jobs will be harder to find and job-finding rates will decrease. If not, there will be little effect. **Unemployment insurance** lowers the cost of job search, lengthening the search process, decreasing job-finding rates, and raising the natural unemployment rate.

The natural unemployment rate can change over time if either the job-losing rate or the job-finding rate changes. For the United States from 1990 through 2002, the average job-losing rate was 2.2 percent per month and the average job-finding rate was 39 percent per month, resulting in a natural rate of unemployment of 5.6 percent. This lower natural rate is consistent with the trends of the last 15 years. The aging of the baby boom generation has reduced turnover, unionization of the workforce has declined, the minimum wage has increased slower than overall wages, and unemployment benefits have not risen in relation to wages. In contrast, for the same period, the European natural rate has not decreased. Unlike the United States, the fraction of the labor force that belong to unions, the minimum wage relative to wages in general, the level of unemployment insurance benefits relative to wages, and the duration of unemployment insurance benefits have not decreased as much, if at all, in Europe.

Unemployment is countercyclical—low in booms and high in recessions. If unemployment is changing, inflows no longer equal outflows. The change in the unemployment rate is the inflow minus the outflow, $l - uf$. The most important source of changes in inflows to unemployment is job destruction. Major fluctuations to unemployment start with a burst of job destruction, caused by factors such as an oil price shock or a financial crisis. Unemployment remains above the natural rate for several years.

Okun's law, named after the late Arthur Okun of the Brookings Institution, is a useful approximation of the cyclical relationship between unemployment and real GDP. It says that, for each percentage point by which the unemployment rate is above the natural rate, real GDP is 3 percent below potential GDP. Okun's law is given by

$$\frac{(Y - Y^*)}{Y^*} = -3(U - U^*), \tag{3-2}$$

Where U is the unemployment rate, U^* is the natural rate of unemployment, Y is GDP, and Y^* is potential GDP. The left-hand side of equation 3–2, called the GDP gap, is the percentage departure of GDP from potential GDP.

The supply and demand framework can be used to understand unemployment. Figure 3–1 shows the actual level of employment (N_R) lower than the equilibrium employment (N^*) determined by the intersection of the labor supply and labor demand curves. This illustrates a recession, with the actual unemployment rate above the unemployment rate that would prevail in normal times.

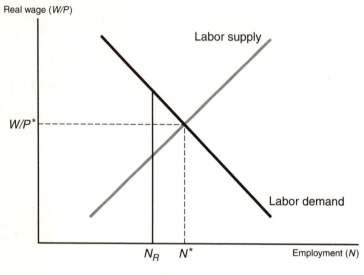

Figure 3–1

When employment is below equilibrium employment, worker and firms face incentives to expand employment. The incentive for employers is the difference between the marginal product of labor (the labor demand schedule) and the real wage. The incentive for workers is the difference between the real wage and the value of the workers' time (the labor supply schedule). These incentives take time to operate, and so recessions, with high unemployment, can last several years.

SELF-TEST

Fill in the Blank

1. The _____ is the number of persons 16 years of age or over who are either working or unemployed.

2. The _____ is the percentage of the labor force that is unemployed.

3. The _____ is the percentage of the working-age population that is in the labor force.

4. The rate of unemployment that prevails during normal times is called the _____.

5. Movements into and out of unemployment are called _____.

6. The duration of a period of unemployment is called a _____ of unemployment.

7. The _____ is the ratio of the number of people who become unemployed in a month to the labor force.

8. The _____ is the fraction of unemployed who leave unemployment during a month.

9. _____ occurs when an employer terminates a position.

10. _____ occurs when a worker loses a job but the employer does not reduce total employment.

11. _____ says that firms want to make their jobs valuable in order to keep their workers from searching for other jobs.

12. _____ is a useful approximation of the cyclical relationship between unemployment and real GDP.

13. The percentage departure of GDP from potential GDP is called the _____.

True-False

14. People are classified as unemployed if they are not working and are looking for work.

15. People 16 years of age or older are classified as either employed or unemployed.

16. If an unemployed person enrolls in school, the unemployment rate decreases.

17. If a student graduates from college and begins to look for a job, the unemployment rate increases.

18. There is not unemployment in normal times when real GDP equals potential GDP.

19. Flows into and out of unemployment are very large.

20. For most people, the duration, or spell, of a period of unemployment is many months.

21. All flows into unemployment are caused by job destruction and job loss without destruction.

22. According to search theory, job seekers take the first job that they are offered.

23. The natural unemployment rate is constant.

24. Unemployment is countercyclical.

25. The most important source of changes in inflows to unemployment is personal transitions.

26. When employment is below equilibrium employment, workers and firms face incentives to expand employment.

Review Questions

27. How is unemployment measured?

28. Why is the unemployment rate never equal to zero?

29. How large are inflows and outflows of unemployment?

30. What is the job-losing rate?

31. What is the job-finding rate?

32. How is unemployment in normal times related to the job-losing rate and the job-finding rate?

33. What are the three categories of flows into unemployment?

34. How do people leave unemployment?

35. What is search theory?

36. What factors contribute to low job-finding rates?

37. Why do many economists believe that the natural unemployment rate for the United States is now lower than it is for European countries?

38. What starts major fluctuations to unemployment?

39. When employment is below equilibrium employment, what are the incentives to expand employment faced by workers and firms?

PROBLEM SET

Worked Problems

1. In a particular month, the job-losing rate l was 3.0 percent and the job-finding rate f was 50 percent.

   a. Suppose that the particular month occurred in normal times, when unemployment does not change from one month to the next. Calculate the unemployment rate u.

   b. Now suppose that unemployment is changing and in the previous month the unemployment rate u was 4.0 percent. Calculate the new unemployment rate.

a. When unemployment does not change from one month to the next, the inflow must equal the outflow and u = l/f. The unemployment rate u = .03 (3 percent)/.5 (50 percent) = .06 (6 percent).

b. If unemployment is changing, inflows no longer equal outflows. The change in the unemployment rate is the inflow minus the outflow, l – uf. Using the preceding numbers, the change in unemployment = .03 (3 percent) – .04 (4 percent) × .5 (50 percent) = .03 – .02 = .01 (1 percent). The new unemployment rate is the previous unemployment rate, .04, plus the change, .01, which equals .05 (5 percent).

2. Looking into our crystal ball, we see the following data:

Year	Unemployment Rate
2011	.05 (5 percent)
2012	.04 (4 percent)
2013	.05 (5 percent)
2014	.06 (6 percent)

a. Assuming that the natural unemployment rate is 6 percent ($U^* = .06$), calculate the GDP gap for each of the unemployment rates from 2011 to 2014.

b. What is the relationship between GDP and potential GDP for these years?

c. If GDP is $2,000 billion in 2013, calculate potential GDP.

a. According to Okun's law, the GDP gap is –3(U – U*).

Year	U	U*	–3(U – U*) (= GDP gap (Y – Y*)/Y*)
2011	.05	.06	.03
2012	.04	.06	.06
2013	.05	.06	.03
2014	.06	.06	.00

b. GDP is above or equal to potential GDP because the unemployment rate is below or at the natural rate for all 4 years.

c. Okun's law states that (Y – Y*)/Y* = GDP gap. To calculate potential output, rearrange terms so that Y* = Y/(1 + GDP gap). For 2013, if Y = 2,000 and the GDP gap (previously calculated) = .03, then Y* = 2,000/1.03 = $1,941.7 billion.

Review Problems

3. In a particular month, the job-losing rate *l* was 2.2 percent and the job-finding rate *f* was 40 percent.

a. Suppose that the particular month occurred in normal times, when unemployment does not change from one month to the next. Calculate the unemployment rate *u*.

b. Now suppose that unemployment is changing and in the previous month the unemployment rate *u* was 8.0 percent. Calculate the new unemployment rate.

c. Explain your answer to Part b in terms of flows.

4. In a particular month, the job-losing rate *l* was 2.0 percent and the job-finding rate *f* was 50 percent.

a. Suppose that the particular month occurred in normal times, when unemployment does not change from one month to the next. Calculate the unemployment rate *u*.

b. Now suppose that unemployment is changing and in the previous month the unemployment rate u was 3.0 percent. Calculate the new unemployment rate.

c. Explain your answer to Part b in terms of flows.

5. In a particular month, the job-losing rate *l* was 3.0 percent and the job-finding rate *f* was 40 percent.

a. Suppose that the particular month occurred in normal times, when unemployment does not change from one month to the next. Calculate the unemployment rate *u*.

b. Now suppose that unemployment is changing and in the previous month the unemployment rate *u* was 10.0 percent. Calculate the new unemployment rate.

c. Does your resulting change in the current unemployment reflect your answer to Part 3b or 4b?

6. In a particular month, the job-losing rate *l* was 2.5 percent and the job-finding rate *f* was 50 percent.

a. Suppose that the particular month occurred in normal times, when unemployment does not change from one month to the next. Calculate the unemployment rate *u*.

b. Now suppose that unemployment is changing and in the previous month the unemployment rate *u* was 4.0 percent. Calculate the new unemployment rate.

7. The following unemployment rate (*U*) data are from the early 1960s.

Year	*U*
1960	.054 (5.4 percent)
1961	.065 (6.5 percent)
1962	.054 (5.4 percent)
1963	.055 (5.5 percent)

a. Assuming that the natural unemployment rate was 5 percent ($U^* = .05$), calculate the GDP gap for each of the unemployment rates from 1960 to 1963.

b. Using the theory of price adjustment discussed in Chapter 1, what pressure was there on prices during these years?

c. Real GDP was $2,834 billion in 1963. Calculate potential GDP. Explain your answer.

8. We now consider the 1980s:

Year	U
1982	.095 (9.5 percent)
1983	.095 (9.5 percent)
1984	.074 (74 percent)
1985	.071 (7.1 percent)

a. Assuming that the natural unemployment rate is 6 percent ($U^* = .06$), calculate the GDP gap for each of the unemployment rates from 1982 to 1985.

b. Using the theory of price adjustment discussed in Chapter 1, what was the pressure on prices during these years?

c. Real GDP was $5,189.3 billion in 1982. Calculate potential GDP.

9. The following are unemployment data from the late 1980s and early 1990s.

Year	U
1988	.054 (5.4 percent)
1989	.052 (5.2 percent)
1990	.054 (5.4 percent)
1991	.066 (6.6 percent)

a. Assuming that the natural unemployment rate is 6 percent ($U^* = .06$), calculate the GDP gap for each of the unemployment rates from 1988 to 1991.

b. Using the theory of price adjustment discussed in Chapter 1, explain why the pressure on prices changed between 1990 and 1991.

c. Real GDP was $7,100.5 billion in 1991. Calculate potential GDP.

10. Finally, we examine the last few years:

Year	U
1999	.042 (4.2 percent)
2000	.04 (4 percent)
2001	.047 (4.7 percent
2002	.058 (5.8 percent)
2003	.06 (6 percent)

a. Assuming that the natural unemployment rate had fallen to 5.5 percent ($U^* = .055$), calculate the GDP gap for each of the unemployment rates from 1999 to 2003.

b. Using the theory of price adjustment discussed in Chapter 1, what pressure was there on prices during these years?

c. Real GDP was $9,817 billion in 2000. Calculate potential GDP.

GRAPH IT

1. Consider the following labor market:

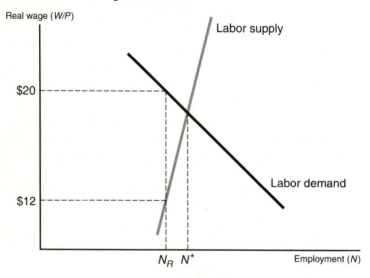

Figure 3–2

If employment is currently at the N_R level, what is the marginal product of labor? What is the real wage at N_R? Is there a profit opportunity for a firm in this situation?

ANSWERS TO THE SELF-TEST

1. Labor force
2. Unemployment rate
3. Labor force participation rate
4. Natural unemployment rate
5. Flows
6. Spell

7. Job-losing rate
8. Job-finding rate
9. Job destruction
10. Job loss without destruction
11. Efficiency wage theory
12. Okun's law
13. GDP gap
14. True.   You need to be both not working and looking for work in order to be considered unemployed.
15. False.   They can also be out of the labor force.
16. True.   You are counted as out of the labor force if in school full time.
17. True.   You are counted as unemployed when you begin to look for a job.
18. False.   The rate of unemployment that prevails during normal times is called the natural unemployment rate.
19. True.   Every month, almost 3 percent of the labor force becomes newly unemployed, and about the same number leave unemployment.
20. False.   For most people, the spell of a period of unemployment is a few weeks.
21. False.   There are also flows into unemployment which are caused by personal transitions, when people start looking for jobs for other reasons.
22. False.   Search theory portrays the activities of job seekers as economically rational, and it is sometimes advantageous to continue to look for a better job.
23. False.   The natural unemployment rate can change over time if either the job-losing rate or the job-finding rate changes.
24. True.   Unemployment is low in booms and high in recessions.
25. False.   The most important source of changes in inflows to unemployment is job destruction.
26. True.   Workers and firms face incentives to expand employment when it is below equilibrium.
27. Unemployment is measured by a national survey of households called the Current Population Survey.
28. The unemployment rate is never equal to zero because people are always entering the labor force, in between jobs, or chronically unemployed.
29. Every month, almost 3 percent of the labor force becomes newly unemployed and about the same number leave unemployment.
30. The job-losing rate is the ratio of the number of people who become unemployed in a month to the labor force.
31. The job-finding rate is the fraction of unemployed who leave unemployment during a month.
32. In normal times, when unemployment does not change from one month to the next, unemployment equals the job-losing rate divided by the job-finding rate.
33. Flows into unemployment are divided into job destruction, job loss without job destruction, and personal transitions.

34. Two-thirds of the outflow is the result of successful job search, and one-third is caused by unemployed workers leaving the labor force.
35. Search theory portrays the activities of job seekers as economically rational.
36. Efficiency wage theory, union wage premiums, minimum wages, and unemployment insurance contribute to low job-finding rates.
37. Several factors have contributed to the differences in the natural unemployment between the United States and Europe. Unionization of the workforce has declined, the minimum wage has increased slower than overall wages for the United States but not Europe.
38. Major fluctuations to unemployment start with a burst of job destruction, caused by factors such as an oil price shock or a financial crisis.
39. The incentive for the employer is the difference between the marginal product for labor and the real wage. The incentive for the workers is the difference between the real wage and the workers' value of time.

SOLUTIONS TO REVIEW PROBLEMS

3. a. The unemployment rate $u = .022/.4 = .055$ (5.5 percent).
   b. The change in the unemployment rate $= .022 - (.08 \times .4) = .022 - .032 = -.01$ (1 percent drop). The new unemployment rate $u =$ previous $u + \Delta u = .08 - .01 = .07$ (7 percent).
   c. The flow into unemployment ($l = .022$) was less than the flow out of unemployment ($fu = .032$). Therefore, the current unemployment rate dropped.
4. a. The unemployment rate $u = .02/.5 = .04$ (4 percent).
   b. The change in the unemployment rate $= .02 - (.03 \times .5) = .02 - .015 = .005$ (.5 percent). The new unemployment rate $u =$ previous $u + \Delta u = .03 + .005 = .035$ (3.5 percent).
   c. The flow into unemployment ($l = .02$) exceeded the flow out ($fu = .015$), so the new unemployment rate increased.
5. a. The unemployment rate $u = .03/.4 = .075$ (7.5 percent).
   b. The change in the unemployment rate $= .03 - (.10 \times .4) = .03 - .04 = -.01$ (−1 percent). The new unemployment rate $u = .10 - .01 = .09$ (9 percent).
   c. The unemployment rate dropped form 10 to 9 percent, so it reflects the result in Part 3b.
6. a. The unemployment rate $u = .025/.5 = .05$ (5 percent).
   b. The change in the unemployment rate $= .025 - (.04 \times .5) = .025 - .02 = .005$ (.5 percent). The new unemployment rate $u =$ previous $u + \Delta u = .04 + .005 = .045$ (4.5 percent).

7. a. The GDP gap is $-3(U - U^*)$. With $U^* = .05$, the gap was

      1960 $-.012$ (-1.2 percent)
      1961 $-.045$ (-4.5 percent)
      1962 $-.012$ (-1.2 percent)
      1963 $-.015$ (-1.5 percent)

  b. With the gap between -1.2 and -4.5 percent, GDP was below potential and there was pressure on prices to fall, although for three of the four years, the gap was quite small.

  c. Rearranging Okun's law, $Y^* = Y/((1 + \text{GDP gap})$. For 1963, with $Y = \$2,834$ and the gap $= -.015$, $Y^* = \$2,877$ billion. With unemployment above normal, current GDP ($Y = \$2,834$) fell short of potential ($Y^* = \$2,877$).

8. a. The GDP gap is $-3(U - U^*)$. With $U^* = .06$, the gap was

      1982 $-.105$ (-10.5 percent)
      1983 $-.105$ (-10.5 percent)
      1984 $-.042$ (-4.2 percent)
      1985 $-.033$ (-3.3 percent)

  b. With the gap between -3.3 and -10.5 percent, GDP was below potential and there was pressure on prices to fall.

  c. Rearranging Okun's law, $Y^* = Y/((1 + \text{GDP gap})$. For 1982, with $Y = \$5,189.3$ and the gap $= -.105$, $Y^* = \$5,798.1$.

9. a. The GDP gap is $-3(U - U^*)$. With $U^* = .06$, the gap was

      1988   .018 (1.8 percent)
      1989   .024 (2.4 percent)
      1990   .018 (1.8 percent)
      1991 $-.018$ (-1.8 percent)

  b. In 1990, GDP was above potential and there was pressure on prices to rise. By 1991, the economy was in a recession, GDP was below potential, and there was pressure on prices to fall.

  c. Rearranging Okun's law, $Y^* = Y/((1 + \text{GDP gap})$. For 1991, with $Y = \$7,100.5$ and the gap $= -.108$, $Y^* = \$7,230.7$.

10. a. The GDP gap is $-3(U - U^*)$. With $U^* = .055$, the gap was

      1999   .039 (3.9 percent)
      2000   .045 (4.5 percent)
      2001   .024 (2.4 percent)
      2002 $-.009$ (-0.9 percent)
      2003 $-.015$ (-1.5 percent)

  b. From 1999 to 2000, GDP was above potential and there was pressure on prices to rise. After the 2001 recession, job creation was unusually sluggish. During 2001–2003, pressure on prices had been downward.

c. Rearranging Okun's law, $Y^* = Y/((1 + \text{GDP gap})$. For 2000, with $Y = \$9,817$ and the gap $= .045$, $Y^* = \$9,394.3$ billion.

ANSWERS TO GRAPH IT

1. The marginal product of labor is 20. The real wage is 12. One added worker is worth 20 to the firm at a cost of 12. The difference of 8 is the profit opportunity. Since it is positive, firms have an incentive to hire more workers beyond N_R.

Part II

Economic Growth

CHAPTER 4 | Long-Run Economic Growth

MAIN OBJECTIVES

The first three chapters have given us much to consider: economic growth, fluctuations, inflation, and employment. These are the central concerns of macroeconomists, and they are all related to one another. In Chapter 4, we assemble the first part of the complete model, called the long-run growth model, to explain the growth path of potential GDP. It simplifies away short-run fluctuations by looking at an economy that is always in full employment because wages and prices are perfectly flexible and focuses on the labor force, capital stock, and technology. Issues involving economic growth are so important, we spend three chapters studying them.

KEY TERMS AND CONCEPTS

The **long-run growth model** is designed to explain differences in growth rates across countries and over time. It describes the economy in a state where supply and demand for both goods and workers are in balance and does not consider short-run economic fluctuations around potential GDP.

The determinants of the long-run growth path of output are **labor**, the people available for work; **capital**, equipment, structures, and other productive facilities; and **technology**, the knowledge about how to use labor and capital to produce goods and services. Technological change increases the productivity of labor and capital. If the marginal productivities of both factors increase in the same proportion so that technological change is **neutral**, it is useful to define technological change as something that increases total factor productivity.

The **production function** shows how much output can be made from given amounts of labor, capital, and technology. In symbols, without being specific about its functional form, the production function can be stated as

$$Y = F(N, K, A), \qquad\qquad (4\text{--}1)$$

where Y is output, N is employment, K is the stock of capital, and A is technology. In order to determine potential GDP, we must calculate the long-run capital stock, labor force, and technology.

Since capital and technology are predetermined by past decisions, we focus on the labor force. The **marginal product of labor**, the additional output produced by one additional unit of work, declines as the amount of employment increases. Profit-maximizing, competitive firms choose the level of employment so that the marginal product of labor equals the **real wage**. The **demand for labor** is a negative function of the real wage because the marginal product of labor declines with increased labor input.

The **supply of labor** is determined by the decisions of individual workers about how much of their time to spend working. It depends on the real wage in two contrasting ways. The **substitution effect** is that, at higher real wages, the incentive to work is stronger and people want to work more. This increases the labor supply. The **income effect** is that higher real wages, by increasing people's income, make them better off. People who are better off choose to spend more time at home and less time in the labor market, which decreases the labor supply. Research indicates that these two effects offset each other. The net effect of the real wage on labor supply is approximately zero, which is illustrated with a very steep labor supply curve. **Full employment**, N^*, is the volume of employment at the intersection of the labor supply and demand schedules, as shown in Figure 4–1. It is the amount people want to work given the real wage that employers are willing to pay. **Potential GDP**, Y^*, is the amount of output produced

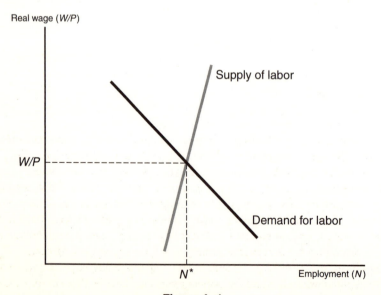

Figure 4–1

at full employment. Y^* is also called the **full-employment level of output**. The **natural rate of unemployment**, U^*, is (as defined in Chapter 3) the amount of unemployment in normal times, when employment is at N^* and GDP is equal to potential, Y^*.

The production function and long-run equilibrium between labor supply and demand together determine full employment and potential GDP. Although it abstracts away from short-run fluctuations, it still describes the economy at a single point in time. We also want to study how the economy, as measured by **GDP per capita**, moves over time. We do this by first considering that, for most of recorded history, economic growth was zero. Thomas Malthus, writing in 1798, accounted for the lack of economic growth by observing that the productivity of labor increases at a diminishing rate when land, capital, and technology are unchanged. This is illustrated by the production function in Figure 4–2.

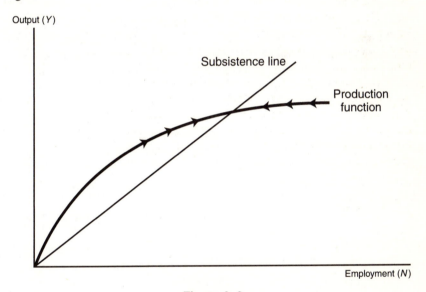

Figure 4–2

The economy is always somewhere on the production function. The exact location is determined by the subsistence line. Along the **subsistence line**, output per worker, Y/N, is constant. Below the subsistence line, output per worker is less than needed for subsistence. With output below the subsistence level, death rates increase as people begin to die of starvation and birth rates decrease because families avoid having children they cannot feed. Both factors lead to population and employment declines. The opposite is true above the subsistence line. Wherever an economy starts, the outcome is **Malthusian stagnation** (the intersection of both lines), where the output per worker is just sufficient to sustain life and the population is constant. With no output growth and no population growth, there is no economic growth.

Malthusian stagnation depicts an extremely pessimistic picture. For the data up until 1800, the theory works well. Despite some technological progress (illustrated with an upward shift of the production function) and population growth, GDP per capita was constant and there was no economic growth. The industrial revolution increased the pace of technological progress, but with fertility rates also increasing, GDP per capita grew slowly at first. The period from 1800–1875 of slowly growing GDP is referred to as the **post-Malthusian regime**. The **demographic transition** occurred afterward, when fertility rates in Western Europe sharply declined around the turn of the century. Combined with continued technological progress, economic growth started to increase sharply starting in the 1920s. For the last 75 years, this period of the **modern growth regime** has been characterized by not only increased technological progress but also fertility reductions. Not all countries have gone through this transition. Many African and Asian countries are still experiencing high birth rates and stagnant growth.

The economy is on a **balanced growth path** if the growth rate of capital equals the growth rate of labor. Along a balanced growth path, net investment is **balanced growth investment**, the amount of investment needed to maintain balanced growth, and equals nK, where n is the growth rate of labor (equal by assumption to the growth rate of capital) and K is the capital stock.

The long-run growth model with the economy on a balanced growth path is often called the **Solow growth model**, after Robert Solow of MIT. Solow's model is sometimes called the **neoclassical growth model**.

Assume, for simplicity, that the economy is closed with no technological change. Define net saving to equal sY, where s is the savings rate and Y is output. We know from Chapter 2 that, whether or not growth is balanced, net saving equals net investment. Since, along a balanced growth path, net investment equals balanced growth investment, Solow's condition for balanced growth is

$$sY = nK, \tag{4-2}$$

which, dividing both sides by N, can be rewritten as

$$sY/N = nK/N, \tag{4-3}$$

where sY/N is saving per workers and nk/N is balanced growth investment per worker.

The Solow growth model is illustrated in Figure 4–3. The intersection of the investment line and the saving curve is the steady-state point. At that point, actual investment, determined by saving, equals balanced growth investment. If the economy starts at the steady state, it will stay there.

An important result of the Solow model is that the balanced growth path is stable. No matter where the economy starts, it converges over time to the same steady state, with the capital stock growing at the same rate as the labor force. Suppose that the economy starts to the left of the steady-state point, so that $sY/N > nK/N$. Actual investment exceeds balanced growth investment, capital

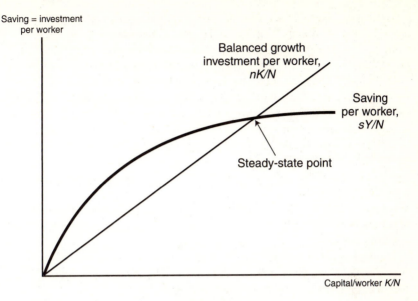

Saving = investment per worker

Balanced growth investment per worker, *nK/N*

Saving per worker, *sY/N*

Steady-state point

Capital/worker *K/N*

Figure 4–3

per worker increases, and the economy moves toward the steady-state point. A similar argument holds if the economy starts to the right of the steady-state point.

Another implication of the Solow model is that, along a balanced growth path, the growth rate of output does not depend on the saving rate. To see this, first note that Equation 4–2 can be rewritten as

$$K/Y = s/n. \qquad (4\text{--}4)$$

Suppose the saving rate increases. Then $s/n > K/Y$ and, according to the stability argument, capital grows faster than labor and the capital-output ratio rises until the economy returns to the balanced growth path. While the long-term growth rate does not change, there is a transition period in which output growth exceeds the balanced growth rate, and so the level of output rises because of the increase in saving. A higher population growth rate lowers the GDP per capital in the Solow growth model, but it does not permanently lower the growth rate.

SELF-TEST

Fill in the Blank

1. The _____ model is designed to explain the path of potential GDP.

2. A convenient rule of thumb, _____, is that a country which is growing at g percent annually doubles its GDP per capita approximately every $70/g$ years.

3. The _____ shows how much output can be made from given amounts of labor, capital, and technology.

4. The additional output that is produced by one additional unit of work is the _____.

5. The two effects of higher real wages on labor supply are the _____ effect and the _____ effect.

6. The _____ is the amount of unemployment when output is equal to potential GDP.

7. A measure of overall productivity is _____ productivity.

8. The three sources of economic growth are growth in _____, _____, and _____.

9. Along the _____, output per worker is constant.

10. _____ occurs in economies when fertility rates decline as income rises.

11. The volume of employment at the intersection of the supply of labor and demand for labor schedules is called _____ employment.

12. The amount of output produced at full employment is called _____ GDP.

13. A _____ is a steady-state growth path, where the growth rates of capital and labor are balanced.

True-False

14. An economy in which wages and prices are perfectly flexible is always exactly at full employment.

15. Higher real wages unambiguously increase the supply of labor.

16. With perfectly flexible prices and wages, the level of output in any one year is determined solely by the labor market.

17. Unemployment is zero when the labor market is in equilibrium.

18. The Malthusian model accurately characterizes long-run economic growth.

19. The Industrial Revolution increased the pace of population growth.

20. Not all countries have yet gone through the demographic transition.

21. The economy is on a balanced growth path if the growth rate of capital equals the growth rate of labor.

22. Solow's condition for balanced growth is that net saving equals net spending.

23. According to the Solow growth model, the economy always moves toward the steady-state point.

24. The Solow model implies that, along a balanced growth path, increasing the saving rate increases the output growth rate.

25. In contrast to the Malthusian model, the Solow growth model can explain economic growth.

26. The economy tends toward the steady state.

Review Questions

27. What determines output in the long-run growth model?

28. Why is the demand for labor a negative function of the real wage?

29. Describe the empirical evidence regarding the effect of the real wage on labor supply?

30. Was Malthus correct?

31. What is the effect of a higher rate of savings on growth?

32. What is the transition period?

33. What are the most important results of the Solow growth model?

34. What happens if the population rate increases in the Solow growth model?

PROBLEM SET

Worked Problems

1. Consider the following long-run growth model:

$$N = 800 + 20(W/P) \quad \text{(Labor supply)}$$
$$N = 2{,}000 - 10(W/P) \quad \text{(Labor demand)}$$
$$Y = 125\sqrt{\bar{N}} \quad \text{(Production function)}$$

   a. What is the level of employment N and the real wage W/P?

   b. What is the level of output Y?

   a. *We first use the labor supply and demand schedules to solve for the real wage:*

$$800 + 20(W/P) = 2{,}000 - 10(W/P)$$
$$30(W/P) = 1{,}200$$
$$(W/P) = 40$$

We then substitute the value for the real wage back into either the labor supply or the labor demand schedule to solve for employment:

$$N = 800 + 20(40) = 1,600$$
$$N = 2,000 - 10(40) = 1,600$$

b. We solve for output using the production function:

$$Y = 125\sqrt{1,600} = 125(40) = 5,000.$$

2. Consider the Solow growth model:

$K = \$2,000$ billion   (Capital stock)
$Y = \$1,000$ billion   (Output)
$n = .02$ (2 percent)   (Labor force growth)

a. What is the saving rate s along a balanced growth path?

b. Suppose that $n = .03$. What is the saving rate s along a balanced growth path?

a. *Along a balanced growth path, sY = nK, so the saving rate s = nK/Y = (.02)2,000/1,000 = .04 (4 percent).*

b. *Along a balanced growth path, s = nK/Y = (.03)2,000/1,000 = .06 (6 percent).*

3. Suppose that GDP per capita is $25,000 in the year 2000, $40,000 in 2015, and the growth rate is constant. What is the annual growth rate?

According to the rule of 70, the growth rate g is

$$g = (40,000/25,000)^{1/15} - 1$$
$$g = 1.0318 - 1 = .0318 \ (3.18 \ percent).$$

Review Problems

4. Consider the following long-run growth model:

$N = 300 + 20(W/P)$ (Labor supply)
$N = 1,500 - 20(W/P)$ (Labor demand)
$Y = 100\sqrt{N}$ (Production function)

a. What is the level of employment N and the real wage W/P?

b. What is the level of output Y?

5. Consider the following long-run growth model:

$N = 525 + 20(W/P)$ (Labor supply)
$N = 1,575 - 10(W/P)$ (Labor demand)
$Y = 100\sqrt{N}$ (Production function)

   a. What is the level of employment N and the real wage W/P?

   b. What is the level of output Y?

6. Consider the Solow growth model:

K = $6,000 billion	(Capital stock)
Y = $2,000 billion	(Output)
s = .03 (3 percent)	(Saving rate)

   a. What is the labor force growth rate n along a balanced growth path?

   b. Suppose that the saving rate rises to .06 (6 percent). What happens to the growth rate of output and the capital-output ratio?

7. Consider the Solow growth model:

K = $4,000 billion	(Capital stock)
Y = $3,000 billion	(Output)
s = .04 (4 percent)	(Saving rate)
g = .01 (1 percent)	(Technology growth)

   a. What is the labor force growth rate n along a balanced growth path?

   b. Suppose that the saving rate falls to .03 (3 percent). What happens to the growth rate of output and the capital-output ratio?

8. Suppose that GDP per capita is $30,000 in the year 2004 and $35,000 in 2014 and the growth rate is constant. What is the annual growth rate?

9. How many years would it take for income to double if the growth rate is 3 percent? 2 percent? 1 percent?

GRAPH IT

1. a. Go back to Problem 1 and draw a diagram showing the labor demand and labor supply schedules.

   b. Graph the production function. Does the production function exhibit diminishing marginal product of labor?

2. Draw a Solow growth analysis figure similar to that in the text's Figure 4.11.

   a. Label on the graph a Point A to represent an economy that starts with less capital per worker compared to the steady-state equilibrium. Explain the transition to the steady state.

   b. Label on the graph a Point B to represent an economy that starts with more capital per worker compared to the steady-state equilibrium. Explain the transition to the steady state.

ANSWERS TO THE SELF-TEST

1. Long-run growth
2. Rule of 70
3. Production function
4. Marginal product of labor
5. Substitution and income
6. Natural rate of unemployment
7. Total factor
8. Labor, capital, and technology
9. Subsistence line
10. Demographic transition
11. Full
12. Potential
13. Balanced growth path
14. True. Wages and prices can adjust instantaneously to offset the effect of disturbances.
15. False. The supply of labor increases because of the substitution effect but decreases because of the income effect.
16. True. With technology and the stock of capital predetermined, the level of output in any one year depends only on employment, which is determined in the labor market.
17. False. It is equal to the natural rate.
18. False. Although Malthusian stagnation characterized most of history, the model proved to be a spectacular failure of predicting growth over the last two centuries.
19. False. It increased the pace of technological process.
20. True. The demographic transition has yet to occur in many African and Asian countries, where birth rates remain high and growth is stagnant.
21. True. Along a balanced growth path, capital and labor growth rates are equal.
22. False. Solow's condition for balanced growth is that net savings equals balanced growth investment.
23. True. The balanced growth path is stable.
24. False. According to the Solow model, the growth rate of output does not depend on the saving rate.
25. True. The engine of growth in per capita GDP is technological progress.
26. True. If the economy starts at a steady rate, it stays there.
27. Output in the long-run growth model is determined by the capital stock, technology, and employment.
28. The demand for labor is a negative function of the real wage because the marginal product of labor declines with increased labor input.

29. Research indicates that the substitution and income effects offset each other, making the net effect approximately zero.
30. Malthus's theory predicts constant per-capita GDP in the long run. Prior to 1800, the theory works well, but the evidence after 1800 is dramatically different. The Industrial Revolution increased the pace of technological progress. Fertility rates also increased so per-capita GDP grew slowly at first. The demographic transition, in which fertility rates decreased in Western Europe, combined with rising technological progress, increased economic growth sharply.
31. In the longer run, the growth rate does not depend on the saving rate. A higher saving rate raises GDP in Solow's analysis, but it does not permanently raise the growth rate.
32. If the economy increases its saving rate, then real output increases. There then is a transition period, during which the growth rate of the economy is greater than the balanced growth rate. The growth rates in the old and new balanced growth paths are the same.
33. The most important implications of the Solow growth model are that the balanced growth path is stable and that the growth rate of output does not depend on the saving rate.
34. A higher population growth rate violates the balanced growth condition in $K/Y > s/n$. The growth rate of the economy during this transition period is less than balanced growth. After the transition period, the growth rate of the economy returns to the balanced growth rate. It lowers the level of GDP per capita, but it does not permanently lower the growth rate.

SOLUTIONS TO REVIEW PROBLEMS

4. a. The real wage $W/P = 30$.
      Full employment $N = 900$.
   b. Output $Y = 3,000$.
5. a. The real wage $W/P = 35$.
      Full employment $N = 1,225$.
   b. Output $Y = 3,500$.
6. a. The labor force growth rate $n = .01$ (1 percent).
   b. Long-term output growth is unchanged. The capital-output ratio K/Y rises to 8.
7. a. The labor force growth rate $n = .02$ (2 percent).
   b. Long-term output growth is unchanged. The capital-output ratio K/Y falls to 1.
8. $g = (35,000/30,000)^{1/10} - 1 = .0155$ (1.55 percent).
9. Years to double $= 70/3 = 23.3$ years; $70/2 = 35$ years; $70/1 = 70$ years.

ANSWERS TO GRAPH IT

1. a.

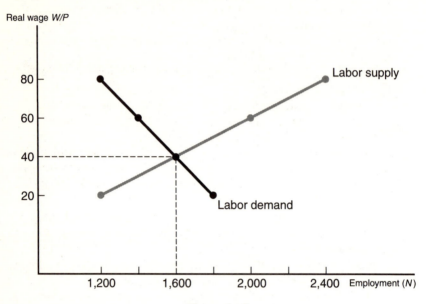

Figure 4–4

b.

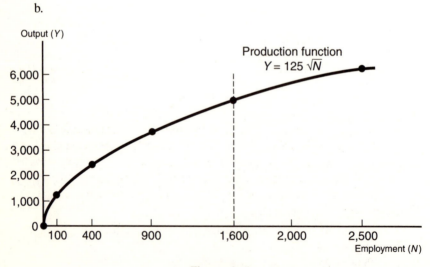

Figure 4–5

N	$Y = 125\sqrt{N}$
100	1,250
400	2,500
900	3,750
1,600	5,000
2,500	6,250

Yes, the production function exhibits a diminishing marginal product of labor.

2.

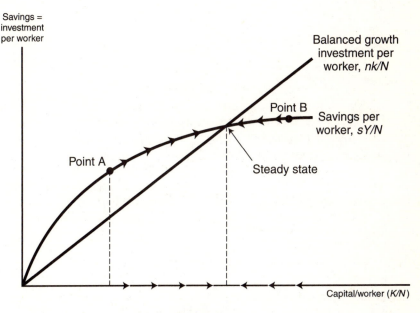

Figure 4–6

Savings per worker, and thus actual investment, exceeds the amount needed to keep the capital per worker constant. Each year, capital per worker increases. The economy gradually approaches the steady-state point. If the economy starts with more capital per worker than the steady-state amount, capital per worker declines each year and the economy approaches the steady state.

CHAPTER 5 | Technology and Economic Growth

MAIN OBJECTIVES

In this chapter, we expand the Solow neoclassical growth model to better incorporate the impact of technology on economic growth. We look at sources of growth and the importance of technology. The Solow model treats technology as exogenous, or determined outside the model. We then consider endogenous growth theory models, where technological change is determined within the model itself. Last, we look at the long-run growth experience of the United States economy and examine productivity growth and the new economy.

KEY TERMS AND CONCEPTS

The **growth accounting formula** provides a framework, which can be used whether or not the economy is in balanced growth, to determine the contributions, of labor, capital, and technology to economic growth. In its simplest form, the formula says that the rate of growth of output equals technology growth plus the weighted rates of growth of labor and capital:

$$\Delta Y/Y = \Delta A/A + .7\Delta N/N + .3\Delta K/K, \qquad (5\text{--}1)$$

where .7 is the share of labor and .3 is the share of capital in national income.

To see how the growth accounting formula helps explain the contribution of technology growth to economic growth, suppose that both labor and capital are growing by 2 percent per year. According to Equation 5–1, output growth is also 2 percent per year. With labor, capital, and output growing at the same rate, output per worker (Y/N) does not change. If, in addition, technology is growing by 2 percent per year, output growth is 4 percent per year. With technology improving, output per worker (*Y/N*) increases even though capital per worker (*K/N*) remains constant.

Endogenous growth theory attempts to provide an explicit theory of technology (*A*). In the neoclassical growth model and the growth accounting formula just described, technological change is **exogenous**, not explained by the model. With endogenous growth theory, technological change is **endogenous**, explained by forces within the model.

A **production function for technology**,

$$\Delta A = T(N_A, K_A, A),\tag{5-2}$$

says that the increase in technology ΔA depends on the amount of labor producing technology N_A, the amount of capital producing technology K_A, and the existing stock of technology A. Because Equation 5–2 shows how labor, capital, and existing technology contribute toward producing new technology, technological change is endogenous.

Technology, as it is used in the production of other technology, is an example of **nonrivalry** (one person's use of the technology does not diminish another person's use of the same technology) and **partial excludability** (the inventor or owner of the technology cannot completely prevent other people from using it). Technology as a good, then, is inherently different from other economic goods, because the same idea can be used over and over again and one firm cannot exclude another firm from using it.

In the neoclassical growth model, because of diminishing returns to labor and capital, economic policy can increase the growth rate only during a transition period. According to endogenous growth theory, if technology production does not have diminishing returns, economic policy that devotes more resources to improving technology increases the growth rate of output in the long run.

Policies to stimulate growth can be directed toward technology growth, capital formation, or labor input. Policies to increase technology growth include tax incentives to encourage research and development. Investment tax credits give firms tax breaks for investment. They are an example of policies to stimulate capital formation. The investment tax credit appears to increase output growth for a few years, after which investment declines to more normal levels.

Policies to increase labor supply have focused on tax cuts and tax reform. Tax cuts, such as President Reagan's 1981 tax cut, have both substitution and income effects. If, as the evidence suggests, the labor supply schedule is steep, the effect on the labor supply of tax cuts is quite small. Tax reforms keep revenue the same, although tax rates are cut, and do not have income effects. The labor supply schedule should shift by the full amount of the substitution effect, and the impact on the growth of output is potentially quite substantial.

The central insight of endogenous growth theory is to explain technological change through a production function for technology (endogenous) rather than leave it unexplained as in the Solow model (exogenous). Endogenous growth theory models, then, allow for the possibility of using government policy to produce permanent changes in long-run growth. However, the evidence for the United States seems to be broadly consistent with the constant long-run growth predictions of the Solow neoclassical model, therefore we observe a **neoclassical growth revival**. Moreover, there appears to be no evidence of **scale effects**, where an increase in the amount of labor producing the technology raises the growth rate of technology and thus the growth rate of output.

The **real wage** is the nominal wage divided by the price level. The real wage is neither procyclical nor countercyclical; it does not fluctuate in a systematic way during recessions or booms. **Productivity** is the amount of output per unit of input. When economists talk about productivity, they generally mean **labor productivity**, output per hour of labor. A broader measure, **total factor productivity**, is output per generalized unit of input. Productivity is procyclical, rising during booms and falling in recessions. Both real wage growth and productivity growth have been lower since the early 1970s than they were in the 1960s. At the end of the 1990s, both productivity growth and real wage growth returned to their 1960s' levels.

The post-1995 acceleration in productivity growth (output per labor hour) coincided with what was popularly called the *New Economy*, because it was dominated by high-technology industries. Productivity growth can be divided into **capital deepening** (growth of capital per hour of labor), **labor quality** (improvements in the measurable skills of workers), and technological change or total factor productivity. The largest source of the post-1995 productivity increase is due to total factor productivity (TFP), but the ability to identify the separate contributing effects of TFP growth in computer-producing industries compared to TFP in other industries is difficult.

SELF-TEST

Fill in the Blank

1. The _____ shows the contributions of labor, capital, and technology to economic growth.

2. _____ attempts to provide an explicit theory of technology.

3. If a variable is _____, then it is determined outside of the model; if a variable is _____, then it is determined within the model.

4. The _____ is the nominal wage divided by the price level.

5. _____ is the broader measure of productivity, which is output per generalized unit of output.

6. Productivity is _____, rising during booms and falling during recessions.

7. When the inventor of a technology cannot completely prevent other people from using it, we say that technology is _____.

8. The technology production function does not exhibit _____ in that an increase to technology increases the growth rate of output in the long run.

9. Policies to increase labor supply have focused on tax _____ and tax _____.

10. Tax _____ keeps revenue neutral.

11. Policies directed toward growth can be directed toward _____ formation, _____ input, and improving _____.

12. _____ occur when an increase in the amount of labor producing the technology raises the growth rate of technology and thus the growth rate of output.

13. Neither _____ nor _____ appear to explain the post-1995 acceleration in productivity growth.

True-False

14. Within the growth accounting formula, the labor share is usually smaller than the capital share in national income.

15. With labor, capital, and output growing at the same rate, output per worker does not change.

16. According to the growth accounting formula, output growth is completely determined by growth of labor and capital.

17. Productivity is the amount of output per unit time.

18. If technology is a nonrival good, then one person's use precludes another person from enjoying the good.

19. Tax cuts unambiguously increase the supply of labor.

20. The neoclassical growth revival describes the renewed interest in the Solow growth model.

21. Real wage growth has increased since the 1970s.

22. There appears to be no evidence of scale effects in the United States data.

23. Endogenous growth theory attempts to explain growth in capital and labor.

24. Total factor productivity in the computer industry relative to other industries is easy to identify.

Review Questions

25. What is the different between the Solow growth model and the endogenous growth model?

26. What determines output in the long-run growth model?

27. What types of policies can the government use to stimulate economic growth?

28. Why can a tax cut and a tax reform have different effects on labor supply?

29. According to the growth accounting formula, what determines output growth?

30. What are the most important results of the Solow growth model?

31. What does it mean to describe technological change as exogenous?

32. What is a production function for technology?

33. According to endogenous growth theory, how can economic policy increase the growth rate of output in the long run?

34. What has happened to productivity growth since the early 1970s?

PROBLEM SET

Worked Problems

1. a. Suppose that the growth rate of technology is 5 percent, the growth rate of employment is 8 percent, and the growth rate of capital is 4 percent. What is the growth rate of real output?

   b. If the growth rate of technology increases by 2 percentage points, what happens to the growth rate of real output?

   a. *According to Equation 5–1 in the Study Guide, the growth rate of real output equals the growth rate of technology plus the weighted growth rates of labor and capital:*

$$\Delta Y/Y = .05 + .7(.08) + .3(.04)$$
$$= .118 \ (11.8 \ percent).$$

   b. *The growth rate of real output will also increase by 2 percentage points to 13.8 percent.*

Review Problems

2. a. Suppose that the growth rate of technology is 5 percent, the growth rate of employment is 4 percent, and the growth rate of capital is 3 percent. What is the growth rate of real output?

   b. If the growth rate of employment increases by 2 percentage points, what happens to the growth rate of real output?

3. a. Suppose that the growth rate of technology is 3 percent, the growth rate of employment is 6 percent, and the growth rate of capital is 6 percent. What is the growth rate of real output?

   b. If the growth rate of capital increases by 3 percentage points, what happens to the growth rate of real output?

ANSWERS TO THE SELF-TEST

1. Growth accounting formula
2. Endogenous growth theory
3. Exogenous; endogenous
4. Real wage
5. Total factor productivity
6. Procyclical
7. Partially excludable
8. Diminishing returns
9. Cuts; reform
10. Reform
11. Capital, labor, technology
12. Scale effects
13. Capital deepening, labor quality
14. False. Typically labor share is .7 and capital share is.3.
15. True. If technology improves, though, output per worker increases.
16. False. Technology also contributes to output growth.
17. False. Productivity is the amount of output per unit of *input*. Generally, economists mean labor productivity here, output per hour of labor.
18. False. Nonrivalry means that a good can be used over and over again or at the same time by one person without diminishing another person's enjoyment of the good.
19. False. Tax cuts have both substitution and income effects.
20. True. The United States' evidence broadly confirms what Solow's growth model predicts.

21. False. Real wage growth has slowed down since the early 1970s but returned to 1960s' levels at the end of the 1990s.
22. True. Scale effects exist where an increase in the amount of labor producing the technology raises the growth rate of technology and thus the growth rate of output.
23. False. Endogenous growth theory attempts to explain growth in technology.
24. False. This uncertainty limits our ability to qauntify the sources of the post-1995 productivity acceleration.
25. Endogenous growth theory attempts to provide an explicit theory of technology whereas the Solow growth model treats technology as exogenous.
26. Output in the long-run growth model is determined by the capital stock, technology, and employment.
27. The government can use policies designed to increase technology and productivity, capital formation, or labor input.
28. A tax cut has both substitution and income effects, while a revenue-neutral tax reform has only substitution effects.
29. The growth accounting formula says that the rate of growth of output equals the rate of growth of technology plus the weighted rates of growth of labor and capital.
30. The most important implications of the Solow growth model are that the balanced growth path is stable and that the growth rate of output does not depend on the saving rate.
31. If technological change is exogenous, it is not explained by the model.
32. A production function for technology describes how the increase in technology depends on the amount of labor producing technology, the amount of capital producing technology, and the existing technology.
33. If technology production does not have diminishing returns, economic policy that devotes more resources to improving technology increases the growth rate of output in the long run.
34. Productivity growth has decreased since the early 1970s but increased in the late 1990s back to 1960s' levels.

SOLUTIONS TO REVIEW PROBLEMS

2. a. The growth rate of real output $\Delta Y/Y = 8.7$ percent.
   b. $\Delta Y/Y$ increases to 10.1 percent.
3. a. $\Delta Y/Y = 9$ percent.
   b. $\Delta Y/Y$ increases to 9.9 percent.

CHAPTER 6 | Growth and the World Economy

MAIN OBJECTIVES

Long-run growth is the single most important determinant of a country's economic well-being. But the greater good of studying economic growth is to both understand and remedy the gap between rich and poor countries. While income inequality has narrowed among industrialized countries, especially among those countries that reduced barriers to trade, the evidence does not extend to the world as a whole.

We develop the augmented Solow growth model to show how it provides a better explanation of the cross-country variation in per-capita income, the speed of conditional convergence, and the difference in capital per worker ratios between rich and poor countries. We study the role of geography and institutions in creating the gap and how the understanding of incentives can help close the gap.

KEY TERMS AND CONCEPTS

The Solow neoclassical growth model of Chapter 4 predicts that, if all countries have the same access to technology and the same production function, then those countries that start out poor should grow faster than those countries that start out rich. The narrowing of the per-capita income gap between rich and poor countries over time is referred to as the **convergence hypothesis**.

Recall from Chapter 4 the production function in the Solow growth model,

$$Y/N = F(K/N, 1, A), \tag{6-1}$$

where output per worker, *Y/N*, is determined by capital per worker, *K/N*, and technology, *A*. If all countries have the same production function and access to technology, then countries with low levels of capital per worker have low levels of income per worker. Since income and capital per worker are closely related to income and capital per person, countries with lower levels of capital per worker are poorer than countries with higher levels of capital per worker.

This situation is not sustainable because the rate of return on capital will be higher for the country with lower levels of capital per worker. Over time, the initially poor country saves more, accumulates capital faster, and grows faster than the initially rich country. Since the two countries are moving toward the same steady state, their incomes per capita converge.

Figure 6–1 depicts two countries with the same production function and access to technology but differing levels of capital per worker. Country A is assumed to be at the steady-state point, where savings is just sufficient to keep capital per worker constant. Country A grows by the exogenous growth rate of technology. Country B starts out with lower income per capita than Country A. Over time, Country B's capital per worker increases relative to Country A. Along the transition path, Country B grows faster than Country A until the per-capita incomes are the same. In this case, the steady-state point is reached and the gap is eliminated; the initially poorer country is said to **catch up** to the initially richer country.

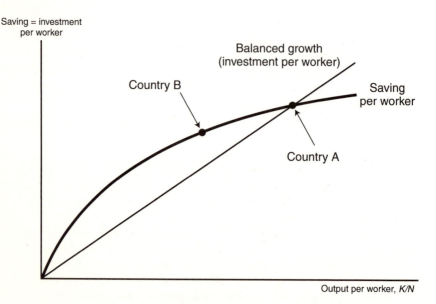

Figure 6–1

The **convergence hypothesis** of the Solow model can be tested using the following equation:

$$\Delta(Y/N)/(Y/N) = a + c(Y/N)(1960), \qquad (6\text{--}2)$$

where $\Delta(Y/N)/(Y/N)$ is the annual growth rate of GDP per capita, $(Y/N)(1960)$ is the initial level of GDP per capita, and a and c are coefficients. Since the convergence hypothesis implies that the growth rate of GDP per capita should be negatively related to the initial level of the GDP per capita, the estimated coefficient c should be negative. For post-1960 data there is strong evidence of convergence among industrial countries, but the evidence does not extend to the world as a whole. When we examine longer spans of data, the picture is actually one of **divergence**, not convergence. Those countries that were relatively poor in 1900 have grown more slowly than those countries that were relatively rich in 1900. **Income inequality**, the gap between rich and poor, has increased in the last century.

Another prediction of the neoclassical Solow growth model is constant steady-state growth. We test the **constant steady-state growth hypothesis** by comparing growth rates before and after a **break date**, that date where the years prior were ones of fairly steady growth rates. While the steady-state growth hypothesis holds for Canada and the United States, it does not generally hold for other advanced countries. These latter countries exhibit the largest changes in long-run growth because they are the ones most affected by world wars. The ratio of their postwar transition period to their prebreak growth rates is higher than countries that reflect constant steady-state growth. This result is logical, given that world wars are about the most exogenous event possible. We conclude that we have to be careful about assuming a country exhibits steady-state growth across time.

We also need to be careful about assuming common steady-state growth across countries. The key assumption for the convergence hypothesis is that the two countries are moving toward the same steady state. If two countries have the same steady state (as in Figure 6–1), then their incomes should converge. But suppose the two countries have different steady states. **Conditional convergence** is the hypothesis that income per capita in a given country, converges to *that country's* steady-state value.

One way this could occur would be if one country increases its savings rate s. That country would experience increased growth during a transition period, an increased steady-state *level* of income, but an unchanged steady-state *growth rate*. Another way this could occur would be if labor force growth rates, n, differ. If n increases, the per-capita income growth decreases in the transition period, decreasing the steady-state *level* of per-capita income but leaving the steady-state *rate of growth* of income per capita unchanged. What we conclude is that the steady-state growth rate of per-capita income depends on technological growth, but the level of per-capita income depends on the saving rates and the labor force growth rates.

Figure 6–2 illustrates conditional convergence. Country A and Country B start on the same balanced growth path. If Country A increases its savings rate at time t, it has a higher growth rate along the transition path. Once the new steady state for Country A is reached, the two countries end up on the same steady-state growth rate, but income per capita is higher in Country A than Country B.

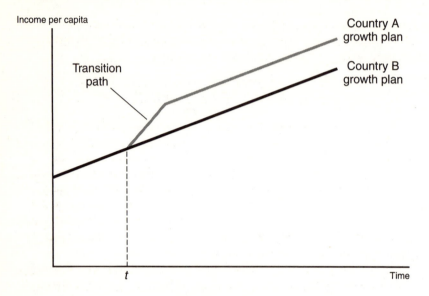

Figure 6–2

Evidence of convergence for the world as a whole is for conditional convergence. The Solow growth model predicts convergence among countries with the same saving rates and population growth rates. This can explain why convergence (without controlling for the determinants of the steady-state) occurs among advanced countries but not for the world as a whole. Saving and population growth rates are much more similar among advanced countries than between advanced and developing countries. Countries move toward their own steady states, but the gap between rich and poor countries does not narrow.

As it stands, the Solow model developed thus far still suffers from the following problems. First, differences in per-capita income between rich and poor countries are too large to be explained by the Solow model. Second, the speed of convergence predicted by the Solow model is twice the rate we actually observe. Third, the model predicts very large differences in rates of return to investment between rich and poor countries. The **augmented Solow model** focuses on both **physical capital** (equipment, structures, and other productive facilities) and **human capital** (schooling and on-the-job training). Accumulating capital, whether by purchasing equipment or attending school, is to forgo current income to receive a higher income in the future. The production function is stated as

$$Y = F(K, H, N, L) = K^{1/3}H^{1/3}N^{1/3}A, \qquad (6\text{--}3)$$

where K is physical capital, H is human capital, L is labor, and A is technology. Divide through by N to get

$$Y/N = (K/N)^{1/3}(H/N)^{1/3}A. \tag{6–4}$$

By incorporating human capital, the augmented Solow model provides a better explanation of the cross-country variation in income per capita. We test for conditional convergence with the following equation:

$$\Delta(Y/N)/(Y/N) = a + c(Y/N)(1960 + \text{(saving rates, population}$$
growth rates, and human capital accumulation). $\tag{6–5}$

When human capital accumulation is included, in addition to savings and population growth rates, the coefficient c becomes more negative. This implies a faster rate of convergence than the previous model, without human capital accumulation. Countries with low GDP per capita in the initial year grow faster than countries with high GDP in the initial year of 1960. Last, the share of physical and human capital in the augmented Solow model is greater than the share of capital in the original Solow model. This helps explain why the difference in capital per worker between rich and poor countries is not as large as would be predicted by the Solow model.

Equations such as Equation 6–5 are called **cross-country growth regressions**, in that variations in saving rates, population growth rates, and other variables are used to explain variation of growth rates across countries. We can also examine the levels of income across countries by considering the following equation:

$$Y/N = a + \text{(saving rates, population growth rates, and other variables).} \tag{6–6}$$

These equations are called **cross-country level regressions**. Variables that enter cross-country growth regressions are used to explain variation of levels of income per capita across countries.

What variables consistently help explain differences in growth rates of income per capital among countries in cross-country growth regressions and differences in levels of income per capita among countries in cross-level regressions? Savings rates, openness to trade, and measures of human capital positively affect growth. Population growth rates, market distortions (such as large underground economy premiums and real exchange rate distortions), and the fraction of primary products in total exports negatively affect growth. The fraction of GDP in mining positively affects growth. Political variables also matter. Rule of law, political rights, and civil liberties positively affect growth while revolutions, military coups, and wars negatively affect growth.

Absolute latitude, or the **distance from the equator**, is another variable positively related to growth. Countries located far from the equator are relatively rich while countries located close to the equator are relatively poor. To what extent geography affects growth directly or indirectly through **social infrastructure** is the subject of recent research. A country's social infrastructure is the institutions and government policies that determine the economic environment within which individuals accumulate skills and firms accumulate capital and produce output.

The **geography hypothesis** is that most of the differences in income per capita can be explained by geographic, climatic, and ecological differences across countries. **Tropical regions** (regions centered near the equator) were poorer than **temperate regions** (regions north or south of the tropics) in the early 1800s due to differences in soil formation and erosion, pests and infectious diseases, water availability, food production, and endowments of energy sources.

Something more than this is needed to explain why tropical regions have grown at a slower rate than temperate regions since the early 1800s. At first pass, we might explain the difference in growth rates by observing that technological innovation has been much higher in temperate climates than in tropical regions throughout the nineteenth and twentieth centuries, but this would be ignoring **technological diffusion**. When countries create technological innovation, it spreads to noninnovating countries, which can then spread economic growth. However, the **ecological divide**, differences in ecological conditions between geographic types of countries, seems to limit the degree to which technological innovations can spread.

The **institutions hypothesis** states that differences in economic performance are caused by the organization of society. Here, geography influences growth through differences in institutions and social infrastructure among countries. Differences in social infrastructure can explain much of the variation of levels of income per capita across countries beyond what differences can be accounted for by physical and human capital.

Among regions colonized by European powers, there has been a **reversal of fortune**. When we use population density and degree of urbanization data as proxies for income per capita, regions that were relatively rich in 1500 are now relatively poor. Regions that were more densely populated in 1500 are now poorer than regions that were more sparsely populated.

This reversal of fortune can be explained by **institutional reversal**. Regions that were densely populated and relatively rich, such as most of Africa and Latin America, were more likely to become *extractive states*. Since these colonies were ones in which the colonizer extracted the colony's resources, the settlers did not create institutions to protect private property or provide limits to government expropriation. According to the institution hypothesis, these early institutions (or lack thereof) persisted and have an important effect on institutions today. Alternatively, settlers of sparsely populated colonies, such as the United States, Australia, and Canada, were more likely to replicate European institutions and create *neo-Europes* with institutions that promoted economic growth, such as protection of private property and checks against government expropriation. The spread of industrial technology in the nineteenth century favored neo-European societies, because they could better take advantage of growth opportunities.

SELF-TEST

Fill in the Blank

1. The _____ of the Solow neoclassical growth model states that, over time, gaps in per-capita income among countries narrow.

2. Poor countries should _____ to rich countries if they possess similar production functions and technology.

3. The convergence hypothesis implies a _____ relation between the beginning level of per-capita GDP and the growth of per-capita GDP.

4. Income inequality, the gap between rich and poor, has _____ in the last century for the world as a whole.

5. The neoclassical Solow growth model also predicts that countries should follow a _____ steady-state growth path.

6. _____ implies a negative relation between beginning levels of per-capita income and subsequent growth rates after the effects of different saving rates and population growth rates have been controlled for.

7. Just as endogenous growth theory focuses on human capital, so too does the _____ Solow growth model.

8. _____ are equations that use variations in saving rates, population growth rates, and other variables to explain variations in growth rates across countries.

9. One of the clearest patterns of cross-country growth across countries is the relation between _____, measured by latitude, and income per capita.

10. Institutions and government policies that determine the economic environment within which individuals accumulate skills and firms accumulate capital and produce output is referred to as the _____.

11. Tropical regions and temperate regions are separated by a _____ in which differences in ecological conditions limit the scope of technical diffusion.

12. The _____ hypothesis states that the differences in economic performance are caused by the organization of society.

True-False

13. Long-run growth is the single biggest determinant to a country's standard of living.

14. Poor countries, on the whole, are catching up to rich countries and narrowing the income gap.

15. The Solow growth model's prediction that poor countries should catch up to rich countries is accurately borne out in the data.

16. A key assumption of the Solow growth model is that countries move toward the same steady state.

17. Allowing countries to be in different steady states helps in understanding the nature of convergence and eliminates all the problems of the Solow growth model.

18. Physical capital is defined as equipment, machines, and other productive facilities.

19. Human capital is straightforward to measure.

20. The augmented Solow model provides a better explanation of the cross-country variation in per-capita income.

21. Savings rates, openness to trade, and measure of capital positively affect growth.

22. Distance from the equator is highly related to income per capita, where countries close to the equator are relatively poor and countries far away are relatively rich.

23. Institutional reversal is the idea that European colonization contributed to a reversal of fortune for countries colonized by Western Europe.

Review Questions

24. What does the Solow growth model predict?

25. What are the assumptions of the Solow growth model?

26. Describe what happened with per-capita income growth rates among the world as a whole.

27. What is the difference between convergence and conditional convergence?

28. What is the break date?

29. What contribution does the augmented Solow model provide to the existing body of research on long-run growth theory?

30. How is human capital like physical capital?

31. What do cross-country growth regressions do?

32. Why is distance from the equator important in explaining per-capita income growth?

33. Compare and contrast the geography hypothesis and the institutions hypothesis.

34. Describe social infrastructure.

35. What variables explain positive levels of per-capita income growth in cross-country growth regressions?

36. Why is debt forgiveness an important policy to study?

PROBLEM SET

Worked Problems

1. Suppose that the production function for both Mexico and the United States is $Y/N = A(K/N)^{1/2}$. If capital per worker, K/N, is $1 million in the United States, technology $A = 10$ for both countries, and output per worker, Y/N, is five times larger in the United States than in Mexico, what is the capital per worker, K/N, in Mexico?

5 × Y/N in Mexico   *= Y/N in United States*
$5 \times A(K/N^{Mexico})^{1/2}$ $= A(K/N^{United\ States})^{1/2}$
$5 \times 10(K/N^{Mexico})^{1/2}$ $= 10(\$1,000,000)^{1/2}$
$(K/N^{Mexico})^{1/2}$ $= \$1,000/5 = \$200$
K/N^{Mexico} $= \$200^2 = \$40,000$ *per worker*

2. Suppose that the average share of physical and human capital in India and the United States is .80, so that the production function is $Y = K^{.8}N^{.2}A$, where K denotes both physical and human capital. If income per worker Y/N is 15 times larger in the United States than in India, what is the physical and human capital per worker, K/N, if the two countries have the same technology?

Divide the production function by N to get

$$Y/N = A(K/N)^{.8}$$

The United States' share is 15 times larger than that of India:

15 × Y/N in India = Y/N in United States
$15 \times A(K/N^{India})^{.8} = A(K/N^{United\ States})^{.8}$
$15\ (K/N^{India})^{.8}$ $= (K/N^{United\ States})^{.8}$
15 $= [(K/N^{United\ States})/(K/N^{India})]^{.8}$
$15^{1/.8}$ $= (K/N^{United\ States})/(K/N^{India})$
29.5 $= (K/N^{United\ States})/(K/N^{India})$

The United States has almost 30 times the physical and human capital per worker of India.

Review Problems

3. Suppose that the production function for both Mexico and the United States is $Y/N = A(K/N)^{.8}$. If capital per worker, K/N, is $1 million in the United States, technology $A = 10$ for both countries, and output per worker, Y/N, is five times larger in the United States than in Mexico, what is the capital per worker, K/N, in Mexico?

4. Suppose that the average share of physical and human capital in India and the United States is .70, so that the production function is $Y = K^{.7}N^{.3}A$, where K denotes both physical and human capital. If income per worker, Y/N, is 10 times larger in the United States than in India, what is the physical and human capital per worker, K/N, if the two countries have the same technology?

GRAPH IT

1. Assume that Country A and Country B are on the same steady-state growth path. What happens when Country A's population growth rate increases? Draw a time-series graph that represents this scenario.

2. Draw two separate time-series graphs. In the first diagram, show two countries demonstrating convergence. In the second diagram, show two countries demonstrating conditional convergence. For each graph, label the countries A and B. Be sure to explain which country is catching up in the first diagram and which country is transitioning in the second diagram.

ANSWERS TO THE SELF-TEST

1. Convergence hypothesis
2. Catch up
3. Negative
4. Increased
5. Constant
6. Conditional convergence
7. Augmented
8. Cross-country growth regressions
9. Distance from the equator
10. Social infrastructure

11. Ecological divide
12. Institutions
13. True.   The slow growth of most of the developing countries over the past 40 years is of great importance to understanding why the gap exists and how to close it.
14. False.   While there is evidence of convergence among advanced countries, the evidence does not extend to the word as a whole.
15. False.   As a result, two strands of research developed in response to these facts: endogenous growth theory (focusing on endogenous technological change) and the neoclassical growth revival.
16. True.   This holds if countries have the same savings and population growth rates.
17. False.   The Solow model still faces problems with differences in income per capita, speeds of conditional convergence, and capital per worker ratios between rich and poor countries.
18. True.
19. False.   Economists use indicators such as secondary school enrollment as a proxy for human capital accumulation.
20. True.   The augmented Solow model also better explains the speed of conditional convergence and the differences in capital per worker ratios between rich and poor than the original Solow model.
21. True.   Cross-country level regressions provide this analysis.
22. True.   Tropical regions have remained poorer than temperate regions since the early 1800s due to the lack of technological diffusion.
23. True.   Densely populated colonies were more likely to be extractive states with bad institutions, whereas sparsely populated colonies were more likely to be neo-European states with good economic institutions.
24. The Solow growth model predicts that countries with less capital per worker will see increased investment in capital until they catch up to countries with higher initial levels of capital per worker. The narrowing of the per-capita income gap between rich and poor countries over time is referred to as convergence.
25. The Solow growth model assumes that all countries have the same access to technology and the same production function.
26. Since 1960, when the vast majority of former colonies achieved independence, income differences between rich and poor nations have not diminished at all. Longer spans of data depict a picture of divergence. Countries that were relatively poor in 1900 have grown more slowly than those relatively rich countries, thereby increasing income inequality in the last century.

27. While two countries with the same saving and labor force growth rates converge or move toward the same steady-state *level* of income per capita (convergence), two countries with different saving and labor force growth rates, once the transition path has passed, grow at the same *rate* but have different steady-state *levels* of income per capita. So while the steady-state *rate* of growth of income per capita depends only on the rate of growth of technological progress, the steady-state *level* of income per capita depends on the saving rate and the labor force growth rate. If you control for differences in saving and labor force growth rates when testing for convergence, you are really testing for conditional convergence.

28. A break date coincides with the timing of an exogenous shock to the economy, such as a war or a stock market collapse. When evaluating the constant steady-state growth hypothesis, economists compare growth rates before and after a break date, omitting the postwar transition period. Wars deplete the capital stock so we expect the capital stock to grow rapidly during a postwar period of rebuilding, which would not coincide with a constant steady-state growth path.

29. The augmented Solow growth model incorporates human capital into the Solow growth model. It provides a better explanation of the cross-country variation in income per capita, the speed of conditional convergence, and the differences in capital per worker ratios between rich and poor countries than the original Solow model.

30. Human capital and physical capital are the same in that, when we devote resources to any type of capital accumulation, we forgo consumption. Why? So that we can produce more income in the future.

31. Cross-country growth regressions explain how variables such as savings rates, population growth rates, market distortions, political variables, and openness to trade affect per-capita growth rates across countries.

32. Distance from the equator, measured by latitude, highlights the role that geography plays, either directly or indirectly, on per-capita income growth. Countries close to the equator have been historically, and remain today, relatively poor when compared to countries far away from the equator.

33. Both hypotheses attempt to explain differences in per-capita income growth. The geography hypothesis posits that differences in per-capita income can be explained by geographic, climatic, and ecological differences across countries. The institutions hypothesis posits that economic performance is determined by the organization of society.

34. Social infrastructure is the institutions and government policies that determine the economic environment within which individuals accumulate skills and firms accumulate capital and produce output. One aspect of

social infrastructure measures a country's degree of openness to the rest of the world. The other aspect of social infrastructure describes the role of government in society (i.e., to what extent law and order exist, bureaucratic quality, corruption, risk of expropriation, and government repudiation of contracts).

35. Savings rates, measures of human capital, rule of law, existence of political rights and civil liberties, openness to trade, and greater distances from the equator are positively related to per-capita income growth.

36. Poor countries use a substantial fraction of their tax revenues to pay interest on their debt. Debt forgiveness would allow these resources to be plowed back into the developing country. However, if the country has a social infrastructure of bad institutions, then debt forgiveness may subsidize irresponsible behavior.

SOLUTIONS TO REVIEW PROBLEMS

3. If the capital per worker of the United States is five times larger than that of Mexico with the same production function:

$5 \times Y/N$ in Mexico $= Y/N$ in United States
$5 \times A(K/N^{Mexico})^{.8} = A(K/N^{United\ States})^{.8}$
$5 \times 10(K/N^{Mexico})^{.8} = 10(\$1,000,000)^{.8}$
$(K/N^{Mexico})^{.8} = \$63,096/5 = \$12,619$
$K/N^{Mexico} = \$12,619/.8 = \$133,748$ per worker.

4. Divide the production function by N to get

$$Y/N = A(K/N)^{.7}$$

Since the income per worker in the United States is 10 times larger than that in India:

$10 \times Y/N$ in India $= Y/N$ in United States
$10 \times A(K/N^{India})^{.7} = A(K/N^{United\ States})^{.7}$
$10(K/N^{India})^{.7} = (K/N^{United\ States})^{.7}$
$10 = [(K/N^{United\ States})/(K/N^{India})]^{.7}$
$26.8 = (K/N^{United\ States})/(K/N^{India})$

The United States has almost 27 times the physical and human capital per worker of India.

ANSWERS TO GRAPH IT

1. Figure 6–3 shows that, if the labor force growth n increases for Country A, the per-capita income growth decreases in the transition period, decreasing the steady-state *level* of per-capita income but leaving the steady-state *rate of growth* of income per capita unchanged.

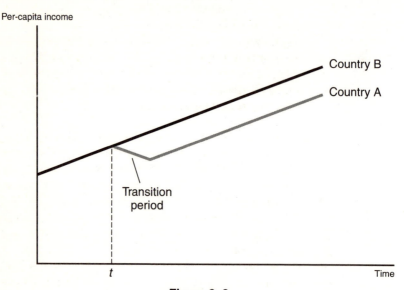

Figure 6–3

2. Figure 6–4 shows two countries converging to the same steady-state level of per-capita income. Here, Country A is catching up to Country B. Figure 6–5 shows two countries demonstrating conditional convergence. Country A is transitioning to a higher level on per-capita income along a parallel growth path to Country B.

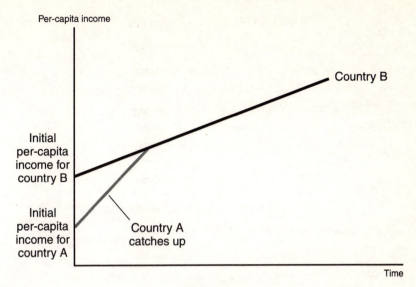

Figure 6–4

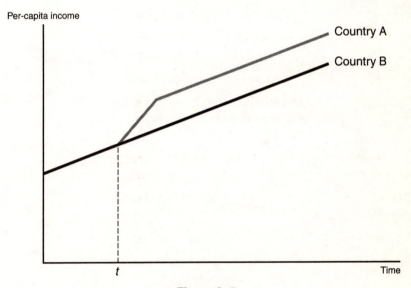

Figure 6–5

Part III

Economic Fluctuations

CHAPTER 7 | Short-Run Fluctuations

MAIN OBJECTIVES

In Chapters 4, 5, and 6, we developed the long-run model to show how potential GDP grows over time. In this chapter and the following two chapters, we shift gears to study fluctuations. We develop the economic fluctuations model by first explaining why changes in spending, or demand, can cause real GDP to depart form its potential growth path. We examine the relationship between spending and income and the concept of spending balance. We ignore for the time being the impact of, among other things, interest rates. You should learn the consumption function and the income identity and know how GDP is determined by combining the two of them through the concept of spending balance. You should also learn how government spending affects GDP through the multiplier and how endogenous net exports affect the analysis of spending balance.

KEY TERMS AND CONCEPTS

Aggregate demand is the total of the spending demands by the various sectors in the economy. These include consumption by households, investment spending by firms, exports by foreigners, and **government spending**. The spending relationships that affect demand add up to the aggregate demand curve.

The **aggregate demand (AD) curve** is illustrated in Figure 7–1, with the price level on the vertical axis and real DGP on the horizontal axis. The aggregate demand curve shows the level of output corresponding to alternative price levels. It will be algebraically derived in Chapter 8. The amount of output generated by the spending process is found at the intersection of the aggregate demand curve and the horizontal line that depicts the existing price level.

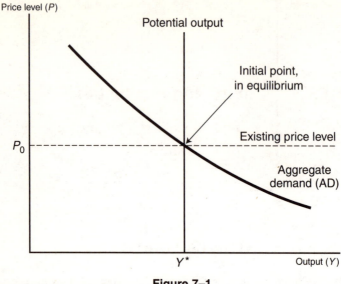

Figure 7–1

Recall that we model prices as unresponsive to current developments; they move only gradually over time.

Shifts of the aggregate demand curve, which can be caused by changes in monetary policy, fiscal policy, consumption, investment, or net exports, cause short-run fluctuations in GDP from its growth path. For example, a leftward shift of the aggregate demand curve is shown in Figure 7–2. Output declines from Y^* to Y' at the existing predetermined price level, P_0.

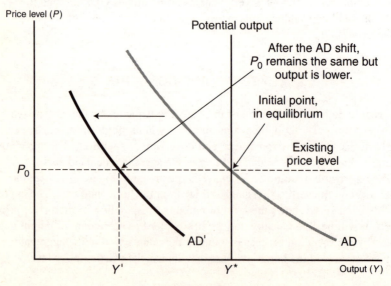

Figure 7–2

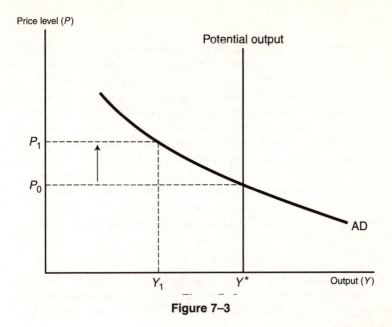

Figure 7–3

Shifts in the price level, such as those caused by changes in the price of oil, also cause fluctuations. In the short run, unemployment can differ from the natural rate and output can be different from potential GDP. A price shock that increases the price level is depicted in Figure 7–3. Output is lower after the price shock that increases prices from P_0 to P_1.

The initial response by firms to changes in demand is to adjust production. Firms normally operate with some excess capacity. When there is an increase in spending demand, they increase production to meet the demand for their goods. If they need additional labor, they can increase the hours per week of their workers, recall laid-off workers, or hire additional workers.

Firms also adjust their prices to changes in demand, but there is a crucial difference between the adjustment of production and the adjustment of prices. Price adjustments are sticky compared to production adjustments. The adjustment of prices occurs gradually, while the adjustment of production and employment occurs almost instantaneously.

The **income identity** says that income (Y) equals the sum of consumption (C), investment (I), government spending (G), and net exports (X),

$$Y = C + I + G + X. \qquad (7–1)$$

It incorporates two important concepts. First, as shown in Chapter 2, income equals GDP. Second, as just discussed, aggregate demand determines GDP. We use the terms output, income, and GDP interchangeably, always represented by the symbol Y.

The consumption function states that consumption depends on disposable income (Y_d), which is equal to income minus taxes,

$$C = a + bY_d. \tag{7–2}$$

There is a subsistence level of consumption, *a*, about which the individual has no choice. If the individual's income is less than *a*, he borrows. At income levels above *a*, he has a choice between consumption and saving. The coefficient *b* is the **marginal propensity to consume**. It measures how much of an additional dollar of disposable income is spent on consumption. For instance, if we set *b* equal to .8, we are saying that 80 cents of each additional dollar of disposable income is spent on consumption. The other 20 cents is saved. Note that the equations that make up the fluctuations model contain both constants and variables. We use lowercase letters for constants and uppercase letters for variables.

If the tax rate is the constant *t*, total tax payments are the tax rate multiplied by income, *tY*. Disposable income Y_d = income – taxes = $Y - tY = (1 - t)Y$. By replacing disposable income Y_d with $(1 - t)Y$, the consumption function can be written

$$C = a + b(1 - t)Y. \tag{7–3}$$

Spending balance occurs at levels of consumption *C* and income *Y* that obey both the consumption function and the income identity. We substitute the consumption function into the income identity, $Y = C + I + G + X$, and solve for income to obtain

$$Y = a + b(1 - t)Y + I + G + X \tag{7–4}$$

$$Y[1 - b(1 - t)] = a + I + G + X$$

$$Y = \frac{1}{1 - b(1 - t)}(a + I + G + X). \tag{7–5}$$

To solve for consumption, substitute back into the consumption function the value of income when spending balance is attained. Because they can be determined inside the model in this case, income and consumption are called **endogenous variables**. Investment, government spending, and net exports cannot be determined *inside* the mode—yet—so they are called exogenous variables, determined *outside* the model.

The concept of spending balance is illustrated in Figure 7–4, with spending on the vertical axis and income on the horizontal axis. The 45-degree line shows where income and spending are equal. The spending line shows how total spending depends on income. Spending balance is attained at the point of intersection of the two lines. The level of income at the point of spending balance is the same as that derived algebraically in Equation 7–5. Figure 7–4 is sometimes called a **Keynesian 45-degree diagram** or a **Keynesian cross diagram**. At income levels below Y_0, spending demands exceed the amount of income. Here, firms respond by increasing production, thereby increasing *Y* to Y_0. At income levels beyond Y_0, spending demands fall short the amount of income. Now, firms respond to the lack of desired spending by decreasing production, which is diagrammed as *Y* falling back to Y_0. This way, production and income are brought into balance with spending at Y_0.

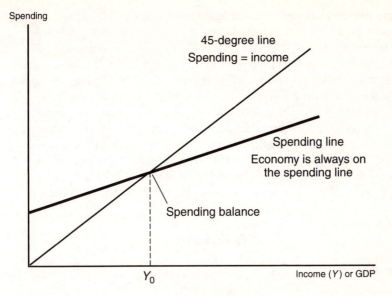

Figure 7–4

The **multiplier** measures how much a change in investment, government spending, or net exports changes income. The formula for the multiplier when investment, government spending, and net exports are exogenous is $1/[1 - b(1 - t)]$. It is greater than 1 because both b and t are between 0 and 1, indicating that an increase in investment, government spending, or net exports has a more than proportional effect on income.

The **net export function** relates net exports to income,

$$X = g - mY, \tag{7–6}$$

where g is a constant and m is a coefficient. Net exports depend negatively on income because, as income rises, spending rises. Since part of this rise in spending is on imported goods, imports rise and net exports fall. The coefficient m, called the **marginal propensity to import**, measures how much of an additional dollar of income is spent on imports.

We now find the value of income at the point of spending balance in an open economy where net exports are endogenous by substituting the net export function, as well as the consumption function, into the income identity, $Y = C + I + G + X$, and solve for income to obtain

$$Y = a + b(1 - t)Y + I + G + g - mY$$
$$Y[1 - b(1 - t) + m] = a + I + G + g$$
$$Y = \frac{1}{1 - b(1 - t) + m}(a + I + G + g). \tag{7–7}$$

The **open-economy multiplier**, which measures the impact of a change in government spending or investment on output in an open economy where net exports are endogenous, is $1/[1 - b(1 - t) + m]$. The open-economy multiplier is smaller when the marginal propensity to import m is larger. If m were zero, so that increases in income did not affect imports, the open-economy multiplier would be the same as in Equation 7–5. With m greater than zero, the open-economy multiplier is smaller than the multiplier with exogenous net exports.

We can begin to analyze the relation between trade deficits and government budget or fiscal deficits. Trade deficits occur when imports are greater than exports. Increases in government spending G, if not matched by tax increases, cause fiscal deficits. According to the multiplier, increases in G also cause income Y to rise. When Y increases, imports rise and trade deficits occur.

SELF-TEST

Fill in the Blank

1. The _____ curve shows the level of output corresponding to alternative price levels.

2. In the short run, firms respond to an increase in demand by producing _____ output rather than raising _____.

3. The income identity says that income is the sum of _____, _____, _____, _____.

4. The _____ is the fraction of an increase in disposable income that is consumed.

5. The _____ is the fraction of an increase in income that is spent on imports.

6. The _____ relates consumption to disposable income.

7. The _____ describes the negative relation between income and net exports. It arises because higher U.S. income causes higher U.S. _____ from other countries.

8. The price level is called _____ because, in the short run, its value is determined by events that have occurred in previous years.

9. _____ is attained at the point of intersection of the 45-degree line and the spending line.

10. A diagram with a 45-degree line and a spending line is sometimes called a _____ or _____ diagram.

11. A _____ occurs when imports are greater than exports.

12. The _____ measures how much a change in investment, government spending, or net exports changes income.

13. The _____ is smaller if the marginal propensity to import is _____.

True-False

14. A leftward shift of the aggregate demand curve causes both output and prices to fall.

15. Firms normally operate at less than 100 percent capacity utilization.

16. If aggregate demand increases, firms increase output before they increase prices.

17. Disposable income is equal to income minus saving.

18. Consumption equals zero if disposable income equals zero.

19. Spending balance means that the government budget deficit is zero.

20. The income identity says that income is equal to consumption.

21. The multiplier is always greater than the marginal propensity to consume.

22. If the tax rate is zero, the multiplier would equal 1.

23. Net exports depend negatively on income.

24. The open-economy multiplier measures the impact of a change in government spending on exports.

25. The open-economy multiplier is smaller than the multiplier when net exports are exogenous.

26. Fiscal and trade deficits are unrelated.

Review Questions

27. What are the four components of aggregate demand?

28. What happens to output and prices following a leftward shift of the aggregate demand curve?

29. What happens to output following a price shock that increases the price level?

30. What does it mean for prices to be sticky?

31. What two concepts are incorporated into the income identity?

32. Why does the consumption function depend on disposable, and not total, income?

33. When does spending balance occur?

34. If aggregate demand is less than output produced, how is spending balance achieved?

35. What is the difference between endogenous and exogenous variables?

36. What is the relation between the government spending and investment multipliers?

37. Why is the open-economy multiplier smaller than the multiplier when net exports are exogenous?

38. Why do increases in income cause trade deficits?

39. Why do trade and fiscal deficits occur together?

PROBLEM SET

Worked Problems

1. Consider an economy described by the following equations:

$$Y = C + I + G + X \quad \text{(Income identity)}$$
$$C = 100 + .9Y_d \quad \text{(Consumption)}$$

with investment I = $200 billion, government spending G = $200 billion, net exports X = $100 billion, and the tax rate t = .2.

a. What is the level of income when spending balance occurs? What is the level of consumption? Taxes?

b. Suppose government spending increases to $300 billion. What is the new level of income?

a. *From the income identity,*

$$Y = C + I + G + X.$$

Using the consumption function, $C = 100 + .9Y_d$, *and the definition of disposable income,* $Y_d = Y - .2Y$,

$$Y = 100 + .9(Y - .2Y) + 200 + 200 + 100$$
$$= 600 + .72Y.$$

Subtract .72Y from both sides of the equation,

$$Y - .72Y = 600,$$

factor out Y,

$$Y(1 - .72) = 600,$$
$$.28Y = 600,$$

and multiply both sides by 1/.28 = 3.571 to obtain the solution,

$$Y = 3.571(600) = \$2,143 \text{ billion.}$$

By solving for income, we automatically derive the multiplier. It is the number, 3.571, that multiplies the exogenous components of consumption, investment, government spending, and net exports, 600, to get income.

Alternatively, we can use the formula

$$\frac{1}{1 - b(1 - t)} = \frac{1}{1 - .9(1 - .2)} = \frac{1}{1 - .72} = \frac{1}{.28} = 3.571$$

to find the multiplier. It is important that you learn how to derive the multiplier rather than just memorize the formula, which is correct only if investment, government spending, and net exports all do not depend on income. Plugging solved Y into the consumption function yields C = 100 + .9(1 − .2)2,143 = 1,643. As a check, Y = C + I + G + X, 2,143 = 1,643 + 200 + 200 + 100. Taxes = tY = .2(2,143) = 428.6.

b. *This can be solved in two ways. One is to recalculate Y using the new level of G, 300.*

$$\begin{aligned} Y &= 100 + .9(Y - .2Y) + 200 + 300 + 100 \\ &= 700 + .72Y. \\ &= 3.571(700) = \$2,500 \text{ billion.} \end{aligned}$$

A second is to use the multiplier to calculate the change in Y,

$$\Delta Y = \text{multiplier} \times \Delta G = 3.571(100) = 357,$$

and then add the change in Y, 357, to the original value of Y, 2,143, to get the new value, \$2,500 billion. It is important that you solve problems in both ways as a check of your calculations.

2. Consider an economy described by the following equations:

$$\begin{aligned} Y &= C + I + G + X && \text{(Income identity)} \\ C &= 100 + .9Y_d && \text{(Consumption)} \\ X &= 100 - .12Y && \text{(Net exports)} \end{aligned}$$

with investment *I* = $200 billion, government spending *G* = $200 billion, net exports *X* = $100 billion, and the tax rate *t* = .2.

a. What is the level of income when spending balance occurs? What is the level of net exports and consumption? What is the multiplier? Compare the multiplier to the multiplier when net exports are exogenous in Problem 1.

b. Suppose government spending increases to $300 billion. What is the new level of income? Does this change the value of the multiplier?

a. *From the income identity,*

$$Y = C + I + G + X.$$

and using the consumption function, $C = 100 + .9Y_d$, *the net export function,* $X = 100 - .12Y$, *and the definition of disposable income,* $Y_d = Y - .2Y$,

$$Y = 100 + .9(Y - .2Y) + 200 + 200 + 100 - .12Y$$
$$= 600 + .6Y.$$

Subtract .6Y from both sides of the equation,

$$Y - .6Y = 600,$$

factor out Y,

$$Y(1 - .6) = 600,$$
$$.4Y = 600,$$

and multiply both sides by 2.5 (the inverse of .4) to obtain the solution,

$$Y = 2.5(600) = \$1,500 \text{ billion}$$
$$X = 100 - .12(1,500) = -80$$
$$C = 100 + .9(1 - .2)1,500 = 1.180.$$

As a check, $Y = C + I + G + X$; $1,500 = 1,180 + 200 + 200 - 80$.

   By solving for income, we automatically derive the multiplier, 2.5. The open-economy multiplier, 2.5, is smaller than the multiplier with exogenous net exports, 3.571, for the same marginal propensity to consume and tax rate.

Alternatively, we can use the formula

$$\frac{1}{1 - b(1 - t) + m} = \frac{1}{1 - .9(1 - .2) + .12} = \frac{1}{.4} = 2.5$$

to find the multiplier.

b. *This can be solved in two ways. One is to recalculate Y using the new level of G, 300.*

$$Y = 100 + .9(Y - .2Y) + 200 + 300 + 100 - .12Y$$
$$= 700 + .6Y.$$

$$= 2.5(700) = \$1,750 \text{ billion}.$$

A second is to use the multiplier to calculate the change in Y,

$$\Delta Y = 2.5 \times \Delta G = 2.5(100) = 250,$$

and then add the change in Y, *250, to the original value of* Y, *1,500, to get the new value, $1,750 billion.*

   No, the spending multiplier remains the same.

Review Problems

3. Consider an economy described by the following equations:

$$Y = C + I + G + X \quad \text{(Income identity)}$$
$$C = 300 + .8Y_d \quad \text{(Consumption)}$$

with investment $I = \$300$, government spending $G = \$100$, net exports $X = \$100$, and the tax rate $t = .2$.

a. What is the level of income when spending balance occurs? What is the multiplier?

b. Consider the same economy, except that investment depends positively on income, so that $I = 300 + .2Y$. What is the level of income and the multiplier now?

c. Returning to the investment equation in Part a, suppose that the tax rate is increased to .4. What happens to income and to the multiplier?

4. Consider an economy described by the following equations:

$$Y = C + I + G + X \quad \text{(Income identity)}$$
$$C = 400 + .9Y_d \quad \text{(Consumption)}$$

with investment $I = \$300$, government spending $G = \$100$, net exports $X = \$100$, and the tax rate $t = .5$.

a. What is the level of income when spending balance occurs? What is the multiplier?

b. Suppose government spending increases to $200. What is the new level of income?

5. Consider an economy described by the following equations:

$$Y = C + I + G + X \quad \text{(Income identity)}$$
$$C = 400 + .9Y_d \quad \text{(Consumption)}$$

with investment $I = \$200$, government spending $G = \$200$, net exports $X = \$100$, and the tax rate $t = .3333$.

a. What is the level of income when spending balance occurs? What is the multiplier?

b. Suppose government spending increases to $300. What is the new level of income?

6. Consider an economy described by the following equations:

$$Y = C + I + G + X \quad \text{(Income identity)}$$
$$C = 300 + .8Y_d \quad \text{(Consumption)}$$
$$X = 100 - .04Y \quad \text{(Net exports)}$$

with investment $I = \$200$, government spending $G = \$200$, and the tax rate $t = .2$.

a. What is the level of income when spending balance occurs? What is the multiplier? Compare your answer to the multiplier in Problem 3.

b. Consider the same economy, except that investment depends positively on income, so that $I = 200 + .2Y$. What is the level of income and the multiplier now?

c. Returning to the investment equation in Part a, suppose that the tax rate is increased to .4. What happens to income and to the multiplier?

7. Consider an economy described by the following equations:

$$Y = C + I + G + X \quad \text{(Income identity)}$$
$$C = 400 + .9Y_d \quad \text{(Consumption)}$$
$$X = 100 - .05Y \quad \text{(Net exports)}$$

with investment $I = \$300$, government spending $G = \$100$, and the tax rate $t = .5$.

a. At what level of income does spending balance occur? What is the multiplier? Compare your answer to the multiplier in Problem 4.

b. Suppose government spending increases from $100 to $200. What is the new level of income?

8. Consider an economy described by the following equations:

$$Y = C + I + G + X \quad \text{(Income identity)}$$
$$C = 400 + .9Y_d \quad \text{(Consumption)}$$
$$X = 200 - .1Y \quad \text{(Net exports)}$$

with investment $I = \$200$, government spending $G = \$200$, and the tax rate $t = .3333$.

a. At what level of income does spending balance occur? What is the multiplier? Compare your answer to the multiplier in Problem 5.

b. Suppose government spending decreases to $100. What is the new level of income?

GRAPH IT

1. a. In the spending/income space, graph Problem 1a.

b. Graph the spending line on the same graph for Problem 1b. What happens to the spending line?

2. a. In the spending/income space, graph the aggregate spending line in Problem 5a. What is different here in comparison to Problem 1a?

   b. Graph the spending line when $\Delta G = 100$ from Problem 5b.

ANSWERS TO THE SELF-TEST

1. Aggregate demand
2. More; prices
3. Consumption, investment, government spending, and net exports
4. Marginal propensity to consume
5. Marginal propensity to import
6. Consumption function
7. Net export function, imports
8. Sticky
9. Spending balance
10. Keynesian 45-degree or Keynesian cross
11. Trade deficit
12. Multiplier
13. Open-economy multiplier, positive
14. False. Output declines at the existing price level because prices are slow to respond in the short run.
15. True. Firms normally operate with some excess capacity.
16. True. This is what it means for prices to be "sticky."
17. False. Disposable income is equal to income minus taxes.
18. False. The positive value of the coefficient a in the consumption function, $C = a + bY_d$, means that, rather than starve if disposable income is zero for 1 year, people will spend some of their savings.
19. False. Spending balance can occur with a positive, negative, or zero government budget deficit.
20. False. The income identity says that income is equal to the sum of consumption, investment, government spending, and net exports.
21. True. The multiplier is greater than 1 and the marginal propensity to consume is less than 1.
22. False. The multiplier would equal $1/(1 - b)$ if the tax rate was zero.
23. True. Imports rise when income rises, lowering net exports.
24. False. The open-economy multiplier measures the impact of a change in government spending on income.
25. True. If the marginal propensity to import is positive, the open-economy multiplier is smaller than the multiplier when net exports are exogenous.
26. False. Increases in government spending cause both fiscal and trade deficits.

27. The four components of aggregate demand are consumption, investment, government spending, and net exports.
28. Output declines at the existing price level.
29. Output is lower after the price shock.
30. Prices are called sticky because they adjust slowly, compared with adjustments in production, to changes in spending demand.
31. The two concepts incorporated into the income identity are that income equals GDP and that aggregate demand determines GDP.
32. The consumption function describes people's choices between consuming and saving. The income available to make such a choice is their after-tax, or disposable, income.
33. Spending balance occurs when the income identity, consumption function, and net export function are satisfied.
34. If a firm produces more output than it can sell, it must either store the additional output, which is costly, or let the output go to waste. The firm is better off by decreasing production, which achieves spending balance.
35. An endogenous variable is determined within the model. An exogenous variable is determined outside the model.
36. The government spending and investment multipliers are equal.
37. The open-economy multiplier is smaller than the multiplier when net exports are exogenous because part of the induced increase in consumption is spent on imports, which do not add to GDP.
38. When income rises, part of the increase is spent on imports, causing trade deficits.
39. Increases in government spending, which cause fiscal deficits, also raise income, causing trade deficits.

SOLUTIONS TO REVIEW PROBLEMS

3. a. $Y = C + I + G + X$ for spending balance to hold.
$$= 300 + .8(Y - .2Y) + 300 + 100 + 100$$
$$= 800 + .64Y$$
$$= 2.777(800) = \$2,222.$$

The government spending multiplier is 2.777. In this case, since neither investment, government spending, nor net exports depends on income, the formula $1/[1 - .8(1 - .2)]$ also gives the correct answer.
   b. $Y = 300 + .8(Y - .2Y) + 300 + .2Y + 100 + 100$
$$= 800 + .84Y$$
$$= 6.25(800) = \$5,000.$$
   The multiplier is 6.25. In this case, since investment depends on income, the formula for the multiplier does not give the correct answer.
   c. $Y = 300 + .8(Y - .4Y) + 300 + 100 + 100$
$$= 800 + .48Y$$
$$= 1.923(800) = \$1,538.$$

The multiplier, 1.923, decreases because higher taxes lower disposable income. Since the multiplier falls and the exogenous variables are unchanged, income decreases.

4. a. $Y = 400 + .9(Y - .5Y) + 300 + 100 + 100$

    $= 900 + .45Y$

    $= 1.818(900) = \$1,636.$

    The multiplier is 1.818.

  b. $Y = \$1,818.$

5. a. $Y = 400 + .9(Y - .3333Y) + 200 + 200 + 100$

    $= 900 + .6Y$

    $= 2.5(900) = \$2,250.$

    The multiplier is 2.5.

  b. $Y = \$2,500.$

6. a. $Y = 300 + .8(Y - .2Y) + 200 + 200 + 100 - .04Y$

    $= 800 + .6Y$

    $= 2.5(800) = \$2,000.$

    The government spending multiplier is 2.5. It is smaller than the multiplier, 2.777, in Problem 3. In this case, since neither investment nor government spending depends on income, the formula $1/[1 - .8(1 - .2) + .04]$ also gives the correct answer.

  b. $Y = 300 + .8(Y - .2Y) + 200 + .2Y + 200 + 100 - .04Y$

    $= 800 + .8Y$

    $= 5(800) = \$4,000.$

    The multiplier is .5. In this case, since investment depends on income, the multiplier formula does not give the correct answer.

  c. $Y = 300 + .8(Y - .4Y) + 200 + 200 + 100 - .04Y$

    $= 800 + .44Y$

    $= 1.79(800) = \$1,429.$

    The multiplier, 1.79, decreases because higher taxes lower disposable income. Since the multiplier falls and the exogenous variables are unchanged, income decreases.

7. a. $Y = 400 + .9(Y - .5Y) + 300 + 100 + 100 - .05Y$

    $= 900 + .4Y$

    $= 1.67(900) = \$1,500.$

    The multiplier is 1.67. It is smaller than the multiplier, 1.818, in Problem 4.

  b. $Y = \$1,667.$

8. a. $Y = 400 + .9(Y - .3333Y) + 200 + 200 + 200 - .1Y$

    $= 1,000 + .5Y$

    $= 2(1,000) = \$2,000.$

    The multiplier is 2. It is smaller than the multiplier, 2.5, in Problem 5.

  b. $Y = \$1,800.$

ANSWERS TO GRAPH IT

1. a.

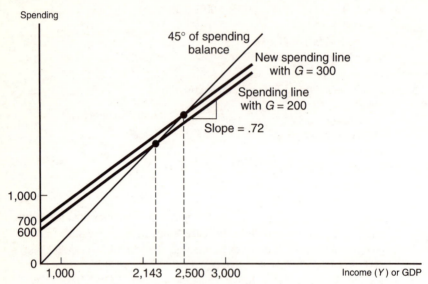

Figure 7–5

The spending line is derived by summing all spending categories:

Aggregate spending = $C + I + G + X$
Aggregate spending = $[100 + .9(1 - .2)Y] + 200 + 200 + 100$
Aggregate spending = $600 + .72Y$

Here 600 is the vertical intercept and .72 is the slope. Having solved the equilibrium level of Y from Part A, we know that the 45-degree line and the spending line intersect at $Y = 2,143$.

b. The spending line shifts up by the $\Delta G = 100$. The slope remains the same since neither t nor the marginal propensity to consume changes. The new spending balance occurs as calculated at $Y = 2,500$, where $\Delta Y = 2,500 - 2,143 = 357$.

2. a.

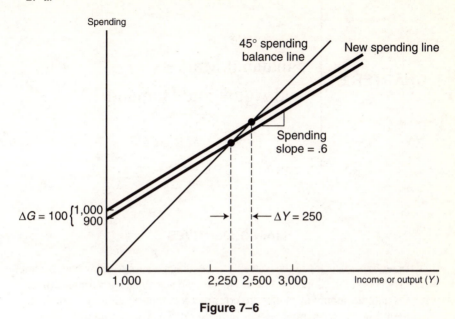

Figure 7–6

The spending line is derived by summing all spending components:

Aggregate spending $= C + I + G + X$
Aggregate spending $= [400 + .9(1 - .33)Y] + 200 + 200 + 100$
Aggregate spending $= 900 + .6Y$

Here the vertical intercept is 900 (300 more than before, which is due to the new C function) and the slope is smaller because the tax rate is higher.

b. The $\Delta G = 100$ shifts the spending line up by that amount. The new spending balance occurs as previously calculated:

$$\Delta Y = \text{multiplier } \Delta G = 2.5(100) = 250.$$
New $Y = 2,500.$

CHAPTER 8 | Financial Markets and Aggregate Demand

MAIN OBJECTIVES

In Chapter 7, we developed the concept of spending balance to show how income is determined in the short run. In this chapter, we add financial variables (interest rates and the supply of money) to construct a complete, although simplified, picture of how the economy operates in the short run. You should understand how the IS-LM framework can be used to analyze monetary and fiscal policy, and how it is summarized by deriving the aggregate demand curve, one of the basic tools of analysis for the remainder of the book.

KEY TERMS AND CONCEPTS

The **investment function** describes the relation between investment and the interest rate,

$$I = e - dR, \tag{8–1}$$

where I is investment and R is the real interest rate. The constant e measures the part of investment that does not depend on interest rates, while the coefficient d measures how much investment falls when the interest rate increases by 1 percentage point. The relationship is negative because most investment purchases are financed by borrowing. Higher interest rates increase the cost of borrowing, resulting in less investment spending.

The **real interest rate**, R, is the nominal interest rate minus the expected rate of inflation. Investment depends on the real interest rate because investors consider expected inflation when determining the cost of borrowing.

The **net export function** depends on the interest rate R as well as income Y,

$$X = g - mY - nR. \tag{8–2}$$

Net exports depend negatively on the interest rate because higher U.S. interest rates encourage foreigners to put their funds into dollars, raising the exchange rate. The higher exchange rate lowers exports and raises imports. The coefficient n measures how much net exports fall when the interest rate increases by 1 percentage point.

Money is the sum of currency used by the Federal Reserve System and checking account balances held by the public. Money is the funds individuals want badly enough for transactions that they are willing to forgo the additional interest they might earn by keeping the funds in another form. The **demand for money** increases with income because, as income rises, people want to make more transactions. It increases with the price level because, as the price level increases, people need more money to make the same real transactions. It decreases with the interest rate because other alternatives for holding financial wealth, such as savings accounts and bonds, pay higher interest rates. The demand for money increases with income, increases with the price level, and decreases with the interest rate, as in the following algebraic expression,

$$M = (kY - hR)P, \tag{8–3}$$

where M is the demand for money, Y is income, R is the interest rate, and P is the price level. The demand for money can also be written in terms of **real money**, money M divided by the price level P,

$$M/P = kY - hR. \tag{8–4}$$

This says that the demand for real money depends positively on real income and negatively on the interest rate.

The **money supply** is determined by the Federal Reserve System. How the Fed manages the money supply is examined in Chapter 14. For now, we assume it picks a certain level, M. In the short-run economic fluctuations model with predetermined prices, the interest rate and, to a lesser extent, income adjust to keep the demand for money equal to its fixed supply. Since the supply of money and the demand for money are always equal, we also use M to represent the money supply.

The economic model described by the income identity, consumption function, investment function, net export function, and money demand is called the **IS-LM framework**. It has two exogenous variables (government spending and the money supply) and five endogenous variables (income, the interest rate, consumption, investment, and net exports). Since prices are sticky and adjust only gradually, they are neither exogenous nor endogenous. We call the price level **predetermined** because, in each period, its value is determined by events that occurred in previous periods.

The **IS curve** shows all the combinations of the interest rate and income that satisfy the income identity, the consumption function, the investment function, and the net export function. It is the set of points for which spending balance occurs. It is downward sloping because lower interest rates cause investment demand to increase, which is consistent with spending balance only if more output is produced. An increase in government spending shifts the IS curve to the right because, for any given level of the interest rate, the increase in G raises Y through the multiplier process. The IS curve is illustrated in Figure 8–1.

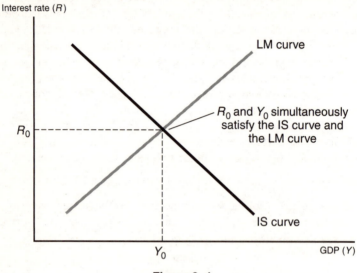

Figure 8–1

The **LM curve**, also illustrated in Figure 8–1, shows all combinations of the interest rate and income that satisfy the money demand relationship for a fixed level of the money supply and a predetermined value of the price level. It slopes upward because, with the nominal money supply fixed by the Fed and the price level predetermined, an increase in income, which increases the demand for money, must be accompanied by an increase in the interest rate, which decreases the demand for money, to keep the demand for money equal to its (fixed) supply.

To satisfy all five relationships of the model, the values of R and Y must be on both the IS curve and the LM curve, that is, at the intersection in Figure 8–1. From this, then, we find the solutions for C, I, and X.

Changes in the money supply are called monetary policy. When the Fed increases the money supply, as shown in Figure 8–2, the LM curve shifts right. This is because, for a fixed P, an increase in M is an increase in real money, M/P. Income rises and the interest rate falls. When the money supply is first increased, there is more money in the economy than people demand. Interest rates fall and investment increases, there is more money in the economy than

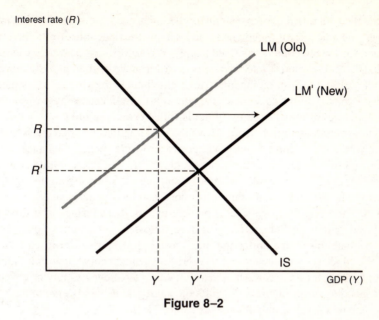

Figure 8–2

people demand. Interest rates fall and investment increases, which raises GDP through the multiplier process.

Changes in government spending, taxes, and transfers are called **fiscal policy**. An increase in government spending, as in Figure 8–3, increases income and increases the interest rate. The increase in government spending increases

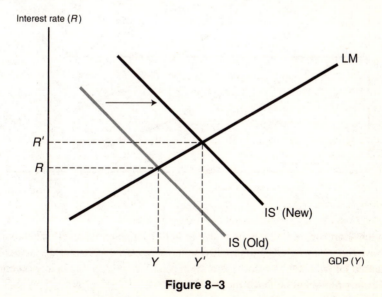

Figure 8–3

income through the multiplier and raises the interest rate because, as GDP increases, the demand for money increases. The interest rate must rise to keep the demand for money equal to its fixed supply. With investment and net exports depending on the interest rate, increases in government spending do not have the full multiplier effect on income. The higher interest rate lowers investment and net exports, offsetting some of the stimulus to GDP caused by government spending. The offsetting negative effect is called **crowding out**.

The **aggregate demand curve** shows the combinations of price levels and output where the IS and LM curves intersect, or where spending balance occurs and money demand equals money supply. It slopes downward because a decrease in prices increases real money, shifting the LM curve to the right, lowering interest rates, increasing investment, and increasing output.

In the short run, the price level is predetermined. It can change over time, but in a given year, the events of that year have almost no impact on the price level. We designate this with a horizontal line drawn at last year's price level, P_0 in Figure 8–4. This, combined with the aggregate demand curve, determines the level of output for this year. An increase in either the money supply or government spending, as in Figure 8–4, shifts the aggregate demand curve to the right. The new level of output changes from Y_0 to Y_1.

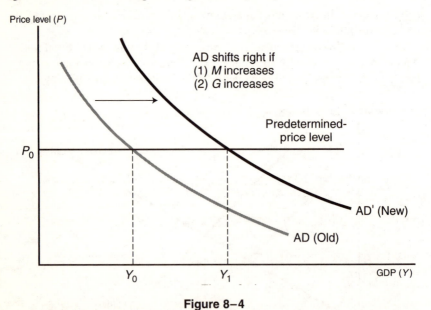

Figure 8–4

In the short run, output can be above or below its potential level. When output is above the potential GDP, unemployment, as we saw in Chapter 3 when we discussed Okun's law, is below the natural rate. When output is below potential GDP, unemployment is above the natural rate.

SELF-TEST

Fill in the Blank

1. The _____ describes the relation between investment and interest rates.

2. Net exports depend on _____ and _____.

3. The real interest rate is the nominal interest rate minus the _____ rate of inflation.

4. The money supply divided by the price level is called _____ money.

5. The demand for money _____ with income, _____ with the price level, and _____ with the interest rate.

6. The IS curve is the combination of _____ and _____ for which spending balance occurs.

7. The LM curve illustrates the condition that the demand and supply of _____ are equal.

8. Fiscal policy is made by the _____.

9. Monetary policy is made by the _____.

10. The offsetting negative effect on GDP, caused by higher interest rates following an increase in government spending is called _____.

11. A(n) _____ in government spending shifts the _____ curve right.

12. If the price level increases, the _____ curve shifts _____.

13. An increase in either the _____ or _____ shifts the aggregate demand curve to the right.

14. In the short run, the price level is _____.

True-False

15. Net exports are negatively related to the interest rate.

16. In the United States, monetary and fiscal policies are determined by different people.

17. Monetary policy shifts both the IS and LM curves.

18. An increase in government spending always causes a more than proportional increase in GDP.

19. Increases in the money supply and in government spending have the same effects on income.

20. Increases in the money supply and in government spending have the same effects on interest rates.

21. Increases in the money supply and in government spending have the same effects on the aggregate demand curve.

22. Prices adjust to keep the demand for money equal to the supply of money in the IS-LM framework.

23. If investment and net exports are very sensitive to interest rates, the LM curve is flat.

24. If the price level decreases, the aggregate demand curve shifts to the right.

Review Questions

25. Why does an increase in the interest rate decrease net exports?

26. What does it mean for the price level to be predetermined

27. When interest rates rise so that the return on financial assets, such as bonds, is high, does this mean that investment is high?

28. What is the relationship between real and nominal interest rates?

29. What are the implications of crowding out for the effectiveness of government spending?

30. What three factors determine the demand for money, and what are their effects?

31. Why does monetary policy shift the LM, but not the IS, curve?

32. Why does fiscal policy shift the IS, but not the LM, curve?

33. If both the money supply and government spending decrease, what happens to output and the interest rate?

34. What conditions are satisfied along the aggregate demand curve?

35. Can anything besides changes in the money supply or government spending shift the aggregate demand curve?

36. Since decreases in the price level and increases in the money supply both shift the LM curve to the right, why does the former cause a movement along the aggregate demand curve while the latter causes it to shift?

37. If government spending is increased, how can the Fed keep GDP from rising?

PROBLEM SET

Worked Problems

1. Consider an economy described by the following equations:

$$Y = C + I + G + X \qquad \text{(Income identity)}$$
$$C = 100 + .9Y_d \qquad \text{(Consumption)}$$
$$I = 200 - 500R \qquad \text{(Investment)}$$
$$X = 100 - .12Y - 500R \qquad \text{(Net exports)}$$
$$M = (.8Y - 2{,}000R)P \qquad \text{(Money demand)}$$

with government spending $G = \$200$ billion, the tax rate $t = .2$, the nominal money supply $M = \$800$ billion, and the predetermined price level $P = 1$.

a. What is the IS curve?

b. What is the LM curve?

c. What are the values of income and the interest rate when spending balance occurs and the demand for money equals the supply of money?

d. What are the values of consumption, investment, and net exports?

a. *We derive the IS curve using the same technique used to solve for income in Problem 2 of Chapter 7.*

$Y = C + I + G + X.$
$Y = 100 + .9(1 - .2)Y + 200 - 500R + 200 + 100 - .12Y - 500R$
$Y = 600 + .6Y - 1{,}000R$
$Y = 1{,}500 - 2{,}500R.$

b. *We derive the LM curve from the equation for money demand, given a fixed level for the money supply and a predetermined value of the price level (1 in this problem):*

$$800 = .8Y + 2{,}000R.$$

Adding 2,000R to both sides of the equation,

$$.8Y = 800 + 2{,}000R,$$

and dividing both sides by .8, we obtain

$$Y = 1,000 + 2,500R.$$

which is the equation for the LM curve.

c. *We compute the values for income and the interest rate by using the IS and LM curves, solving for R, and then solving for Y. Combining the two equations,*

$$IS = LM$$
$$Y = Y$$
$$1,500 - 2,500R = 1,000 + 2,500R,$$

adding 2,500R and subtracting 1,000 from both sides,

$$500 = 500R,$$
$$R = .10 \ (10 \ percent).$$

Substituting the value for R into either the IS or LM curve, Y = \$1,250 billion. To verify, substitute into both the IS and LM equations.

d. *We determine the values for consumption, investment, and net exports by substituting the computed values of R and Y into the consumption, investment, and net export equations:*

$$C = 100 + .9Y_d$$
$$= 100 + .9(1 - .2)1,250 = \$1,000 \ billion.$$
$$I = 200 - 500R$$
$$= 200 - 50 = \$150 \ billion.$$
$$X = 100 - .12Y - 500R$$
$$= 100 - 150 - 50 = -\$100 \ billion.$$

2. Derive the aggregate demand curve and show by how much an increase in government spending or real money of $100 billion increases GDP in Problem 1. Compare your answer for government spending to the government spending multiplier in Problem 2 of Chapter 7.

To derive the effects of increases in government spending and real money on income, start with the equation for the LM curve, do not substitute a specific value for real money, and solve for output:

$$M/P = .8Y - 2,000R$$

$$Y = 1.25(M/P) + 2,500R.$$

Now use the income identity, substitute the consumption, investment, and net export equations, but not a specific value for government spending, and solve for 2,500 times the intereest rate:

$$Y = 100 + .9(1 - .2)Y + 200 - 500R + G + 100 - .12Y - 500R$$
$$Y = 400 + .6Y - 1,000R + G$$
$$1,000R = 400 - .4Y + G$$
$$2,500R = 1,000 - Y + 2.5G.$$

Substitute the spending balance equation into the LM curve, and solve for Y:

$$Y = 1.25(M/P) + 1,000 - Y + 2.5G$$
$$2Y = 1.25(M/P) + 1,000 + 2.5G$$
$$Y = .625(M/P) + 500 + 1.25G.$$

An increase in government spending of 100 raises real GDP by 125. An increase in the money supply of 100, with the price level constant, raises real GDP by 62.5.

In Problem 7.2, with the government spending multiplier equal to 2.5, an increase in government spending of $100 billion raised real GDP by $250 billion. The only difference between the two models is that investment and net exports now depend on the interest rate. This is an example of crowding out. Government spending, in this problem, is only half as effective when the effects of interest rates on investment and net exports are included.

Review Problems

3. Consider an economy described by the following equations:

$Y = C + I + G + X$	(Income identity)
$C = 300 + .8Y_d$	(Consumption)
$I = 200 - 1,500R$	(Investment)
$X = 100 - .04Y - 500R$	(Net exports)
$M = (.5Y - 2,000R)P$	(Money demand)

   with government spending $G = \$200$, the tax rate $t = .2$, the nominal money supply $M = \$550$, and the predetermined price level $P = 1$.

   a. What is the IS curve?

   b. What is the LM curve?

   c. What are the values of income and the interest rate when spending balance occurs and the demand for money equals the supply of money?

4. Derive the aggregate demand curve and show by how much an increase in government spending or real money increases GDP in Problem 3. Compare your answer for government spending to the government spending multiplier in Problem 6 of Chapter 7.

5. Consider an economy described by the following equations:

$$Y = C + I + G + X \qquad \text{(Income identity)}$$
$$C = 400 + .9Y_d \qquad \text{(Consumption)}$$
$$I = 300 - 2{,}000R \qquad \text{(Investment)}$$
$$X = 100 - .05Y - 1{,}000R \qquad \text{(Net exports)}$$
$$M = (.4Y - 1{,}000R)P \qquad \text{(Money demand)}$$

with government spending $G = \$100$, the tax rate $t = .5$, the nominal money supply $M = \$180$, and the predetermined price level $P = 1$.

a. What is the IS curve?

b. What is the LM curve?

c. What are the values of income and the interest rate when spending balance occurs and the demand for money equals the supply of money?

6. Derive the aggregate demand curve and show by how much an increase in government spending or real money increases GDP in Problem 5. Compare your answer for government spending to the government spending multiplier in Problem 7 of Chapter 7.

7. Consider an economy described by the following equations:

$$Y = C + I + G + X \qquad \text{(Income identity)}$$
$$C = 400 + .9Y_d \qquad \text{(Consumption)}$$
$$I = 200 - 1{,}800R \qquad \text{(Investment)}$$
$$X = 200 - .1Y - 200R \qquad \text{(Net exports)}$$
$$M = (.8Y - 3{,}000R)P \qquad \text{(Money demand)}$$

with government spending $G = \$200$, the tax rate $t = .3333$, the nominal money supply $M = \$1{,}104$, and the predetermined price level $P = 1$.

a. What is the IS curve?

b. What is the LM curve?

c. What are the values of income and the interest rate when spending balance occurs and the demand for money equals the supply of money?

8. Derive the aggregate demand curve and show by how much an increase in government spending or real money increases GDP in Problem 7. Compare your answer for government spending to the government spending multiplier in Problem 8 of Chapter 7.

GRAPH IT

1. Graph the IS and LM curves from Problem 1 using the equilibrium values of R and Y you solved for in Part c. Line up the AD curve you derived in Problem 2 directly under your graph of the IS and LM curves. Last, graph the AD curve from Problem 2 when G increases by $100 billion, M stays at $800 billion, and the price level remains at $P = 1$. How does the increase in government spending affect the equilibrium point in the IS/LM space?

2. Go back to Graph It Problem 1, only this time (instead of G increasing by $100) let M increase by $100 to $M = 900$. Show graphically what happens.

ANSWERS TO THE SELF-TEST

1. Investment function
2. Income and the interest rate
3. Expected
4. Real
5. Increases with income, increases with the price level, and decreases with the interest rate
6. Interest rates and income
7. Money
8. President and Congress
9. Federal Reserve System
10. Crowding out
11. Increase, IS
12. LM, back or left
13. Money supply or government spending
14. Predetermined
15. True.   Increases in the interest rate raise the exchange rate, lowering net exports.
16. True.   Monetary policy is determined by the Federal Reserve System. Fiscal policy is determined by Congress and the president.
17. False.   Monetary policy shifts the LM curve. Fiscal policy shifts the IS curve.
18. False.   This is correct only if investment and net exports do not depend on the interest rate.
19. True.   Increases in either the money supply or government spending raise income.
20. False.   Increases in the money supply lower interest rates, while increases in government spending raise them.
21. True.   They both shift the aggregate demand curve to the right.

22. False. Interest rates and, to a lesser extent, output adjust.
23. False. The sensitivity of investment and net exports to interest rates affects the slope of the IS curve, not the LM curve.
24. False. A decrease in the price level causes a movement along the aggregate demand curve, not a shift of the curve.
25. An increase in the interest rate raises the exchange rate, making U.S. goods more expensive compared to foreign goods. This decreases exports and increases imports, decreasing net exports.
26. The price level is called predetermined because, in each period, its value is determined by events that occurred in previous periods.
27. No. Investment is spending on items such as factories and houses and has nothing to do with the return on financial assets.
28. The real interest rate equals the nominal interest rate minus the expected rate of inflation.
29. Crowding out decreases the effectiveness of government spending.
30. The demand for money increases with income and the price level, and decreases with the interest rate.
31. Monetary policy changes the supply of money, shifting the LM curve. The IS curve depends on spending balance, which is unaffected by the money supply.
32. Fiscal policy, changes in government spending or taxes, affects spending balance, shifting the IS curve. The LM curve depends on the supply of and demand for money, which are unaffected by spending balance.
33. Since both the IS and LM curves shift to the left, output decreases. You cannot say what happens to the interest rate without knowing the magnitudes of the decreases and the coefficients of the consumption, investment, net export, and money demand equations.
34. Spending balance occurs and the demand for money equals the supply of money.
35. Yes. Changes in the exogenous component of consumption (a), investment (e), or net exports (g) shift the aggregate demand curve by shifting the IS curve.
36. The aggregate demand curve is drawn with P and Y on the axes. A shift of the curve can be caused only by a variable, such as M, that is not on one of the axes. Changes in variables on the axes, P and Y, cause shifts along the curve. For the LM curve, neither P nor M is on the axes, so both can cause shifts of the curve.
37. Using coordinated monetary policy, the Fed can lower the money supply. This shifts the LM curve to the left, raising interest rates and preventing output from rising.

SOLUTIONS TO REVIEW PROBLEMS

3. a. The IS curve is derived from the condition for spending balance:

$$Y = 300 + .8(Y - .2Y) + 200 - 1{,}500R + 200 + 100 - .04Y - 500R$$
$$= 800 + .6Y - 2{,}000R$$
$$= 2{,}000 - 5{,}000R.$$

   b. The LM curve is derived from the condition that the demand for money equal the supply of money with a predetermined price level:

$$550 = .5Y - 2{,}000R$$
$$Y = 1{,}100 + 4{,}000R.$$

   c. Using the IS and LM curves,

$$2{,}000 - 5{,}000R = 1{,}100 + 4{,}000R$$
$$900 = 9{,}000R, \ R = .10 \ (10 \ \text{percent}).$$

   Substituting back into either the IS or LM curve, $Y = \$1{,}500$.

4. Staring with the LM curve,

$$M/P = .5Y - 2{,}000R,$$
$$Y = 2(M/P) + 4{,}000R.$$

   Using the condition for spending balance,

$$Y = 300 + .8(Y - .2Y) + 200 - 1{,}500R + G + 100 - .04Y - 500R$$
$$4{,}000R = 1{,}200 - .8Y + 2G.$$

   Substituting the spending balance condition into the LM curve,

$$Y = 2(M/P) + 1{,}200 - .8Y + 2G$$
$$= 1.11(M/P) + 666.7 + 1.11G.$$

   An increase in government spending has less effect on output than in the earlier problem because of crowding out.

5. The technique for this problem is the same as for Problem 3.

   a. $Y = 400 + .9(Y - .5Y) + 300 - 2{,}000R + 100 + 100 - .05Y - 1{,}000R$
$$= 900 + .4Y - 3{,}000R$$
$$= 1{,}500 + 5{,}000R.$$

   b. $180 = .4Y - 1{,}000R$
$$Y = 450 + 2{,}500R.$$

   c. $R = .14$ (14 percent), $Y = \$800$.

6. The technique for this problem is the same as for Problem 4.
   From the LM curve,

$$Y = 2.5(M/P) + 2,500R.$$

From the condition for spending balance,

$$2,500R = 666.67 - .5Y + .83G.$$

Substituting the spending balance condition into the LM curve,

$$Y = 1.67(M/P) + 444.5 + .55G.$$

This illustrates that crowding out can cause an increase in government spending to have a less than proportionate effect on income, a result that is not possible if investment and net exports do not depend on the interest rate.

7. The technique for this problem is the same as for Problem 3.

   a. $Y = 400 + .9(Y - .3333Y) + 200 - 1,800R + 200 + 200 - .1Y - 200R$
      $= 1,000 + .5Y - 2,000R$
      $= 2,000 - 4,000R.$

   b. $1,104 = .8Y - 3,000R$
      $Y = 1,380 + 3,750R.$

   c. $R = .08$ (8 percent), $Y = \$1,680.$

8. The technique for this problem is the same as for Problem 4.
   From the LM curve,

$$Y = 1.25(M/P) + 3,750R.$$

From the condition for spending balance,

$$3,750R = 1,500 - .94Y + 1.875G.$$

Substituting the spending balance condition into the LM curve,

$$Y = .64(M/P) + 773.2 + .97G.$$

Government spending is less effective because of crowding out.

ANSWERS TO GRAPH IT

1. The IS curve shifts right when government spending increases to $G = 300$. This also shifts the AD curve right. Crowding out is the result of the interest rate rising. The new equilibrium is found by computing values of R and Y using the new IS curve ($Y = 1,750 - 2,500R$) and the LM curve ($Y = 1,000 + 2,500R$). Now, $R = .15$ and $Y = \$1,375$ billion is the new equilibrium.

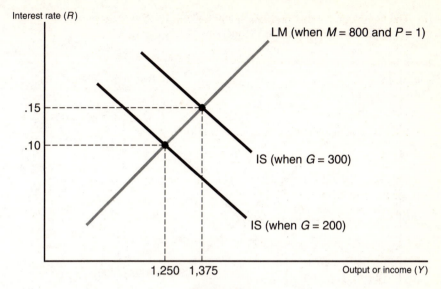

Figure 8–5

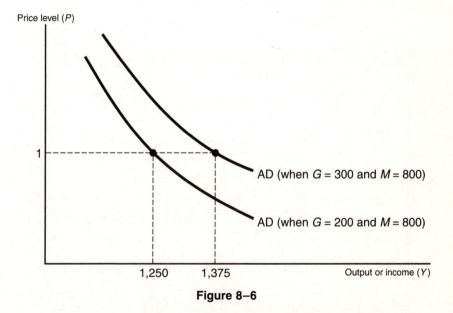

Figure 8–6

2. The LM curve shifts right when *M* increases to $900 billion. This also shifts the AD curve right. Expansionary monetary policy puts pressure on interest rates to fall in the short run, thereby stimulating investment and net exports. The new equilibrium is obtained by setting the old IS and new

LM curves ($Y = 1,125 + 2,500R$) and solving for $R = .075$. Substituting in $R = .075$ into both IS and LM functions yields $Y = 1,312.50$.

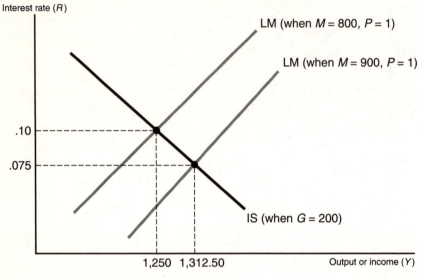

Figure 8–7

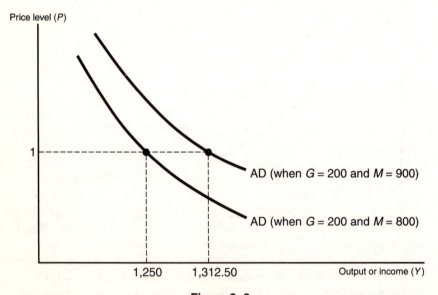

Figure 8–8

CHAPTER 9

The Economic Fluctuations Model

MAIN OBJECTIVES

The economic fluctuations model has two components: the aggregate demand curve developed in Chapter 8 and the price adjustment process developed in this chapter. You should understand how the adjustment process takes the economy from a position where GDP is either above or below potential GDP back to that point. You should understand how shocks, or disturbances to the economy, affect the model. You should understand the dynamic effects of monetary and fiscal policies in the fluctuations model and the crucial role that expectations of inflation play in the price adjustment process.

KEY TERMS AND CONCEPTS

The process of **price adjustment** describes the transition from the short to the long run. There are two aspects of price adjustment. First, if firms and workers expect inflation to occur, they will write contracts and set prices in accord with their expectations. An important factor that determines expected inflation is the rate of inflation that prevailed over the past few years. The process by which past inflation gets translated into expected inflation, and then into actual inflation, is called **inflationary momentum**.

The second aspect of price adjustment is the state of the labor market. Prices rise when output is above potential GDP and unemployment is below the natural rate and fall when output is below potential GDP and unemployment is above the natural rate. The rate of inflation is the rate of change of the price level, and can be expressed as

$$\pi = (P - P_{-1})/P_{-1}, \tag{9-1}$$

where π is the rate of inflation, P is the current price level, and P_{-1} is the last period's price level (the subscript -1 indicates the previous period). When prices are rising, the inflation rate is positive. When prices are falling, the inflation rate is negative.

The interaction between the aggregate demand curve and the process of price adjustment produces a **dynamic model**, where the variables change from one year to the next. Because prices are **predetermined**, fixed in the short run but variable in the long run, the current price level, P, is based on the recent past level of output, Y_{-1}. Given the price level, output is determined by the aggregate demand schedule. The current level of output then determines next year's price level, and so on.

The **Phillips curve** is an algebraic formulation of price adjustment,

$$\pi = \pi^e + f(Y_{-1} - Y^*)/Y^*, \tag{9-2}$$

where π^e is the expected rate of inflation, Y^* is potential GDP, Y_{-1} is last period's GDP, and f is a positive coefficient. It says that inflation equals expected inflation plus a term that is positive if output is greater than potential and negative if output is less than potential. Prices are predetermined because the current price level is determined by the last period's output Y_{-1}, not by current output Y. Incorporating expectations of inflation into the Phillips curve makes it possible for inflation to be positive even if output is below potential GDP.

If inflation were fairly constant form year to year, the best forecast of current inflation π would be last period's inflation π_{-1}. The price adjustment equation would become

$$\pi = \pi_{-1} + f(Y_{-1} - Y^*)/Y^*. \tag{9-3}$$

When inflation is variable, other factors such as previous years' inflation rates and expectations of future money supply growth would also influence expected inflation.

The price adjustment equation with expected inflation equal to last period's inflation, Equation 9–3, has three important properties. First, the only way to reduce inflation is to have a recession. Output must be below potential GDP for inflation to be less than last period's inflation. Second, the larger the gap between actual and potential GDP, the greater the increase in the inflation rate (or decrease in the inflation rate if the gap is negative). Third, if output is permanently above potential GDP, inflation will rise without bound; this is called the **accelerationist** or **natural rate property**.

Aggregate demand and price adjustment can be combined to anlayze the short- and long-run effects of monetary and fiscal policy. For the moment, assume that expected inflation is always zero. Suppose that, beginning with output equal to potential GDP, the Fed increases the money supply. In the short run, with predetermined prices, the stimulus to aggregate demand lowers interest rates and raises output above potential, as described in Chapter 8. This causes inflation, as can be seen from the price adjustment equation, 9–1. The inflation causes prices to rise over time, decreasing real money and output. As output falls toward potential, the rate of inflation decreases. In the long run, output returns to potential GDP with zero inflation at the original interest rate and a higher price level. Monetary policy is neutral in the long run because all real variables—GDP, consumption, investment, net exports, and interest rates—return to their original levels. Monetary policy is not neutral in the short run. It has a powerful effect on output before prices have time to adjust.

Fiscal policy, such as an increase in government spending, looks very similar to monetary policy. Output rises above potential in the short run. This causes inflation, which increases prices and drives output back to potential in the long run. There are, however, important differences between monetary and fiscal policy. Fiscal policy raises interest rates in the short run. As prices rise, real money falls and interest rates keep rising. In the long run, potential output is attained with both higher prices and higher interest rates. The sum of investment and net exports is decreased by the same amount that government spending is increased. This is called **complete crowding out**. Even though fiscal policy does not change real output in the long run, it is not neutral because it changes investment, net exports, and interest rates.

Expansionary monetary and fiscal policies are illustrated in Figure 9–1. Both expansionary policies shift the aggregate demand curve to the right. In the short run, output rises along the predetermined price line. Over time, prices rise and output falls along the aggregate demand curve until, in the long run, output returns to potential.

The preceding description of monetary and fiscal policy is incomplete because it ignores the impact of expected inflation. Incorporating expected inflation into the Phillips curve does not affect either the short-run or the long-run

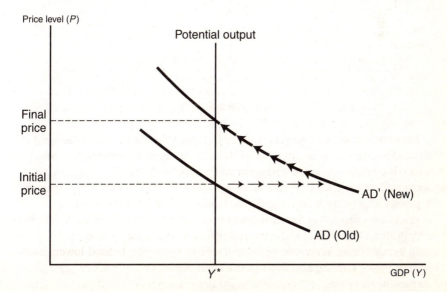

Figure 9–1

results. What it does change is the transition between the short and long run. With expected inflation always equal to zero, past inflation influences current inflation only because, by raising current prices, it affects the difference between actual and potential output. With expected inflation equal to last period's inflation, as in Equation 9–3, past inflation also influences current inflation directly.

The major difference for monetary and fiscal policy is that the transition from the short to the long run is no longer smooth. Inflation increases as output falls toward potential, where prices overshoot their long-run level. Output overshoots as well when it falls below potential, causing a recession that finally brings inflation down. Prices fall and output rises as the economy cycles back to the long run. Prices and output are said to overshoot their long-run levels. The cyclical movement of prices and output along the aggregate demand curve in response to expansionary policy is shown in Figure 9–2.

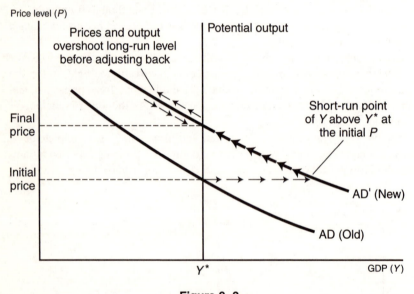

Figure 9–2

Economic shocks or **disturbances** are events other than policy changes that move the economy away from potential GDP. An **aggregate demand disturbance** is one that shifts the aggregate demand curve. Examples of aggregate demand disturbances are changes in investment, net exports, and money demand. A **price disturbance** is an event that shifts the price adjustment curve. Examples of price disturbances are increases in the price of imported oil and widespread anticipation of inflation by firms that leads them to increase prices.

In the short run, aggregate demand disturbances change output without affecting prices. In the absence of a policy response, the analysis of aggregate demand disturbances is exactly the same as the analysis of monetary and fiscal policy depicted in Figure 9–2. For instance, an increase in investment demand shifts the aggregate demand curve to the right, raising output above potential in the short run. Over time, prices rise and output falls until potential GDP is again attained. Another example is an increase in money demand, which has exactly the same effects as a decrease in the money supply.

Price disturbances affect both output and prices in the short run. Consider a positive price shock, such as an oil price shock, that shifts up the price adjustment curve. In the short run, the price level rises, dropping output below potential GDP. If there is no policy response, the process of price adjustment causes prices to fall slowly and output to rise until potential output is eventually restored at the original price level. The economy is in a recession until potential GDP is attained. The path taken by the economy following a price disturbance is illustrated in Figure 9–3.

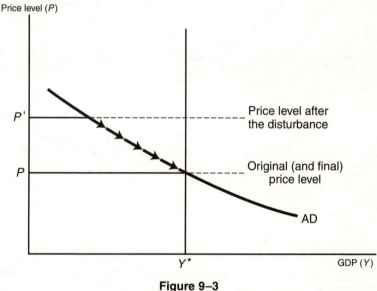

Figure 9–3

The response of monetary and fiscal policy to aggregate demand and price shocks is a very important part of macroeconomics. **Discretionary policy** is a one-time change in a monetary and fiscal policy in response to a specific shock or disturbance. Chapter 16 considers **monetary policy rules**, which is a systematic response of monetary policy to economic conditions. Shocks are considered undesirable because they cause fluctuations in real GDP and in inflation. Suppose that an increase in money demand shifts the aggregate demand curve to the left. With no policy response, there will be a recession until falling prices raise real money sufficiently to restore potential GDP. Instead of allowing the economy to suffer through the recession, the Fed can increase the money supply to meet the additional demand for money. This immediately shifts the aggregate demand curve to the right, restoring potential output. Shifts to investment demand can be similarly counteracted.

Figure 9–4 shows how monetary and fiscal policy can be used to counter the effects of a negative aggregate demand shock, such as the ones just described. Following the shock, real GDP falls. Timely action by the Fed to increase the money supply (and therefore lower interest rates) or by the president and Congress to increase government spending or lower taxes could offset the reduction in GDP. When policy attempts to mitigate the length and severity of aggregate demand shocks, we call this a **countercyclical stabilization policy**.

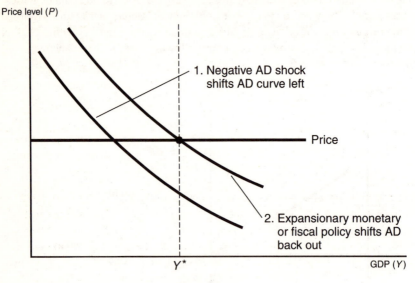

Figure 9–4

Accommodative monetary policy is an increase in the money supply in response to a *price disturbance*. A policy that holds the money supply constant is called **nonaccommodative**. A price disturbance increases the price level and decreases output below potential in the short run. This presents the Fed with several difficult choices. While accommodative policy, as shown in Figure 9–5, returns output quickly to potential by increasing AD with expansionary monetary policy, it has the cost of further increasing the price level to P_1. Nonaccommodative policy, however, causes a sustained recession until prices fall back to P_0. Therefore, with a price shock, there is a trade-off between the stability of the price level (nonaccommodative) and the stability of real GDP (accommodative).

We can look at the long-run effects of fiscal policy on not only the total amount of GDP but also the components, or shares, of GDP. Recall form Chapter 2 that GDP equals the sum of consumption, investment, government spending, and net exports,

$$Y = C + I + G + X, \qquad (9\text{–}4)$$

where Y is GDP, C is consumption, I is investment, G is government spending, and X is net exports. Since fiscal policy does not affect GDP in the long run, an

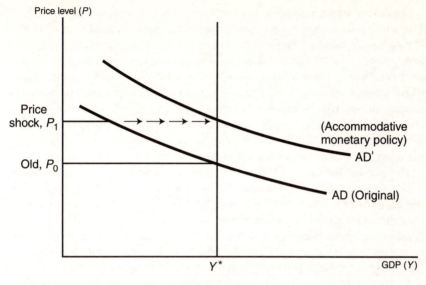

Figure 9–5

increase in government spending must cause a decrease in **nongovernment purchases**, $C + I + X$, of exactly the same amount. The term **crowding out** is used to describe this process.

We can also consider the shares of GDP represented by different components of spending. Dividing both sides of Equation 9–4 by Y,

$$1 = \frac{C}{Y} + \frac{I}{Y} + \frac{G}{Y} + \frac{X}{Y}. \tag{9–5}$$

The shares of the different components of spending must sum to 1. If government purchases as a share of GDP increase, the share of nongovernment purchases in GDP must decrease by the same amount. This is another illustration of crowding out.

We look at three periods of expansion (1961–1969, 1982–1990, and 1991–2000) to see if the model predicts the effect of policy changes. During these times, income taxes were lowered and, indeed, consumption shares increased and net export shares fell. Also, the share of government purchases fell, which caused a rise in investment shares.

Consumption, investment, and net exports all depend negatively on interest rates. When the interest rate rises, firms have to pay more to finance their investment of machines and equipment and consumers have to pay more to finance their consumption of automobiles and other durables, decreasing both consumption and investment. Net exports depend negatively on the interest rate because higher U.S. interest rates encourage foreigners to put their funds into dollars, raising the exchange rate. The higher exchange rate lowers exports and raises imports, decreasing net exports.

134 | Chapter 9

The **interest-rate sensitivity** of consumption, investment, and net exports determines how a decrease in nongovernment purchases, caused by an increase in government spending is distributed among the three components. Consumption is less sensitive to interest rates than investment or net exports because a large percentage of consumption consists of nondurables and services, neither of which is much affected by interest rates. When government spending increases, causing interest rates to rise, investment and net exports fall more than consumption. This analysis also illustrates the close positive relation between the budget deficit, which is caused by an increase in government purchases if not matched by a tax increase, and the trade deficit, a fall in net exports.

The long-run behavior of the inflation rate is explained by long-run behavior of the price level. For this, we examine long-run equilibrium in the money market. **Money market equilibrium** occurs when the supply of money equals the demand for money. Since the money supply is determined by the Fed, the demand for money must adjust to achieve equilibrium. In the long run, with output equal to potential GDP and the interest rate determined by the income identity, only the price level adjusts to equilibrate the money market.

Neutrality of money, also called the **classical dichotomy**, means that changes in the money supply have no influence on output or the interest rate. This can be illustrated using the money demand function,

$$M = (kY^* - hR^*)P, \tag{9--6}$$

where Y^* is potential GDP and R^* is the long-run interest rate. When the Fed increases the money supply, the price level increases in proportion while output and the interest rate are unchanged. Another implication from Equation 9–6 is that an increase in government spending, which raises the interest rate, causes the price level to rise to offset the fall in money demand. A further implication is that an increase in potential GDP, holding the money stock constant, causes the price level to fall.

Inflation is the rate of increase of the price level. If potential GDP is constant, inflation is equal to the rate of growth of the money supply. In a growing economy, where potential GDP increases over time, the rate of inflation is less than the money supply growth. Empirical evidence indicates that, since 1973, money growth has been about 2 percentage points above inflation for a sample of industrialized countries. Although changes in the money supply do not directly affect the supply of productive factors, some economists believe that higher inflation reduces productivity. In that case, monetary policy can affect potential GDP by affecting the rate of inflation.

SELF-TEST

Fill in the Blank

1. The economic fluctuations model has two components: _____ and _____.

2. _____ describes the process by which past inflation causes current inflation.

3. Prices are _____ because they are fixed in the short run but variable in the long run.

4. The relationship between the rate of inflation and the deviation of real GDP from potential is called the _____ curve.

5. The rate of inflation forecasted by workers and firms is the _____ rate of inflation.

6. The long-run decrease in investment and net exports when government spending increases is called _____.

7. Monetary policy is determined by _____.

8. Economic _____ or _____ are events other than policy changes that move the economy away from potential GDP.

9. A shock to investment, net exports, or money demand is an _____.

10. Policies that increase the money supply in response to price shocks are called _____ policies. Holding the money supply constant in response to a price shock is called a _____ policy.

11. In the long run, an increase in government spending causes _____ to decrease by exactly the same amount.

12. The property that changes in the money supply do not affect output or interest rate is called the _____ or the _____.

13. _____ is the rate of increase in the price level.

True-False

14. In the short run, output can be below or above its potential level.

15. In the short run, unemployment can be above or below the natural rate.

16. When output equals potential GDP, inflation is zero.

17. When inflation equals expected inflation, output is equal to last period's GDP.

18. The current price level does not depend on the current level of output.

19. Expected inflation is always equal to lasts year's inflation.

20. If expected inflation is equal to last year's inflation, output can be permanently raised above potential only by having inflation increase without bound.

21. Aggregate demand disturbances do not affect output in the long run.

22. Price shocks do not affect the price level in the long run.

23. An oil price increase is an example of an aggregate demand disturbance.

24. Net exports depend negatively on interest rates.

25. The interest-rate sensitivity of consumption is greater than that of investment or net exports.

26. Neutrality of money implies that, when the Fed raises the money supply, the price level increases in proportion.

Review Questions

27. How is output determined in the short run?

28. How is output determined in the long run?

29. What is the relation between output and unemployment?

30. What is inflationary momentum?

31. What does it mean for prices to be predetermined?

32. What is the accelerationist property?

33. If there is no expected inflation, describe what happens to GDP and prices when the Fed increased the money supply.

34. How does expected inflation change your answer to Question 33?

35. What happens to GDP and prices when government spending is increased if there is no expected inflation? How does your answer change if there is expected inflation?

36. Describe the effects of a negative aggregate demand disturbance, such as a decrease in investment demand, with no change in policy.

37. How can countercyclical stabilization policy be used to counter the effects of a negative aggregate demand disturbance?

38. Describe the effects of a positive price shock with no change in policy.

39. How can accommodative monetary policy be used in response to a price shock?

PROBLEM SET

Worked Problems

1. Suppose the economy has the aggregate demand curve

$$Y = 500 + 1.25G + .625(M/P)$$

and the price adjustment schedule

$$\pi = (Y_{-1} + 1{,}250)/1{,}250 + \pi^e.$$

Government spending is $200 billion and the money supply is $800 billion.

a. Assume that expected inflation, π^e, is always zero. Starting from $P_0 = .8$, describe the path of the economy until GDP is within 1 percent of its long-run value.

b. Assume that $\pi^e = \pi_{-1}$. Describe the path of the economy, again starting from $P_0 = .8$ with zero inflation. How does your answer differ from that of Part a?

a. *Notice that* $Y^* = 1{,}250$ *from the price adjustment schedule. The initial level of output,* Y_0, *is found from the aggregate demand curve by setting* $P_0 = .8$ *and using the given values for government spending and the money supply:*

$$Y_0 = 500 + 1.25(200) + .625(800)/.8$$
$$= \$1{,}375 \ billion.$$

The inflation rate, π_1, *is found from the price adjustment curve,*

$$\pi_1 = (1{,}375 - 1{,}250)/1{,}250 = .1 \ (10 \ percent),$$

$P_1 = P_0(1 + \pi)$ *is the formula you need to determine next year's price level:*

$$P_1 = .8 + .8(.1) = .88.$$

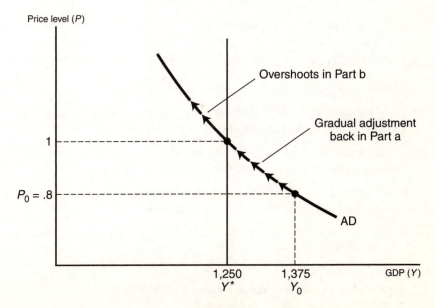

Figure 9–6

Y_1 *can now be determined by substituting* P_1 *into the aggregate demand curve, and so on. The complete answer follows:*

Year	π	P	Y
0	.000	.80	$1,375
1	.100	.88	1,318
2	.055	.93	1,289
3	.031	.96	1,271
4	.017	.98	1,262

Output is initially above potential GDP. Prices rise and output falls smoothly until potential GDP is attained with P = 1.

b. *The technique for this part is the same as for Part a except that, when computing inflation, last year's inflation needs to be incorporated. This does not affect* π_1, *since* $\pi_0 = 0$, *but* $\pi_2 = .055 + \pi_1 = .155$, *and so on. This affects the rest of the answer.*

Year	π	P	Y
0	.000	.80	$1,375
1	.100	.88	1,318
2	.155	1.02	1,242
3	.149	1.17	1,177
4	.088	1.27	1,143
5	.002	1.27	1,143
6	−.084	1.16	1,180
7	−.140	1.00	1,250

Output is initially above potential GDP. As previously, prices begin to rise and output falls, but now output falls below potential. This causes prices first to stop rising, then to fall. Output recovers to potential. The numerical answer gives only the first part of the cycle because inflation does not equal zero when output equals potential GDP.

2. Using the same model as in Problem 1, increase government spending by $50 billion starting from potential GDP with the price level *P* = 1.

   a. Calculate the paths of inflation, the price level, and GDP for the first 5 years, in the case where expected inflation is always zero.

   b. Perform the same calculations, this time for 10 years, in the case where expected inflation equals last period's inflation.

   a. *Initially, in Year 0, GDP equals potential with* π = 0 *and* P = 1. *The increase in government spending first affects output, which can be calculated from the aggregate demand curve with* G = $250 billion:

   $$Y_1 = 500 + 1.25(250) + .625(800)/1$$
   $$= \$1,313 \text{ billion.}$$

The inflation rate, π_2, is found from the price adjustment curve,

$$\pi_2 = (1{,}313 - 1{,}250)/1{,}250 = .05 \text{ (5 percent)},$$

and determines the next year's price level:

$$P_2 = 1 + 1(.05) = 1.05.$$

Y_2 can now be determined by substituting P_2 into the aggregate demand curve, and so on. The complete answer is presented in the following table:

Year	π	P	Y
0	.000	1.00	$1,250
1	.000	1.00	1,313
2	.050	1.05	1,289
3	.031	1.08	1,275
4	.020	1.10	1,266
5	.013	1.11	1,261

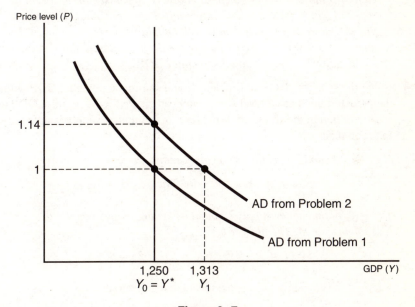

Figure 9–7

The increase in government spending shifts the aggregate demand curve to the right. In the short run, output increases above potential with unchanged prices. Over time, prices rise and output falls smoothly until potential GDP is restored.

b. *The technique for this part is the same as for Part a except that, when computing inflation, last year's inflation needs to be incorporated. This does not affect π_2, since $\pi_1 = 0$, but $\pi_3 = .031 + \pi_2 = .081$, and so on. This affects the rest of the answer.*

Year	π	P	Y
0	.000	1.00	$1,250
1	.100	1.00	1,313
2	.050	1.05	1,289
3	.081	1.14	1,253
4	.083	1.23	1,217
5	.057	1.30	1,197
6	.015	1.32	1,191
7	−.032	1.28	1,204
8	−.069	1.19	1,232
9	−.083	1.09	1,271
10	−.066	1.02	1,303

Output is initially above potential GDP. As previously, prices begin to rise and output falls, but now output falls below potential. This causes prices first to stop rising, then to fall. Output recovers to potential. The numerical answer gives only part of the cycle because inflation does not equal zero when output equals potential GDP.

3. Using the same model as in Problem 1, and starting at potential GDP with the predetermined price level $P = 1$, suppose the Fed wants to raise GDP to $1,300 billion in the short run. What level of the money supply is necessary to accomplish this?

For $G = 200$ and $P = 1$, the aggregate demand curve is

$$Y = 750 + .625M.$$

The level of the money supply is found by setting output Y equal to 1,300 and solving for M. The answer is

$$M = (1,300) - 750)/.625 = 550/.625 = 880.$$

4. Suppose the economy has the aggregate demand curve

$$Y = 500 + 1.25G + .625(M/P) + Z_d$$

and the price adjustment schedule

$$\pi = (Y_{-1} - Y^*)/Y^*,$$

where Z_d is an aggregate demand shock. Potential GDP $Y^* = \$1,250$ billion, government spending $G = \$200$ billion, and the money supply $M = \$800$ billion.

a. Starting at potential output with the price level $P = 1$ and inflation $\pi = 0$, an aggregate demand disturbance $Z_d = -\$100$ billion occurs in the first year. No further shocks occur ($Z_d = -\$100$ billion in all future years). Describe the path of the economy until GDP is within 1 percent of its long-run value.

b. How can the Fed offset the aggregate demand disturbance and keep output equal to potential GDP?

a. *In the first year output decreases by 100 (the amount of the aggregate demand disturbance) to $1,150 billion. The inflation rate π_2 is found from the price adjustment curve,*

$$\pi_2 = (1,150 - 1,250)/1,250 = -.08 \; (-8 \; percent),$$

and determines the price level:

$$P_2 = 1 + 1(-.08) = .92.$$

Output is found from the aggregate demand curve using the given values for government spending, the money supply, and the aggregate demand disturbance:

$$Y_2 = 500 + 1.25(200) + .625(800)/.92 - 100$$
$$= \$1,193 \; billion.$$

The inflation rate π_3 can be computed by substituting Y_2 into the price adjustment curve, and so on. It takes 5 years to return to within 1 percent of potential GDP:

Year	π	P	Y
0	.000	1.00	$1,250
1	.000	1.00	1,150
2	-.080	.92	1,193
3	-.045	.88	1,219
4	-.025	.86	1,233
5	-.014	.85	1,240

The aggregate demand disturbance lowers output potential at an unchanged price level. Over time, prices fall and output rises until potential GDP is restored.

b. *In order to offset the shock, the money supply should b e increased so that $.625 \, (\Delta M/P) = -Z_d$. The money supply is therefore raised by 160 to $960 billion.*

5. Suppose the economy had the aggregate demand curve

$$Y = 500 + 1.25G + .625(M/P)$$

and the price adjustment schedule

$$\pi = (Y_{-1} - Y^*)/Y^* + Z_p,$$

where Z_p is a price shock. Potential GDP $Y^* = \$1,250$ billion, government spending G is $200 billion, and the money supply M is $800 billion.

a. Starting at potential output with the price level $P = 1$ and inflation $\pi = 0$, a price disturbance of 10 percent occurs in the first year ($Z_p = .1$). No further shocks occur ($Z_p = 0$ in all future years). Describe the path of the economy until GDP is within 1 percent of its long-run value.

b. Suppose that, starting in the first year, the Fed increases the money supply by 5 percent. Compare the new path of prices and output to the original path.

a. *The first year's price level is raised from 1 to 1.1 by the 10 percent price disturbance. Output is found from the aggregate demand curve,*

$$Y_1 = 500 + 1.25(200) + .625(800)/1.1$$
$$= \$1,250 \text{ billion,}$$

which determines the inflation rate π_2, and so on:

Year	π	P	Y
0	.000	1.00	$1,250
1	.100	1.10	1,205
2	−.036	1.06	1,222
3	−.023	1.04	1,233
4	−.014	1.03	1,238

The price disturbance raises prices and lowers output below potential. Over time, prices fall and output rises until potential GDP is restored.

b. *The technique for this part is the same as for Part a except that, starting in Year 1, the new money supply is substituted in the aggregate demand curve. The accommodative policy restores output to within 1 percent of potential in 3 years at the cost of a higher price level:*

Year	π	P	Y
0	.000	1.00	$1,250
1	.100	1.10	1,227
2	−.018	1.08	1,236
3	−.011	1.07	1,242

6. Consider the following long-run model:

$Y^* = C + I + G + X$	(Income identity)
$C = 3,000$	(Consumption)
$I = 1,000 - 1,500R$	(Investment)
$X = 500 - 1,000R$	(Net exports)

with potential output $Y^* = \$5,000$ billion and government spending $G = \$750$ billion.

a. What is the interest rate R?

b. What are the levels of consumption C, investment I, and net exports X?

c. What are the shares of consumption C, investment plus net exports $I + X$, and government purchases G?

d. What if G increases to $800 billion?

a. *We solve for the interest rate by substituting the equations for consumption, investment, and net exports, as well as the values for potential output and government spending, into the income identity:*

$$Y^* = C + I + G + X$$
$$5,000 = 3,000 + 1,000 - 1,500R + 750 + 500 - 1,000R$$
$$5,000 = 5,250 - 2,500R$$
$$R = .1 \ (10 \ percent)$$

b. *Substitute the interest rate from Part a into the consumption, investment, and net export equations:*

$$C = 3,000$$
$$I = 1,000 - 1,500(.1) = 850$$
$$X = 500 - 1,000(.1) = 400$$

c. *Dividing both sides of the income identity by* Y^*,

$$1 = \frac{C}{Y^*} + \frac{I+X}{Y^*} + \frac{G}{Y^*}$$

$$1 = \frac{3,000}{5,000} + \frac{1,250}{5,000} + \frac{750}{5,000} = .6 + .25 + .15.$$

The share of consumption $= .6$, *investment plus net exports* $= .25$, *and government purchases* $= .15$.

d. *Substitute* $G = 800$ *into the income identity:*

$$5,000 = 3,000 + 1,000 - 1,500R + 800 + 500 - 1,000R$$
$$5,000 = 5,300 - 2,500R$$
$$R = .12 \ (12 \ percent)$$

Now, we use R *to calculate* $C, I, and \ X:$

$$C = 3,000$$
$$I = 1,000 - 1,500(.12) = 820$$
$$X = 500 - 1,000(.12) = 380$$

Then calculate the shares as in Part c:

$$1 = \frac{3,000}{5,000} + \frac{1,200}{5,000} + \frac{800}{5,000} = .6 + .24 + .16.$$

The share of government purchases increases by 1 percent to .16 matched by a decrease in the share of investment plus net exports by 1 percent to .24. Because consumption does not depend on the interest rate, its share is unchanged.

Review Problems

7. Suppose the economy has the aggregate demand curve

$$Y = 667 + 1.11G + 1.11(M/P)$$

and the price adjustment schedule

$$\pi = (Y_{-1} + 1,500)/1,500 + \pi^e.$$

Government spending is $200 and the money supply is $550.

   a. Assume that expected inflation, πe, is always zero. Starting from $P_0 = 1.4$, describe the path of the economy until GDP is within 1 percent of its long-run value.

   b. Assume that $\pi^e = \pi_{-1}$. Describe the path of the economy, again starting from $P_0 = 1.4$, with zero inflation. How does your answer differ from that of Part a?

   c. Increase the money supply by $100 starting from potential GDP with the price level $P = 1$. Calculate the paths of inflation, the price level, and GDP for the first 5 years, in the case where expected inflation is always zero.

   d. Perform the same calculations as for Part c, this time for 7 years, in the case where $\pi^e = \pi_{-1}$.

8. Suppose the economy has the aggregate demand curve

$$Y = 445 + .55G + 1.67(M/P)$$

and the price adjustment schedule

$$\pi = .8(Y_{-1} - 800)/800 + \pi^e.$$

Government spending is $100 and the money supply is $180.

   a. Assume that expected inflation, π^e, is always zero. Starting from $P_0 = .8$, describe the path of the economy until GDP is within 1 percent of its long-run value.

b. Assume that $\pi^e = .4\pi_{-1}$. Describe the path of the economy, again starting from $P_0 = .8$, with zero inflation. How does your answer differ from that of Part a?

c. Decrease government spending by $20 and the money supply by $20 starting from potential GDP with the price level $P = 1$. Calculate the paths of inflation, the price level, and GDP for the first 5 years, in the case where expected inflation is always zero.

d. Perform the same calculation as in Part c, this time for 7 years, in the case where $\pi^e = .4\pi_{-1}$.

9. Suppose the economy has the aggregate demand curve

$$Y = 734 + 1.21G + .64(M/P)$$

and the price adjustment schedule

$$\pi = (Y_{-1} + 1,680)/1,680 + \pi^e.$$

Government spending is $200 and the money supply is $1,100.

a. Assume that expected inflation, π^e, is always zero. Starting from $P_0 = .8$, describe the path of the economy until GDP is within 1 percent of its long-run value.

b. Assume that $\pi^e = \pi_{-1}$. Describe the path of the economy, again starting from $P_0 = .8$, with zero inflation. How does your answer differ from that of Part a?

10. Suppose the economy has the aggregate demand curve

$$Y = 667 + 1.11G + 1.11(M/P)$$

with potential GDP $Y^* = \$1,500$ billion, government spending $G = \$200$ billion, and the money supply $M = \$550$ billion. Starting at potential GDP with the predetermined price level $P = 1$, suppose the Fed wants to lower GDP to $1,400 billion in the short run. What level of the money supply is necessary to accomplish this?

11. Suppose the economy has the aggregate demand curve

$$Y = 667 + 1.11G + 1.11(M/P) + Z_d$$

and the price adjustment schedule

$$\pi = (Y_{-1} - Y^*)/Y^*,$$

where Z_d is an aggregate demand shock. Potential GDP $Y^* = \$1,500$, government spending $G = \$200$, and the money supply $M = \$550$.

a. Starting at potential output with the price level $P = 1$ and inflation $\pi = 0$, an aggregate demand disturbance $Z_d = -\$150$ occurs in the first year. No further shocks occur ($Z_d = -\$150$ in all future years). Describe the path of the economy until GDP is within 1 percent of its long-run value.

b. How can the Fed offset the aggregate demand disturbance and keep output equal to potential GDP?

12. Suppose the economy has the aggregate demand curve

$$Y = 667 + 1.11G + 1.11(M/P)$$

and the price adjustment schedule

$$\pi = (Y_{-1} - Y^*)/Y^* + Z_p,$$

where Z_p is a price shock. Potential GDP $Y^* = \$1,500$, government spending $G = \$200$, and the money supply $M = \$550$.

a. Starting at potential output with the price level $P = 1$ and inflation $\pi = 0$, a price disturbance of 15 percent occurs in the first year ($Z_p = .15$). No further shocks occur ($Z_p = 0$ in all future years). Describe the path of the economy until GDP is within 1 percent of its long-run value.

b. Suppose that, starting in the first year, the Fed increases the money supply by 4 percent. Compare the new path of prices and output to the original path.

13. Suppose the economy has the aggregate demand curve

$$Y = 445 + .55G + 1.67(M/P)$$

with potential GDP $Y^* = \$800$ billion, government spending $G = \$100$ billion, and the money supply $M = \$180$ billion. Starting at potential GDP with the predetermined price level $P = 1$, suppose the Fed wants to raise GDP to $900 billion in the short run. What level of the money supply is necessary to accomplish this?

14. Suppose the economy has the aggregate demand curve

$$Y = 445 + .55G + 1.67(M/P) + Z_d$$

and the price adjustment schedule

$$\pi = (Y_{-1} - Y^*)/Y^*,$$

where Z_d is an aggregate demand shock. Potential GDP $Y^* = \$800$, government spending $G = \$100$, and the money supply $M = \$180$.

a. Starting at potential output with the price level $P = 1$ and inflation $\pi = 0$, an aggregate demand disturbance $Z_d = -\$50$ occurs in the first year. No further shocks occur ($Z_d = -\$50$ in all future years). Describe the path of the economy until GDP is within 1 percent of its long-run value.

b. How can the Fed offset the aggregate demand disturbance and keep output equal to potential GDP?

15. Suppose the economy has the aggregate demand curve

$$Y = 445 + .55G + 1.67(M/P)$$

and the price adjustment schedule

$$\pi = (Y_{-1} - Y^*)/Y^* + Z_p,$$

where Z_p is a price shock. Potential GDP $Y^* = \$800$, government spending $G = \$100$, and the money supply $M = \$180$.

a. Starting at potential output with the price level $P = 1$ and inflation $\pi = 0$, a price disturbance of 10 percent occurs in the first year ($Z_p = .1$). No further shocks occur ($Z_p = 0$ in all future years). Describe the path of the economy until GDP is within 1 percent of its long-run value.

b. Suppose that, starting in the first year, the Fed increases the money supply by 5 percent. Compare the new path of prices and output to the original path.

16. Suppose the economy has the aggregate demand curve

$$Y = 734 + 1.21G + .64(M/P)$$

with potential GDP $Y^* = \$1,680$ billion, government spending $G = \$200$ billion, and the money supply $M = \$1,100$ billion. Starting at potential GDP with the predetermined price level $P = 1$, suppose the Fed wants to lower GDP to $\$1,600$ billion in the short run. What level of the money supply is necessary to accomplish this?

17. Consider the following long-run model:

$$
\begin{array}{lll}
Y^* = C + I + G + X & \text{(Income identity)} \\
C = 2,000 & \text{(Consumption)} \\
I = 500 - 1,000R & \text{(Investment)} \\
X = 200 - 3,000R & \text{(Net exports)}
\end{array}
$$

with potential output $Y^* = \$3,000$ billion and government spending $G = \$900$ billion.

a. What is the interest rate?

b. What are the levels of consumption, investment, and net exports?

c. If government spending decreases to $\$700$ billion, what is the new interest rate?

18. In Problem 17, what are the shares of consumption C, investment plus net exports $I + X$, and government purchases G in GDP if

   a. $G = \$900$ billion as in Parts a and b.

   b. G decreases to $700 billion as in part c.

19. Add the following equation for money demand to the long-run model of Problem 17:

$$M = (1.2Y^* - 2{,}000R)P,$$

with potential output $Y^* = \$3{,}000$ billion and government spending $G = \$900$ billion, and the money supply $M = \$3{,}300$ billion.

   a. What is the price level?

   b. If the money supply decreases to $2,970 billion, what are the new price level and interest rate?

20. Consider the following long-run model:

$$
\begin{aligned}
Y^* &= C + I + G + X &&\text{(Income identity)} \\
C &= 1{,}500 &&\text{(Consumption)} \\
I &= 500 - 1{,}000R &&\text{(Investment)} \\
X &= 100 - 1{,}250R &&\text{(Net exports)}
\end{aligned}
$$

with potential output $Y^* = \$2{,}200$ billion and government spending $G = \$280$ billion.

   a. What is the interest rate?

   b. What are the levels of consumption, investment, and net exports?

   c. If government spending decreases to $325 billion, what is the new interest rate?

21. In Problem 20, what are the shares of consumption C, investment plus net exports $I + X$, and government purchases G in GDP if

   a. $G = \$280$ billion as in Parts a and b.

   b. G decreases to $325 billion as in part c.

22. Add the following equation for money demand to the long-run model of Problem 20:

$$M = (Y^* - 5{,}000R)P,$$

with potential output $Y^* = \$2{,}200$ billion, government spending $G = \$280$ billion, and the money supply $M = \$2{,}160$ billion.

   a. What is the price level?

   b. If the money supply decreases to $2,340 billion, what are the new price level and interest rate?

GRAPH IT

1. Draw the AD shift from Problem 10. Is this expansionary or contractionary monetary policy?

2. Draw the AD shift from Problem 13. Is this expansionary or contractionary monetary policy?

3. Draw the AD and price adjustment lines in Problem 15, using subscripts for Y and P to reflect your time path adjustment. Draw one graph without an accommodative policy from Part a and one graph with an accommodative policy from Part b.

4. Plot the price adjustment path that results from the AD shock in Problem 11a.

ANSWERS TO THE SELF-TEST

1. Aggregate demand and the price adjustment process
2. Inflationary momentum
3. Predetermined
4. Phillips
5. Expected
6. Complete crowding out
7. The Federal Reserve System
8. Shocks or disturbances
9. Aggregate demand disturbance
10. Accommodative and nonaccommodative
11. Nongovernment purchases
12. Neutrality of money or classical dichotomy
13. Inflation
14. True.   In the short run, aggregate demand determines output at a predetermined price. It is only over time that price adjustment moves output toward potential GDP.
15. True.   In the short run, with sticky prices, unemployment can be above or below its long-run, natural rate.
16. False.   When output equals potential GDP, inflation is equal to expected inflation.
17. True.   When output equals last period's GDP, the second term of the Phillips curve, Equation 9–2, is zero, leaving inflation equal to expected inflation.
18. True.   Current prices are affected by past, but not current, output. This is what is meant by prices being predetermined.

19. False. Other factors, such as people's expectations of future monetary policy, also influence expected inflation.
20. True. The rate of inflation would have to increase each year to keep inflation above expected inflation and output above potential output.
21. True. In the long run, output is equal to potential GDP, which is unaffected by aggregate demand disturbances.
22. True. Unless there is a policy response, prices return to their original level in the long run.
23. False. An oil price increase is a price shock.
24. True. Increases in the interest rate raise the exchange rate, lowering net exports.
25. False. Both investment and net exports are more sensitive to interest rates.
26. True. An increase in the level of money supply, which affects neither potential GDP nor the interest rate, causes the price level to increase in proportion.
27. In the short run, output is determined by the intersection of the aggregate demand curve and the predetermined price level.
28. In the long run, output is determined by potential GDP
29. When output is above (below) potential GDP, unemployment is below (above) the natural rate. Unemployment equals the natural rate when output equals potential GDP.
30. Inflationary momentum is the process by which past inflation affects inflationary expectations, which in turn causes current inflation.
31. Prices are predetermined because they are fixed in the short run but variable in the long run.
32. The accelerationist property is that, if real GDP is kept above potential permanently, inflation increases without bound.
33. An increase in the money supply shifts the aggregate demand curve to the right. In the short run, output increases and the price level is unchanged. Over time, prices rise and output falls. In the long run, output returns to potential at a higher price level. Money is neutral in the long run—consumption, investment, net exports, and interest rates return to their original levels.
34. Since prices are predetermined, expectations of inflation do not change the short-run results. Once prices begin to rise, people expect more inflation, which in turn increases actual inflation. Price adjustment is no longer smooth. Prices and output cycle before the long run is attained. The results for the long run are also unaffected by expectations of inflation.
35. An increase in government spending also shifts the aggregate demand curve to the right. Output increases with an unchanged price level in the short run. Over time, prices rise and output falls. In the long run, output

returns to potential at a higher price level. There is complete crowding out in the long run. The higher interest rate causes investment and net exports to decrease by the same amount that government spending increased. Expectations of inflation affect the transition from the short to the long run, but they do not change either the short-run or long-run results.

36. In the short run, output declines at an unchanged price level. Over time, prices fall and output increases until potential GDP is restored.
37. Expansionary fiscal or monetary policy can be used to shift the aggregate demand curve to the right, restoring potential GDP without a prolonged recession.
38. In the short run, prices rise and output falls. Over time, prices fall and output increases until potential GDP is restored.
39. Accommodative monetary policy, increasing the money supply in response to a price shock, shortens the recession at the cost of increasing the price level.

SOLUTIONS TO REVIEW PROBLEMS

7. a.

Year	π	P	Y
0	.000	1.40	$1,325
1	−.117	1.24	1,382
2	−.079	1.14	1,423
3	−.051	1.08	1,453
4	−.031	1.05	1,472

b.

Year	π	P	Y
0	.000	1.40	$1,325
1	−.117	1.24	1,382
2	−.196	1.00	1,500
3	−.196	.80	1,652
4	−.095	.72	1,732
5	.060	.76	1,692
6	.188	.90	1,565
7	.231	1.11	1,439

c.

Year	π	P	Y
0	.000	1.00	$1,500
1	.000	1.00	1,611
2	.074	1.07	1,561
3	.041	1.11	1,537
4	.024	1.14	1,524
5	.016	1.16	1,512

d.

Year	π	P	Y
0	.000	1.00	$1,500
1	.000	1.00	1,611
2	.074	1.07	1,561
3	.115	1.19	1,494
4	.111	1.32	1,435
5	.067	1.41	1,401
6	.001	1.41	1,400
7	−.067	1.32	1,437

8. a.

Year	π	P	Y
0	.000	.80	$876
1	.076	.86	849
2	.049	.90	833
3	.033	.93	823
4	.023	.95	816

b.

Year	π	P	Y
0	.000	.80	$876
1	.076	.86	849
2	.079	.93	824
3	.056	.98	806
4	.030	1.01	798
5	.009	1.02	795

c.

Year	π	P	Y
0	.000	1.00	$800
1	.000	1.00	756
2	−.044	.96	768
3	−.032	.93	777
4	−.023	.91	783
5	−.017	.89	788

d.

Year	π	P	Y
0	.000	1.00	$800
1	.000	1.00	756
2	−.044	.96	768
3	−.050	.91	782
4	−.038	.88	794
5	−.021	.86	799
6	−.010	.85	803
7	−.001	.85	804

9. a.

Year	π	P	Y
0	.000	.80	$1,856
1	.105	.88	1,773
2	.055	.93	1,734
3	.032	.96	1,709
4	.017	.98	1,697

b.

Year	π	P	Y
0	.000	.80	$1,856
1	.105	.88	1,773
2	.160	1.02	1,666
3	.151	1.17	1,575
4	.089	1.27	1,529
5	−.001	1.27	1,529
6	−.091	1.15	1,586
7	−.056	1.09	1,625

10. The money supply $M = (1,400 − 889)/1.11 = 460$

11. a.

Year	π	P	Y
0	.000	1.00	$1,500
1	.000	1.00	1,350
2	−.100	.90	1,417
3	−.055	.85	1,457
4	−.029	.83	1,479
5	−.014	.82	1,485

b. The money supply should be increased by $135 to $685.

12. a.

Year	π	P	Y
0	.000	1.00	$1,500
1	.015	1.15	1,420
2	−.053	1.09	1,450
3	−.034	1.05	1,469
4	−.021	1.03	1,483

a.

Year	π	P	Y
0	.000	1.00	$1,500
1	.015	1.15	1,441
2	−.039	1.11	1,464
3	−.024	1.08	1,475
4	−.017	1.06	1,487

The accommodative policy mitigates the recession at the cost of a higher price level.

13. The money supply $M = (900 - 500)/1.67 = 239.5$.

14. a.

Year	π	P	Y
0	.000	1.00	$800
1	.000	1.00	750
2	-.062	.94	771
3	-.037	.91	782
4	-.022	.89	788
5	-.015	.88	793

b. The money supply should be increased by $30 to $210.

15. a.

Year	π	P	Y
0	.000	1.00	$800
1	.010	1.10	773
2	-.033	1.06	783
3	-.022	1.04	790
4	-.013	1.03	793

b.

Year	π	P	Y
0	.000	1.00	$800
1	.010	1.10	787
2	-.016	1.08	792

The accommodative policy mitigates the recession at the cost of a higher price level.

16. The money supply $M = (1,600 - 976)/.64 = 975$.

17. a. $R = .15$.
    b. $C = 2,000$
       $I = 500 - 1,000(.15) = 350$
       $X = 200 - 3,000(.15) = -250$.
    c. $R = .1$.

18. a. The share of $C = .67$, $I + X = .03$, and $G = .30$.
    b. The share of G decreases to .23, $I + X$ increases to .10, and C is unchanged at .67.

19. a. $P = 1$.
    b. $P = .9$, $R = .15$.

20. a. $R = .08$.
    b. $C = 1,500$
       $I = 500 - 1,000(.08) = 420$
       $X = 100 - 1,250(.08) = 0$.
    c. $R = .1$.

21. a. The share of $C = .68$, $I + X = .19$, and $G = .13$.
    b. The share of G increases to .15, $I + X$ decreases to .17, and C is unchanged at .68.

22. a. $P = 1.2$.
    b. $P = 1.3$, $R = .08$.

ANSWERS TO GRAPH IT

1. The Fed is conducting contractionary monetary policy. Interest rates will rise in the short run, reducing investment and net export spending.

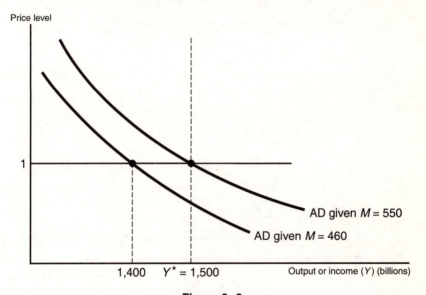

Figure 9-8

2. Here the Fed is driving down interest rates in the short run by increasing the money supply. This is expansionary monetary policy.

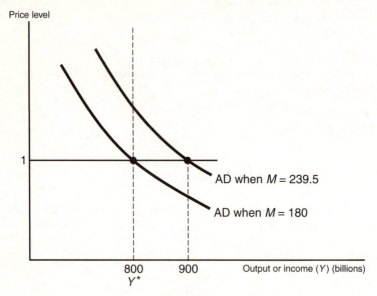

Figure 9–9

3.

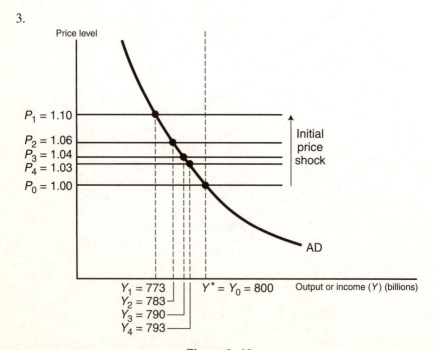

Figure 9–10

This scenario has no monetary or fiscal accommodative policy. The accommodative policy follows:

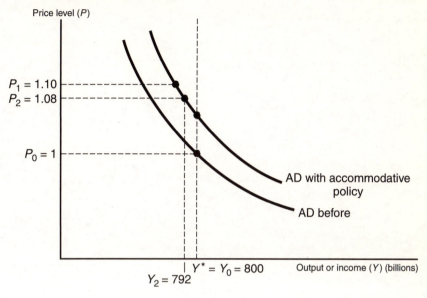

Figure 9–11

4.

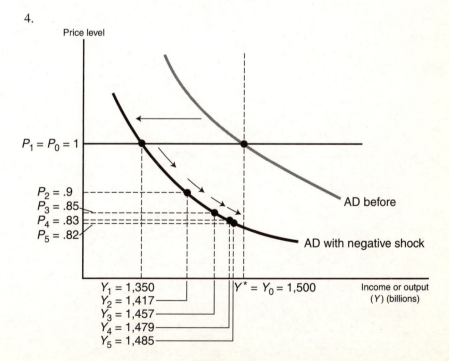

Figure 9–12

Part IV

The Microfoundations of Macroeconomics

CHAPTER 10 | Consumption Demand

MAIN OBJECTIVES

The simple consumption function discussed in Chapter 7, which says that people consume a constant fraction of their current disposable income, is an incomplete description of consumer behavior. This chapter develops a more complete description by examining the empirical evidence regarding consumption and relating consumption not only to current income but to expectations of future income and interest rates as well. You should learn the more sophisticated consumption model. Also, you should understand the implications of this model for the IS-LM analysis developed in Chapter 8 and price adjustment developed in Chapter 9. Indeed, a habit you should begin in this chapter is always to consider the impact of any new details on the complete model developed in Chapters 7, 8, and 9.

KEY TERMS AND CONCEPTS

Consumption is spending by households. Macroeconomists break consumption into three broad categories: durable goods, which are consumed over a number of years, such as automobiles; nondurable goods, which are consumed during the year that they are purchased, such as laundry detergent; and services, or professional attention, such as a visit to the barber or the doctor.

The central relationship between consumption and GDP is that, over the long run, **consumption expenditures** and GDP grow at about the same rate, but over short-run business cycles, consumption expenditures fluctuate less than GDP. These fluctuations would be even smaller if we measured true consumption rather than consumption expenditures, so that consumer durables would be counted as providing consumption over the years that they are used rather than being considered fully consumed during the period in which they are purchased.

One reason that consumption fluctuates less than GDP in the short run is because consumption depends on personal disposable income, which itself fluctuates less than GDP. Depreciation, taxes, and retained earnings by corporations are all part of GDP but not part of disposable income, while transfers from the government, such as unemployment insurance and social security, are part of disposable income but not part of GDP. Disposable income does not fall as much as GDP during recessions because tax collections decline while transfers increase. Tax collections and transfers are called **automatic stabilizers** because of their built-in stabilizing effect on disposable income.

The **Keynesian consumption function** discussed in Chapter 7 relates consumption to current disposable income,

$$C = a + bY_d, \tag{10--1}$$

where b, the **marginal propensity to consume**, has been measured at about .94 for the United States.

While this equation fits the data fairly well, there are aspects of consumption that it cannot explain. For example, the simple Keynesian consumption function overpredicted consumption through the 1980s and early 1990s and underpredicted consumption during the expansion of the 1990s. A more systematic problem is that, on average, fluctuations in consumption are not only smaller than fluctuations in GDP, they are smaller than fluctuations in disposable income: While the **long-run marginal propensity to consume** is equal to .94, the **short-run marginal propensity to consume** is equal to .72. If consumption actually followed the simple Keynesian consumption function, the short- and long-run marginal propensities to consume would be equal.

Two theories of consumption were developed during the 1950s in response to the defects in the simple Keynesian consumption function. The **life-cycle theory**, developed by Franco Modigliani, is based on a family's planning consumption over its entire lifetime and incorporates assets into the Keynesian consumption function:

$$C = b_1 Y_d + b_2 A, \tag{10--2}$$

where A is assets held by the family and b_1 and b_2 are coefficients. Empirical work by Albert Ando of the University of Pennsylvania and Franco Modigliani found that, as predicted by the life-cycle theory, holdings of assets influence consumption.

The **permanent-income theory**, developed by Milton Friedman, postulates that consumption depends not on current income but on a measure of a family's average long-run, or permanent, income:

$$C = b_p Y_p, \tag{10--3}$$

where Y_p is permanent income and b_p is a coefficient. Empirical tests by Friedman, using a weighted average of current and past incomes as a proxy for permanent income, demonstrated that his formulation fit the data better than the simple Keynesian consumption function.

Both the life-cycle and permanent-income theories are **forward-looking theories** of consumption. The most important aspect of forward-looking theories is that expected future, as well as current, income influences consumption. Families face an **intertemporal budget constraint**: They cannot have significantly negative assets. This constraint limits their consumption, but within it they can choose a wide range of consumption plans.

Without further assumptions, the forward-looking theory allows for such a wide range of consumption plans that it cannot be tested. Therefore, economists qualify it by assuming that most people prefer to keep their consumption fairly smooth from year to year, rather than have their consumption fluctuate with their yearly income. Other factors come into play in determining which smooth consumption path a family will choose. For instance, the **bequest motive**, which describes parents' preferences for assets at the end of their lifetimes, must also be known in order to determine whether the family will choose a high or low smooth consumption path.

The most important proposition of the forward-looking theory of consumption is the difference between the **marginal propensity to consume out of a temporary change in income** and the **marginal propensity to consume out of a permanent change in income**. Consider a tax cut that raises disposable income. If the tax cut is permanent, the increase in disposable income is also permanent and consumption increases by the marginal propensity to consume times the change in income. If the tax cut is temporary, disposable income returns to its original level once the tax cut ends. A family's lifetime disposable income increases much less than if the tax cut were permanent, which causes consumption to increase much less than under a permanent cut.

Another feature of the forward-looking theory of consumption involves **anticipated changes in income**. Suppose a permanent tax cut was announced one year in advance. With the announcement, people would know that their lifetime disposable income had increased and would immediately raise their consumption. The increase in consumption would occur before the tax cut actually took place.

The forward-looking theory of consumption has been extensively tested in recent years. The most compelling evidence in favor of the forward-looking theory as opposed to the simple Keynesian theory is that the short-run marginal propensity to consume is smaller than the long-run marginal propensity to consume. Additional evidence comes from examining temporary changes in policy such as the tax surcharge of 1968, the tax rebate and social security bonus of 1975, and the tax rebates of 1992 and 2001. In all cases, the response to consumption to the change in disposable income was small.

Recent empirical work on the forward-looking theory, using rational expectations to measure future income, raises some interesting questions. This research indicates that consumption is more responsive to temporary changes in income than the forward-looking theory predicts, although clearly not as responsive as in the simple Keynesian theory. Other research involving individual family histories, using panel or longitudinal surveys, produces the same result. Refinements to the forward-looking model incorporate **precautionary saving** and **liquidity**

constraints. Precautionary saving is the idea that, with uncertain future labor income and impatience, consumers put more weight on their current situation than on their expectation of future happenings. With liquidity constraints, some consumers cannot borrow as easily as the forward-looking model suggests. Both ideas explain why the marginal propensity to consume out of disposable income is higher than predicted by earlier models of the forward-looking theory.

Real interest rates may also influence consumption. If the real interest rate is positive, as it generally is, people have an incentive to defer spending. On the other hand, consumption today is preferred to consumption in the future, and this is measured by the **rate of time preference**. If the real interest rate is greater than the rate of time preference, people shift some of their consumption toward the future. These effects, like all relative price changes, are theoretically ambiguous. Higher real interest rates also raise income, which would tend to increase consumption. Indeed, the effects of real interest rates on consumption have not been strongly confirmed empirically.

The issues raised in this chapter have conflicting effects on the slope of the IS curve. Forward-looking consumers have a smaller marginal propensity to consume out of disposable income than is predicted by the Keynesian consumption function, making the multiplier smaller and the IS curve steeper than it seemed in Chapter 8. On the other hand, higher real interest rates decrease consumption, making GDP more sensitive to the interest rate and the IS curve flatter than in Chapter 8. Which effect dominates is an empirical question.

The forward-looking theory of consumption also has implications for shifts in the IS curve due to tax changes. If a tax cut is permanent, the IS curve shifts much more than if it is temporary. Expectations of future tax cuts also shift the IS curve.

SELF-TEST

Fill in the Blank

1. Over short-run business cycles, consumption expenditures fluctuate _____ than GDP.

2. Changes in taxes and transfers that cause disposable income to fluctuate less than GDP are called _____.

3. The short-run marginal propensity to consume is _____ than the long-run marginal propensity to consume.

4. The forward-looking theory of consumption combines the _____ and _____ theories.

5. The _____ limits the amount of consumption by a family over a period of years.

6. The forward-looking theory of consumption assumes that most people prefer to keep a _____ consumption path.

7. The forward-looking theory of consumption predicts that the effects of tax changes differ depending on whether they are _____ or _____.

8. Consumers are _____ if they cannot borrow as easily as the forward-looking model suggests.

9. If consumers are uncertain that an increase in permanent income will actually materialize, they will hold _____.

10. The _____ is the relative price between present and future consumption.

11. The _____ measures the preference for consumption today over consumption in the future.

12. Forward-looking consumers have a _____ marginal propensity to consume than is predicted by the Keynesian consumption function.

13. According to the forward-looking theory, anticipated tax changes shift the _____.

True-False

14. Consumption fluctuates less than consumption expenditures.

15. The relation between consumption expenditures and GDP is the same over short-run business cycles as over the long run.

16. Automatic stabilizers decrease fluctuations in disposable income.

17. According to the simple Keynesian consumption function, the short-run marginal propensity to consume is equal to the long-run marginal propensity to consume.

18. The intertemporal budget constraint means that, in any single year, a family cannot consume more than its disposable income.

19. People choose a smooth consumption path because of the bequest motive.

20. The simple Keynesian consumption function predicts that consumption will respond equally to temporary and permanent tax cuts.

21. The forward-looking theory of consumption predicts that consumption will respond equally to temporary and permanent tax cuts.

22. According to the forward-looking theory, the announcement of a tax cut one year in the future increases consumption immediately.

23. If consumers are liquidity constrained, consumption would respond more to temporary changes in income than the forward-looking theory predicts.

24. Real interest rates strongly influence consumption.

25. If consumption is negatively related to the real interest rate, the IS curve is flatter.

26. According to the forward-looking theory, the IS curve is steeper than it seemed in Chapter 8.

Review Questions

27. What is the difference between consumption and consumption expenditures?

28. What is the most important reason that consumption fluctuates less than GDP.

29. What is the major piece of evidence against the simple Keynesian consumption function?

30. What is the basic difference between the forward-looking theory of consumption and the simple Keynesian consumption function?

31. What does the forward-looking theory assume about people's preferences for steady versus erratic consumption?

32. Describe the early empirical evidence on the permanent-income and the life-cycle theories.

33. Why did the 1968 tax surcharge and the tax rebates of 1975, 1992, and 2001 provide support for the forward-looking theory?

34. What is the recent empirical evidence that points out defects in the forward-looking theory?

35. How does the idea of precautionary saving help refine the forward-looking theory?

36. Why does consumption depend on the real interest rate?

37. Why does the forward-looking theory of consumption affect the slope of the IS curve?

38. Why do temporary tax changes cause smaller shifts of the IS curve than permanent tax changes?

39. Why do expectations of future tax cuts shift the IS curve?

PROBLEM SET

Worked Problems

1. Suppose that consumption is of the form

    $$C = 500 + .8Y_p,$$

    where Y_p is permanent disposable income. Suppose also that consumers estimate their permanent disposable income by a simple average of disposable income in the current and past years:

    $$Y_p = .5(Y_d + Y_{d-1}),$$

    where Y_d is current disposable income.

    a. Suppose that disposable income Y_d is equal to $5,000 billion in Years 1 and 2. What is consumption in Year 2?

    b. What are the short- and long-run marginal propensities to consume?

    c. Suppose that disposable income increases to $6,000 billion in Year 3 and then remains at $6,000 billion in all future years. What is consumption in Years 3 and 4 and all remaining years? Explain why consumption responds the way it does to an increase in income.

    a. *Permanent income in Year 2 = .5(5,000 + 5,000) = $5,000 billion. Consumption in Year 2 = 500 + .8(5,000) = $4,500 billion.*

    b. *The short-run marginal propensity to consume (the coefficient that relates consumption, C, to disposable income, Y_d) = (.8)(.5) = .4. The long-run marginal propensity to consume (the coefficient that relates C to permanent income, Y_p) = .8.*

    c. *Permanent income in Year 3 = .5(6,000 + 5,000) = $5,500 billion. Consumption in Year 3 = 500 + .8(5,500) = $4,900 billion. Permanent income in Year 4 and all remaining years = .5(6,000 + 6,000) = $6,000 billion. Consumption in Year 4 and all remaining years = 500 + .8(6,000) = $5,300 billion. Consumption responds less in Year 3 than in Year 4 and thereafter because the short-run marginal propensity to consume is smaller than the long-run marginal propensity to consume.*

2. Suppose that consumption is given by

    $$C = 100 + .9Y_d - 1,000R$$

    rather than by the consumption function in Problem 1 of Chapter 8. Add this consumption function to the other three equations of the IS-LM model:

$$Y = C + I + G + X \qquad \text{(Income identity)}$$
$$I = 200 - 500R \qquad \text{(Investment)}$$
$$X = 100 - .12Y - 500R \qquad \text{(Net exports)}$$
$$M = (.8Y - 2,000R)P \qquad \text{(Money demand)}$$

with government spending G = $200 billion, the tax rate t = .2, the nominal money supply M = $800 billion, and the predetermined price level P = 1.

a. What is the IS curve? Compare it with the IS curve in Problem 1 of Chapter 8.

b. Derive the aggregate demand curve and calculate the effect of increases in government spending or real money on GDP. Compare your answer with Problem 2 of Chapter 8.

a. *As in Chapter 8, the IS curve is derived by substituting consumption, investment, net exports, and government spending into the income identity:*

$$Y = 1,500 - 5,000R.$$

It is flatter than the IS curve in Chapter 8, Y = 1,500 – 2,500R, because consumption depends negatively on the interest rate.

b. *The aggregate demand curve is calculated as in Chapter 8. From the LM curve,*

$$Y = 1.25(M/P) + 2,500R.$$

From the condition for spending balance, we can derive the IS curve with the G variable.

$$2,500R = 500 - .5Y + 1.25G.$$

Substituting the spending balance condition into the LM curve, we derive the aggregate demand curve:

$$Y = .83(M/P) + 333 + .83G.$$

Because the IS curve is faller, increases in government spending have less effect on GDP than in Chapter 8, while increases in real money have more effect.

Review Problems

3. Suppose that consumption is of the form

$$C = 200 + .9Y_p,$$

where Y_p is permanent disposable income. Suppose also that consumers estimate their permanent disposable income by a weighted average of disposable income in the current and past years:

$$Y_p = .7Y_d + .3Y_{d-1},$$

where Y_d is current disposable income.

a. Suppose that disposable income Y_d is equal to $6,000 in Years 1 and 2. What is consumption in Year 2?

b. Suppose that disposable income increases to $7,000 in Year 3 and then remains at $7,000 in all future years. What is consumption in Years 3 and 4 and all remaining years?

c. What are the short- and long-run marginal propensities to consume? How do they explain your answer to Part b?

4. Suppose that consumption is of the form

$$C = 300 + .9Y_p,$$

where Y_p is permanent disposable income. Suppose also that consumers estimate their permanent disposable income by a weighted average of disposable income in the current and past 2 years:

$$Y_p = .6Y_d + .3Y_{d-1} + .1Y_{d-2},$$

where Y_d is current disposable income.

a. Suppose that disposable income Y_d is equal to $8,000 in Years 1, 2, and 3. What is consumption in Year 3?

b. Suppose that disposable income increases to $9,000 in Year 4 and then remains at $9,000 in all future years. What is consumption in Years 4, 5, and 6 and all remaining years?

c. What are the short- and long-run marginal propensities to consume?

5. Suppose that consumption is given by

$$C = 300 + .8Y_d - 1{,}000R$$

rather than by the consumption function in Problem 3 of Chapter 8. Completing the IS-LM model,

$Y = C + I + G + X$	(Income identity)
$I = 200 - 1{,}500R$	(Investment)
$X = 100 - .04Y - 500R$	(Net exports)
$M = (.5Y - 2{,}000R)P$	(Money demand)

with government spending $G = 200$, the tax rate $t = .2$, the nominal money supply $M = 550$, and the predetermined price level $P = 1$.

a. What is the IS curve? Compare it with the IS curve in Problem 3 of Chapter 8.

b. Derive the aggregate demand curve and calculate the effect of increases in government spending or real money on GDP. Compare your answer with Problem 4 of Chapter 8.

6. Suppose that consumption is given by

$$C = 400 + .9Y_d - 1,500R$$

rather than by the consumption function in Problem 5 of Chapter 8. Completing the IS-LM model,

Y	$= C + I + G + X$	(Income identity)
I	$= 300 - 2,000R$	(Investment)
X	$= 100 - .05Y - 1,000R$	(Net exports)
M	$= (.4Y - 1,000R)P$	(Money demand)

with government spending $G = \$100$, the tax rate $t = .5$, the nominal money supply $M = \$180$, and the predetermined price level $P = 1$.

a. What is the IS curve? Compare it with the IS curve in Problem 5 of Chapter 8.

b. Derive the aggregate demand curve and calculate the effect of increases in government spending or real money on GDP. Compare your answer with Problem 6 of Chapter 8.

7. Suppose that consumption is given by

$$C = 400 + .9Y_d - 1,750R$$

rather than by the consumption function in Problem 7 of Chapter 8. Completing the IS-LM model,

Y	$= C + I + G + X$	(Income identity)
I	$= 200 - 1,800R$	(Investment)
X	$= 200 - .1Y - 200R$	(Net exports)
M	$= (.8Y - 3,000R)P$	(Money demand)

with government spending $G = \$200$ billion, the tax rate $t = .3333$, the nominal money supply $M = \$1,104$ billion, and the predetermined price level $P = 1$.

a. What is the IS curve? Compare it with the IS curve in Problem 7 of Chapter 8.

b. Derive the aggregate demand curve and calculate the effect of increases in government spending or real money on GDP. Compare your answer with Problem 8 of Chapter 8.

GRAPH IT

1. Sketch an IS-LM diagram. Compare two cases: one in which consumption depends negatively on the interest rate and one where the consumption function does not depend on the interest rate. Which case yields a more effective expansionary monetary policy? How do we judge effectiveness?

ANSWERS TO THE SELF-TEST

1. Less
2. Automatic stabilizers
3. smaller
4. Permanent-income and life-cycle
5. Intertemporal budget constraint
6. Smooth
7. Temporary or permanent
8. Liquidity constrained
9. Precautionary savings
10. Real interest rate
11. Rate of time preference
12. Smaller
13. IS curve
14. True.   Consumption expenditures count consumer durables such as automobiles, when they are purchased rather than over the time they are used.
15. False. Over the long run, consumption expenditures and GDP grow at about the same rate, but over short-run business cycles, consumption expenditures fluctuate less than GDP.
16. True.   Automatic stabilizers, such as taxes, which fall during recessions, and transfers, which rise during recessions, are the reason that disposable income fluctuates less than GDP.
17. True.   The simple Keynesian consumption function is that consumption depends on current disposable income, which equates the short- and long-run marginal propensities to consume.
18. False. The intertemporal budget constraint limits consumption over a period of many years, not for any single year.
19. False. People choose a smooth consumption path because they prefer steady to erratic consumption. The bequest motive determines which smooth path they choose.
20. True.   They both raise current disposable income by the same amount.
21. False. A temporary tax cut causes only a small increase in lifetime disposable income and so causes only a small increase in consumption.

22. True.   The announcement of a future tax cut increases lifetime disposable income and, to maintain a smooth consumption path, consumption increases immediately.
23. True.   Liquidity-constrained consumers are not able to borrow sufficiently to smooth consumption as much as the forward-looking theory predicts.
24. False.   The effects of real interest rates on consumption have not been strongly confirmed empirically.
25. True.   A negative relation between consumption and the real interest rate makes GDP more sensitive to the interest rate and the IS curve flatter.
26. False.   The forward-looking theory incorporates two conflicting factors, making the total effect ambiguous.
27. The distinction applies only to consumer durables. Consumption expenditure occurs when the good, such as a car, is purchased. Consumption occurs as the car is used up.
28. The most important reason why consumption fluctuates less than GDP is that consumption depends on disposable income, which itself fluctuates less than GDP.
29. The short-run marginal propensity to consume is less than the long-run marginal propensity to consume.
30. The simple Keynesian consumption function depends only on current disposable income, while the forward-looking theory depends on both current and expected disposable income.
31. It assumes that people prefer steady rather than erratic consumption.
32. Milton Friedman found that the permanent-income formulation of the consumption function fit the data better than the simple Keynesian formulation. Albert Ando and Franco Modigliani found that, as predicted by the life-cycle theory, assets as well as disposable income influence consumption.
33. All were temporary. As predicted by the forward-looking theory, none had much effect on consumption.
34. Recent empirical evidence, assuming rational expectations, finds that consumption is more sensitive to temporary changes in income than would be predicted by the forward-looking theory. Studies using individual family histories find the same result.
35. When making consumption decisions, people do not know with certainty their lifetime earnings. This leads to impatience; consumers then discount expected future income by more than the interest rate. This helps explain why the marginal propensity to consume out of disposable income is higher than predicted by the forward-looking theory.
36. The real interest rate, as the relative price between present and future consumption, influences the choice of whether to consume more today or more tomorrow.

37. According to the forward-looking theory, the multiplier is smaller than in Chapter 8, making the IS curve steeper, but consumption depends on real interest rates, making the IS curve flatter.
38. Temporary tax changes have less effect on consumption than permanent tax changes, causing smaller shifts of the IS curve.
39. Expectations of future tax cuts increase consumption, shifting the IS curve.

SOLUTIONS TO REVIEW PROBLEMS

3. a. Permanent income in Year 2 = .7(6,000) + .3(6,000) = $6,000. Consumption in Year 2 = 200 + .9(6,000) = $5,600.
   b. Permanent income in Year 3 = .7(7,000) + .3(6,000) = $6,700. Consumption in Year 3 = 200 + .9(6,700) = $6,230. Permanent income in Year 4 and all remaining years = $7,000. Consumption in Year 4 and all remaining years = 200 + .9(7,000) = $6,500.
   c. The short-run marginal propensity to consume = (.9)(.7) = .63. The long-run marginal propensity to = .9. In Part b, consumption in Year 3 increases by $630, the short-run marginal propensity to consume, .63, times the change in disposable income, $1,000. Consumption in Year 4 and thereafter increases by $900, the long-run marginal propensity to consume, .9, times the change in income.
4. a. Consumption in Year 3 = $7,500.
   b. Consumption in Year 4 = $8,040, in Year 5 = $8,310, and in Year 6 and in all subsequent years = $8,400.
   c. The short-run marginal propensity to consume = .54. The long-run marginal propensity to consume = .9.
5. a. The IS curve is $Y = 2,000 - 7,500R$. It is flatter than the IS curve in Chapter 8.
   b. The aggregate demand curve is $Y = 1.3(M/P) + 523 + .87G$. Because the IS curve is flatter, increases in government spending have less effect on GDP than in Chapter 8, while increases in real money have more effect.
6. a. The IS curve is $Y = 1,500 - 7,500R$. It is flatter than the IS curve in Chapter 8.
   b. The aggregate demand curve is $Y = 1.88(M/P) + 334 + .42G$. Because the IS curve is flatter, increases in government spending have less effect on GDP than in Chapter 8, while increases in real money have more effect.
7. a. The IS curve is $Y = 2,000 - 7,500R$. It is flatter than the IS curve in Chapter 8.
   b. The aggregate demand curve is $Y = .83 (M/P) + 533 + .67G$. Because the IS curve is flatter, increases in government spending have less effect on GDP than in Chapter 8, while increases in real money have more effect.

ANSWERS TO GRAPH IT

1.

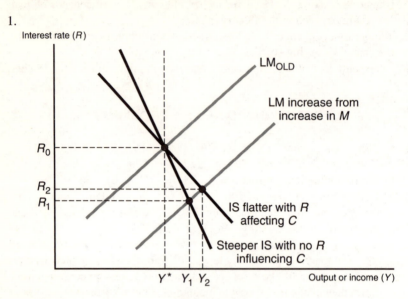

Interest rate (R)

LM_{OLD}

LM increase from increase in M

R_0

R_2
R_1

IS flatter with R affecting C

Steeper IS with no R influencing C

Y^* Y_1 Y_2

Output or income (Y)

Figure 10–1

Initially we observe R_0 and Y^*. Expansionary monetary policy shifts the LM curve right. When consumption depends negatively on the interest rate, a drop in interest rates not only stimulates investment and net exports but also consumption. Income increases by more to Y_2, and with income changes being our criteria for effectiveness, we say monetary policy is more effective when C depends negatively on R.

CHAPTER 11 | Investment Demand

MAIN OBJECTIVES

Investment is the most volatile component of aggregate demand. Chapter 11 expands the simple investment demand function of Chapter 8 by examining the microeconomic underpinnings of investment behavior. You should learn how investment, influenced by the forward-looking behavior of firms, depends in a systematic way on output as well as on interest rates. You should also be able to explain these effects on investment in the IS-LM framework.

KEY TERMS AND CONCEPTS

Investment is the flow of newly produced capital goods. It consists of three subcategories: **nonresidential fixed investment**, or business purchases of new plant and equipment; **residential fixed investment**, or construction of new houses and apartments; and **inventory investment**, or increases in stocks of goods produced but not yet sold.

The **desired capital stock** is the amount of factories, equipment, and supplies that firms desire. It is determined by equating the **marginal cost** and the **marginal benefit** of employing more capital. Firms need to be forward-looking in order to determine the marginal benefit.

The rental price of capital is the cost of using capital for 1 year. It depends on the real price of new equipment, the real interest rate, and the rate of depreciation:

$$R^K = (R + d)P^K, \tag{11--1}$$

where R^K is the rental price of capital, R is the interest rate, d is the rate of depreciation, and P^K is the price of new equipment.

Since the rental price of capital is the cost of using capital, the desired capital stock declines if the rental price of capital rises. The desired capital stock increases if planned output rises, because it is generally advantageous to use more of both capital and labor to produce additional output. It also increases if the wage rises, because a higher wage lowers the cost of capital relative to labor. Algebraically,

$$K^* = k(W/R^K)Y, \tag{11-2}$$

where K^* is the desired capital stock, W is the wage, R^K is the rental price of capital, Y is output, and k is a coefficient.

The **investment function** shows the amount of investment a firm will undertake during the year. If there is no depreciation, investment equals the change in the actual capital stock, $K - K_{-1}$. If there are no lags in the investment process, so that firms can attain their desired capital stock within 1 year, investment can be written as the difference between the desired capital stock and last year's capital stock,

$$I = K^* - K_{-1} = r(W/R^K)Y - K_{-1}, \tag{11-3}$$

where I is investment. The investment function shows that investment depends positively on the wage rate and output and negatively on the rental price of capital. Since the rental price of capital rises with the real interest rate, investment depends negatively on the interest rate.

The **accelerator** describes the relation between investment and output. If the desired capital stock is attained within one year, this year's capital stock, K, depends on this year's output, Y, and so last year's capital stock, K_{-1}, depends on last year's output, Y_{-1}. Then the level of investment, I, which is the change in the capital stock, ΔK, depends on the change in output, Y. When output accelerates—when its change gets bigger—investment increases.

A large part of investment serves to replace, rather than add to, the capital stock. The **rate of depreciation** is the fraction of the capital stock that wears out each year. If a constant fraction d of the existing capital stock wears out each year, the net investment function, Equation 11–3, can be changed into a gross investment function by adding d times K_{-1} to the right-hand side of the equation.

While net investment, the change in the capital stock, depends on the change in output, replacement investment is related to the level of the capital stock and depends on the level of output. Thus investment depends on both the level and the change in output.

Lags in the investment function prevent the capital stock from being adjusted to its desired level immediately. For many investment projects, such as building a new factory, there is a lag of several years between the decision to invest and the completion of the project. These lags can be modeled by modifying the investment function,

$$I = s(K^* - K_{-1}), \tag{11-4}$$

where *s* is the fraction of the difference between the desired and actual capital stock that can be changed within 1 year. Studies indicate that the value of *s* is between one-tenth and one-third.

Taxes can have a substantial influence on investment. Taxation of capital discourages investment, while investment incentives increase investment. If *u* is the tax rate on rental income, so that after-tax rental incomes $(1 - u)R^K$, and *z* is the investment incentive, so that the cost of purchasing a machine is $(1 - z)P^K$, the rental price of capital becomes

$$R^K = \frac{(R + d)(1 - z)P^K}{1 - u}. \tag{11-5}$$

Compared with Equation 11–1, the net effect of taxation and investment incentives is to multiply the rental price of capital by $(1 - z)/(1 - u)$.

Three types of tax policies are used to increase investment. The **investment tax credit** would add .1 to the variable *z* in Equation 11–5. A permanent investment tax credit raises the desired capital stock, causing positive net investment as firms increase their capital. **Write-offs** are depreciation deductions for fixed investment. When these are accelerated, *z* rises and the rental price of capital falls, increasing investment. **Capital gains taxes** are one of the determinants of the interest rate *R*. A lower capital gains tax rate stimulates investment. The **Tax Reform Act of 1986**, which included an elimination of the investment tax credit and a reduction of write-offs, raised the rental price of capital by about 10 percent.

The effect of tax and subsidy policies on investment depends on whether the changes are temporary or permanent. In general, temporary policies are more effective than permanent policies for stimulating the economy. For example, a 1-year investment tax credit during a recession would stimulate investment as businesses pushed up the start of investment projects in order to take advantage of the credit before it expired.

Anticipated tax changes can have perverse effects. For instance, expectations of an increase in the investment tax credit 1 year from now decreases current investment as firms wait for the tax credit to come into effect before starting investment projects. Expectations of the elimination of the investment tax credit can explain why investment rose at the end of 1985, just before the credit was eliminated, then fell in early 1986.

Residential investment can be analyzed in much the same way as business investment. One difference is that the annual rate of depreciation for business equipment is about 10 percent, while the rate of depreciation for houses is about 2 percent. Consequently, the real interest rate is a much larger fraction of the rental price of housing than it is of the rental price of business capital, and residential investment is much more sensitive to fluctuations in interest rates than business investment. Monetary policy, through its effect on interest rates, has a very large effect on residential construction.

Inventory investment can also be analyzed like business investment. The **pipe-line function** describes inventories that are an intrinsic part of the production process, such as automobile parts held by a car manufacturer. The **buffer-stock function** describes finished goods that are ready for sale, such as automobiles held by a car dealer. About two-thirds of inventories are held for the pipeline function, with the other third for the buffer-stock function

   Investment depends positively on real GDP and negatively on the real interest rate. In terms of the IS-LM framework, the dependence of investment on GDP increases the multiplier, raising the intercept of the IS curve and making it flatter. Because of lags in the investment process, the response of investment to changes in interest rates is small in the very short run and increases over time. This makes the IS curve close to vertical in the very short run but flatter over longer periods.

SELF-TEST

Fill in the Blank

1. The three categories of investment spending are _____, _____, and _____.

2. Fluctuations in investment are _____ than fluctuations in real GDP.

3. The cost of capital to a firm is measured by the _____ of capital.

4. Firms invest if their actual capital stock differs from their _____ capital stock.

5. The desired capital stock depends on the _____, _____, and _____.

6. If there is no depreciation, investment is the change in the _____.

7. Investment depends _____ on the wage rate, _____ on the rental price of capital, and _____ on output.

8. The _____ shows the amount of investment a firm will undertake during the year.

9. The _____ is the fraction of the capital stock that wears out each year.

10. _____ in the investment function prevent the capital stock from being adjusted to its desired level immediately.

11. The accelerator describes the effect of the _____ of output on the _____ of investment.

12. The two functions of inventories are the _____ and _____ functions.

13. Three types of tax policies used to increase investment are the
    _____, _____, and _____.

True-False

14. Investment is the least volatile component of aggregate demand.

15. The rental price of capital increases if the rate of depreciation rises.

16. The desired capital stock increases when output rises.

17. Investment is high when wages are high.

18. When the price of new equipment rises, investment is high.

19. The actual capital stock is always equal to the desired capital stock.

20. Gross investment is equal to the change in the capital stock.

21. The accelerator describes the effect of the level of output on the change of investment.

22. The Jobs and Growth Tax Relief Reconciliation Act of 2003 lowered the capital gains tax rate.

23. Anticipated and unanticipated tax credits have the same effects on investment.

24. Temporary and permanent tax credits are equally effective for stimulating investment.

25. Monetary policy has more effect on residential investment than on business fixed investment.

26. Inventory investment tends to be closely related to changes in production.

Review Questions

27. Why do firms need to be forward looking when they determine their desired capital stock?

28. How is the rental price of capital determined?

29. What are the determinants of the desired capital stock?

30. Why does investment depend negatively on the real interest rate?

31. Why does the level of investment depend on the change of output?

32. Why does the level of investment depend on the level of output?

33. Why are there lags in the investment process?

34. What is the relation between the stock market and investment?

35. Describe how the tax system influences investment.

36. What policies could the government use to stimulate investment?

37. Why is residential investment very sensitive to fluctuations in the interest rate?

38. What is the relation between the interest sensitivity of investment and the slope of the IS curve?

39. Why do lags in the investment process make the IS curve steeper in the very short run?

PROBLEM SET

Worked Problems

1. Suppose that the demand for investment is given by

$$I = .5(K^* - K_{-1}),$$

where K^* is the desired stock of capital given by

$$K^* = .025(Y/R),$$

where Y is output and R is the interest rate. Assume that there is no depreciation.

a. Calculate the desired capital stock in Year 1 if output is $1,000 billion and the interest rate is .1 (10 percent).

b. What is the level of investment in Year 1 if the capital stock in Year 0 was $150 billion?

c. Assuming that output and the interest rate are constant, what is investment in Years 2 and 3 and all subsequent years?

a. *The desired capital stock $K^* = .025(1,000)/.1 = $250 billion.*

b. *Investment $I_1 = .5(250 - 150) = $50 billion. The long-run marginal propensity to consume (the coefficient that relates C to permanent income, Y_p) = .8.*

c. *The relation between current and previous stocks of capital is $K = K_{-1} + I$. In this problem, $K_1 = K_0 + I_1$. The capital stock K_1 increases by I_1 to $200 billion. Since the desired capital stock K^* is unchanged,*

$$I_2 = .5(250 - 200) = $25 \text{ billion.}$$

Similarly,

$$I_3 = .5(250 - 225) = $12.5 \text{ billion.}$$

Investment decreases by one-half each year and eventually approaches zero.

2. Suppose that investment is given by

$$I = 200 - 500R + .2Y$$

rather than by the investment function in Problem 1 of Chapter 8. Add this investment function to the other equations of the IS-LM model:

$$Y = C + I + G + X \quad \text{(Income identity)}$$
$$C = 100 + .9Y_d \quad \text{(Consumption)}$$
$$X = 100 - .12Y - 500R \quad \text{(Net exports)}$$
$$M = (.8Y - 2{,}000R)P \quad \text{(Money demand)}$$

with government spending $G = \$200$ billion, the tax rate $t = .2$, the nominal money supply $M = \$800$ billion, and the predetermined price level $P = 1$.

a. What is the IS curve? Compare it with the IS curve in Problem 1 of Chapter 8.

b. Derive the aggregate demand curve and calculate the effect of increases in government spending or real money on GDP. Compare your answer with Problem 2 of Chapter 8.

a. *As in Chapter 8, the IS curve is derived by substituting consumption, investment, net exports, and government spending into the income identity:*

$$Y = 3{,}000 - 5{,}000R.$$

Because investment depends positively on income, the multiplier is greater than in the sample problem of Chapter 8. This makes the IS curve flatter.

b. *The aggregate demand curve is calculated as in Chapter 8. From the LM curve,*

$$Y = 1.25(M/P) + 2{,}500R.$$

From the condition for spending balance,

$$2{,}500R = 1{,}000 - .5Y + 2.5G.$$

Substituting the condition for spending balance into the LM curve, we derive the aggregate demand curve,

$$Y = .83(M/P) + 667 + 1.67G.$$

Because of the larger multiplier, increases both in government spending and in real money have more effect on GDP than in the model used in Chapter 8.

Review Problems

3. Suppose that the demand for investment is given by

$$I = .2(K^* - K_{-1}),$$

where K^* is the desired stock of capital given by

$$K^* = .01(Y/R),$$

where Y is output and R is the interest rate. Assume that there is no depreciation.

    a. Calculate the desired capital stock in Year 1 if output is \$2,000 and the interest rate is .05 (5 percent).

    b. What is the level of investment in Year 1 if the capital stock in Year 0 was \$200?

    c. Assuming that output and the interest rate are constant, what is investment in Years 2 and 3 and all subsequent years?

4. Answer Problem 3 if the interest rate is .10 (10 percent).

5. Suppose that investment is given by

$$I = 200 - 1,500R + .2Y$$

rather than by the investment function in Problem 3 of Chapter 8. Complete the IS-LM model:

$$
\begin{aligned}
Y &= C + I + G + X &&\text{(Income identity)}\\
C &= 300 + .8Y_d &&\text{(Consumption)}\\
X &= 100 - .04Y - 500R &&\text{(Net exports)}\\
M &= (.5Y - 2,000R)P &&\text{(Money demand)}
\end{aligned}
$$

with government spending $G = \$200$, the tax rate $t = .2$, the nominal money supply $M = \$550$, and the predetermined price level $P = 1$.

    a. What is the IS curve? Compare it with the IS curve in Problem 3 of Chapter 8.

    b. Derive the aggregate demand curve and calculate the effect of increases in government spending or real money on GDP. Compare your answer with Problem 4 of Chapter 8.

6. Suppose that investment is given by

$$I = 300 - 2,000R + .1Y$$

rather than by the investment function in Problem 5 of Chapter 8. Completing the IS-LM model:

$$Y = C + I + G + X \qquad \text{(Income identity)}$$
$$C = 400 + .9Y_d \qquad \text{(Consumption)}$$
$$X = 100 - .05Y - 1{,}000R \qquad \text{(Net exports)}$$
$$M = (.4Y - 1{,}000R)P \qquad \text{(Money demand)}$$

with government spending $G = \$100$, the tax rate $t = .5$, the nominal money supply $M = \$180$, and the predetermined price level $P = 1$.

a. What is the IS curve? Compare it with the IS curve in Problem 5 of Chapter 8.

b. Derive the aggregate demand curve and calculate the effect of increases in government spending or real money on GDP. Compare your answer with Problem 6 of Chapter 8.

7. Suppose that investment is given by

$$I = 200 - 1{,}800R + .1Y$$

rather than by the investment function in Problem 7 of Chapter 8. Complete the IS-LM model:

$$Y = C + I + G + X \qquad \text{(Income identity)}$$
$$C = 400 + .9Y_d \qquad \text{(Consumption)}$$
$$X = 200 - .1Y - 200R \qquad \text{(Net exports)}$$
$$M = (.8Y - 3{,}000R)P \qquad \text{(Money demand)}$$

with government spending $G = \$200$, the tax rate $t = .3333$, the nominal money supply $M = \$1{,}104$, and the predetermined price level $P = 1$.

a. What is the IS curve? Compare it with the IS curve in Problem 7 of Chapter 8.

b. Derive the aggregate demand curve and calculate the effect of increases in government spending or real money on GDP. Compare your answer with Problem 8 of Chapter 8

GRAPH IT

1. Suppose that GDP is currently at potential output and Congress passes investment tax credits. Sketch this situation on an IS-LM diagram. Is this new equilibrium sustainable?

ANSWERS TO THE SELF-TEST

1. Nonresidential fixed investment, residential fixed investment, and inventory investment
2. Greater
3. Rental price
4. Desired
5. Wage rate, level of output, and rental price of capital
6. Actual capital stock
7. Positively, negatively, and positively
8. Investment function
9. Rate of depreciation
10. Lags
11. Change of output on the level of investment
12. Pipeline and buffer stock
13. Investment tax credit, write-offs, and capital gains taxes
14. False. Investment is the most volatile component of aggregate demand.
15. True. Higher depreciation raises the rental cost of capital, which increases the rental price.
16. True. With higher output, firms want to use more capital in production.
17. True. High wages cause firms to substitute away from labor toward capital, which raises the desired capital stock and investment.
18. False. An increase in the price of new equipment raises the rental price of capital, which lowers the desired capital stock and investment.
19. False. Lags in the investment process can cause the actual and desired capital stock to differ.
20. False. Net investment is equal to the change in the capital stock. Gross investment also includes investment to replace depreciated capital.
21. False. The accelerator describes the effect of the change of output on the level of investment.
22. True. The act of 2003 lowered the maximum capital gains tax rate from 20 to 15 percent. This is expected to stimulate investment.
23. False. An unanticipated tax credit raises investment immediately. An anticipated tax credit first decreases investment while firms wait for the credit to occur.
24. False. Temporary tax credits are more effective because they cause businesses to push up the start of investment projects.
25. True. Residential investment is more sensitive to interest rates than business fixed investment.
26. True. Most inventory investment is for the pipeline function, which closely follows changes in production.
27. Firms determine their desired capital stock by equating the marginal benefits of capital to the rental cost of capital. They need to be forward looking in order to determine the marginal benefits.

28. The rental price of capital is the price of new equipment multiplied by the sum of the real interest rate plus the rate of depreciation.
29. The determinants of the desired capital stock are the wage rate, the level of output, and the rental price of capital.
30. A higher real interest rate raises the renal price of capital, lowering the desired capital stock and investment.
31. In a world without depreciation, the level of investment is the change in the capital stock. Since the level of the capital stock depends on the level of output, the change in the capital stock depends on the change in output.
32. Replacement investment, the fraction of investment that serves to replace the depreciated capital stock, depends on the level of the capital stock and thus on the level of output.
33. Much investment spending, such as building new factories, takes time and cannot be completed within 1 year.
34. Increases in stock prices raise investment and decreases in stock prices reduce investment spending. Firms undertake investment because they hope to increase future profits. Market participants want to share in this, thereby bidding up the stock price. This relation is complicated with asymmetric information and the double taxation of dividend income.
35. Taxation of capital decreases investment. Tax incentives for investment, such as the investment tax credit, write-offs, and reduction in capital gains taxes, stimulate investment.
36. Investment tax credits, tax credits for house purchases, accelerated depreciation of capital, and cuts in the capital gains tax rate are examples of government policies that would stimulate investment.
37. Because the rate of depreciation of houses is slow, the interest rate is a large fraction of the rental price of housing, and residential investment is very sensitive to fluctuations in the interest rate.
38. The greater is the interest sensitivity of investment, the flatter the IS curve.
39. Lags in the investment process make investment very insensitive to interest rates in the very short run, making the IS curve steeper in the very short run than it is otherwise.

SOLUTIONS TO REVIEW PROBLEMS

3. a. The desired capital stock $K^* = .01(2,000)/.05 = \$400$.
   b. Investment $I_1 = .2(400 - 200) = \$40$.
   c. The capital stock K_1 increases by 40 to 240. Since the desired capital stock K^* is unchanged,

$$I_2 = .2(400 - 240) = \$32.$$
$$I_3 = .2(400 - 272) = \$25.6.$$

Investment decreases by one-fifth each year and eventually approaches zero.

4. a. The desired capital stock $K^* = .01(2,000)/.1 = \$200$.
    b. Investment $I_1 = .2(400 - 400) = 0$ since the actual capital stock equals the desired capital stock.
    c. Investment equals zero in all subsequent years.
5. a. The IS curve is $Y = 4,000 - 10,000R$. It is flatter than the IS curve in Chapter 8.
    b. The aggregate demand curve is $Y = 1.43(M/P) + 857 + 1.43G$. Because the multiplier is larger, increases in both government spending and real money have more effect on GDP than in Chapter 8.
6. a. The IS curve is $Y = 1,800 - 6,000R$. It is flatter than the IS curve in Chapter 8.
    b. The aggregate demand curve is $Y = 1.76(M/P) + 470 + .58G$. Because the multiplier is larger, increases in both government spending and real money have more effect on GDP than in Chapter 8.
7. a. The IS curve is $Y = 2,500 - 5,000R$. It is flatter than the IS curve in Chapter 8.
    b. The aggregate demand curve is $Y = .71(M/P) + 857 + 1.07G$. Because the multiplier is larger, increases in both government spending and real money have more effect on GDP than in Chapter 8.

ANSWERS TO GRAPH IT

1.

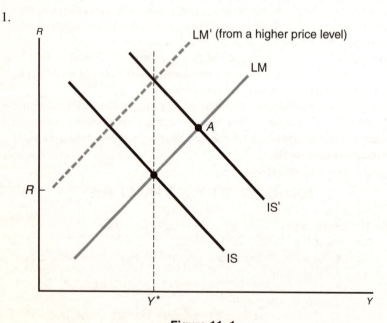

Figure 11–1

Point A, the new equilibrium, is not sustainable. Eventually prices will rise to bid away the positive GDP gap.

CHAPTER 12

Foreign Trade and the Exchange Rate

MAIN OBJECTIVES

Issues involving foreign trade and the exchange rate play a central role in the performance of the U.S. economy. The unprecedented trade deficit and roller-coaster ride of the dollar during the 1980s and 1990s led to proposals for protectionism and exchange-rate stabilization. Chapter 12 discusses the causes of trade imbalances and exchange-rate fluctuations, considers the effects of these foreign influences on the U.S. economy, and analyzes whether proposals for protectionism and exchange-rate stabilization do more harm than good.

KEY TERMS AND CONCEPTS

Exports are sales of goods and services to the rest of the world. Imports are purchases of goods and services from the rest of the world. The terms of trade is the ratio of the price of exports to the price of imports. **Net exports** are exports minus imports. There is a **trade surplus** when exports are greater than imports and a **trade deficit** when imports are greater than exports. A trade deficit must be financed by borrowing from abroad. This borrowing is called a **capital inflow**.

The **exchange rate** is the price of one currency in terms of another. For the United States, it is the amount of foreign currency that can be bought with 1 dollar, for example, 100 Japanese yen. If more foreign currency can be bought with 1 dollar, say, 110 yen, then we say that the dollar rises or **appreciates** with respect to that currency. If less foreign currency can be bought with 1 dollar, then the dollar falls, or **depreciates**.

Currencies are traded in the **foreign exchange market**, which is a worldwide network of banks rather than a single organized market. For a variety of reasons,

188 | *Chapter 12*

the major industrialized countries fixed exchange rates prior to 1971. Today's international monetary system is called a **floating** or **flexible exchange-rate system** because there is a free market in foreign exchange. The **trade-weighted exchange rate** is an average of several different exchange rates, each weighted by the amount of trade with the United States. It measures the exchange rate between the United States and the rest of the world.

The **real exchange rate** is a measure of the relative price of goods produced in the United States compared to the price of goods produced in the rest of the world (ROW),

$$\text{Real exchange rate} = EP/P_w, \qquad (12–1)$$

where E is the trade-weighted exchange rate, P is the U.S. price level, and P_w is the ROW price level. When the real exchange rate is high, foreigners have to pay more for goods produced in the United States compared with goods produced in the rest of the world. The exchange rate E is sometimes called the **nominal exchange rate**. Recall, in the short run, both U.S. and ROW price levels are predetermined. The real exchange rate, EP/P_w, varies with the exchange rate (E). In the long run, prices are flexible and the real exchange rate is constant. **Purchasing power parity** is a theory proposing that the real exchange rate is constant. It does not hold for the short run but does for the long run. The theory of long-run purchasing power parity is that there is a constant long-run level of the real exchange rate.

The **net export function** relates net exports to real income and the real exchange rate,

$$X = g - mY - n(EP/P_w), \qquad (12–2)$$

where g is a constant and m and n are coefficients. Net exports depend negatively on real income because, as domestic income rises, our imports increase. The coefficient m is called the **marginal propensity to import**. Net exports depend negatively on the real exchange rate because a higher real exchange rate makes our goods more expensive relative to foreign goods. This increases our imports and decreases our exports.

To complete our theory, we now need to explain what determines the real exchange rate in the short run. Here, real interest rates play a key role. When the U.S. interest rate rises in comparison to other interest rates, U.S. assets become more attractive and the dollar appreciates. The positive relation between the real exchange rate and the U.S. interest rate can be expressed as

$$EP/P_w = q + vR, \qquad (12–3)$$

where q is a constant and v is a coefficient. Combining the equation for the real exchange rate with the net export function enables us to derive the open-economy IS curve, which was discussed in Chapter 8.

The **open-economy IS curve** differs from what the IS curve would be in a closed economy, in two ways. First, net exports depend negatively on income, which makes the open-economy multiplier, $1/[1 - b(1 - t) + m]$, smaller than the closed-economy multiplier and the IS curve steeper. This reduction in the size of the multiplier is called **leakage**. Second, as can be seen by combining Equations 12–2 and 12–3, net exports depend negatively on the interest rate. This makes the IS curve flatter. The LM curve is the same as for a closed economy.

Expansionary monetary policy lowers interest rates, causes the exchange rate to depreciate, and stimulates net exports as well as investment in the short run. Over time, if output was pushed beyond potential, prices rise and output falls toward potential. In the long run the real exchange rate returns to parity and the nominal exchange rate depreciates by the increase in the price level. Monetary policy is neutral in the long run.

Expansionary fiscal policy increases interest rates, causes the exchange rate to appreciate, increases the trade deficit (or reduces the trade surplus), and raises output above potential in the short run. Hence, the increase in government spending crowds out export industries as well as investment. The government budget deficit is partially financed by the capital inflow from abroad. Over time, prices rise and output falls toward potential. In the long run, the interest rate and real exchange rate are permanently higher.

Changes in the exchange rate have an immediate impact on the price level for a small country by changing the price of imports. The situation is quite different for the United States Importers tend to keep the dollar price of their goods stable through swings in the exchange rate. For the large U.S. economy, movements in the exchange rate do not create price shocks.

Protectionist policies include **tariffs** on imports, **quotas** on the quantity of imports, and outright **bans** on some imports. They help domestic producers by lessening foreign competition but hurt consumers by raising prices on imported goods. The effects on prices are sticky for tariffs but immediate for quotas. Protection stimulates net exports and shifts the IS curve outward, raising interest rates and the exchange rate. Protectionist policies also invite retaliation by our trading partners, which would undo any benefits and reduce the welfare of all involved nations.

The Fed can **stabilize** the exchange rate by using monetary policy to keep the interest rate constant, which would make the LM curve perfectly flat. In that case monetary policy could not be used for other goals, such as preventing fluctuations in unemployment or prices. With a flat LM curve, fiscal policy becomes more powerful but spending disturbances, such as investment shocks, that shift the IS curve cause large movements in GDP.

In the long run, with flexible prices the behavior of exchange rates, price levels, and monetary policy is determined by purchasing power parity,

$$PE = P_w, \tag{12–4}$$

where P is the domestic price level, E is the exchange rate, and P_w is the world price level. Also remember from Chapter 9, the price level P is simply proportional to the money supply in the long run. A fixed exchange-rate system locks monetary policy into defending a fixed E. If world prices rise by 50 percent over a decade, then the money supply (and thereby the domestic price level) must also rise by 50 percent. If there is steady foreign inflation, the domestic inflation rate must adjust to equal the world inflation rate.

A floating exchange-rate system permits different countries to have different inflation rates, even in the long run, as long as the rate of appreciation of the currency is equal to the difference between the foreign inflation rate and the home inflation rate:

$$\pi_w - \pi = \Delta E/E, \tag{12-5}$$

where π_w is the world inflation rate, π is home inflation, and $\Delta E/E$ is the rate of appreciation. Inflation rate differentials then determine the long-run behavior of the exchange rate. The behavior of actual exchange rates and exchange rates for the decade following the breakdown of the Bretton Woods System comes very close to this theoretical prediction.

SELF-TEST

Fill in the Blank

1. The _____ is the ratio of the price of exports to the price of imports.

2. Net exports are _____ minus _____.

3. Exchange rates are _____ when they are determined by market forces.

4. When the United States runs a trade deficit, the amount we borrow from abroad is the _____.

5. The nominal exchange rate adjusted for changes in purchasing power between the United States and the ROW is the _____.

6. The theory that the real exchange rate is constant in the long run is called _____.

7. The net export function says that net exports depend negatively on _____ and _____.

8. The coefficient that describes how much imports rise when income rises is the _____.

9. The differences between U.S. and ROW interest rates is called the _____.

10. The reduction in the size of the multiplier because net exports depend negatively on income is called _____.

11. Protectionist measures include _____, _____, and
_____ on imports.

12. The Fed can limit exchange-rate fluctuations by using monetary policy to
_____ the exchange rate.

True-False

13. Appreciation of the dollar occurs when the exchange rate rises.

14. Since the exchange rate is flexible, the United States is powerless to affect it.

15. The theory of long-run purchasing power parity says that the nominal
exchange rate is constant.

16. Movements in nominal and real exchange rates are unrelated.

17. When domestic income rises, net exports fall.

18. When the real exchange rate appreciates, net exports fall.

19. The exchange rate and interest rate are negatively correlated.

20. The open-economy LM curve is steeper than what the LM curve would be
in a closed economy.

21. For an open economy, monetary policy is not neutral in the long run
because increases in the money supply depreciate the exchange rate.

22. Changes in the exchange rate have an immediate impact on the U.S. price
level.

23. The Fed can stabilize the exchange rate and allow interest rates to fluctuate.

24. The money supply of a small country is endogenous under fixed exchange
rates.

25. In the long run, with floating exchange rates, inflation rates are the same in
all countries.

Review Questions

26. Compare the slope of the open-economy IS curve to what the IS curve
would be in a closed economy.

27. What are the short- and long-run effects of a decrease in government
spending?

28. What are the short- and long-run effects of a decrease in the money
supply?

29. What is the relation between the government budget deficit and capital inflow from abroad?

30. Why does the exchange rate appreciate when the interest rate rises?

31. Briefly describe today's international monetary system.

32. Why do changes in the exchange rate have different impacts on the price level of the United States than they do for a small country?

33. Why do protectionist measures help domestic producers but hurt consumers?

34. How does the Fed stabilize the exchange rate?

35. Why does exchange-rate stabilization increase fluctuations of GDP in response to spending disturbances?

36. Why can't monetary policy be used to stabilize both the exchange rate and prices?

PROBLEM SET

Worked Problems

1. Consider the following macroeconomic model:

Y	$= C + I + G + X$	(Income identity)
C	$= 100 + .8Y_d$	(Consumption)
I	$= 300 - 1,000R$	(Investment)
X	$= 195 - .1Y - 100(EP/P_w)$	(Net exports)
EP/P_w	$= .75 + 5R$	(Real exchange rate)
M	$= (.8Y - 2,000R)P$	(Money demand)

with government spending $G = \$200$ billion, the tax rate $t = .25$, and the money supply $M = \$800$ billion. The U.S. price level P is predetermined at 1 and the ROW price level P_w is always equal to 1.

a. What are the IS curve, the LM curve, and values of Y, R, and E predicted by this model?

b. Derive the aggregate demand curve. Calculate the effect of an increase in government spending of $50 billion on Y, R, and E.

a. *The IS curve is derived by substituting the values for* C, I, G, *and* X *into the income identity*

$$Y = 1,440 - 3,000R.$$

The LM curve is derived by equating money supply and demand:

$$Y = 1,000 + 2,500R.$$

Values for Y and R are found from the IS and LM curves:

$$Y = \$1,200 \text{ billion}, \quad R = .08 \text{ (8 percent)}$$

With $P = P_w = 1$, $E = EP/P_w = .75 + 5(.08) = 1.15$.

b. The aggregate demand curve is calculated as in Chapter 8. From the LM curve,

$$Y = 1.25(M/P) + 2,500R.$$

From the condition for spending balance,

$$2,500R = 867 - .83Y + 1.67G.$$

Substituting the spending balance condition into the LM curve, we derive the aggregate demand curve:

$$Y = .68(M/P) + 474 + .91G.$$

If G increases by $50 billion to $250 billion,

$$Y = 474 + .68(800) + .91(250) = \$1,246 \text{ billion}.$$

The interest rate can be calculated from the LM curve:

$$R = [Y - 1.25(M/P)]/2,500$$
$$= [1,246 - 1.25(800)]/2,500 = .098 \text{ (9.8 percent)}.$$

With $P = P_w = 1$, $E = 1.24$.

2. Assume that prices in Problem 1 adjust according to the price adjustment equation

$$\pi = .5(Y_{-1} - Y^*)/Y^*,$$

where π is the rate of inflation and potential output Y^* is equal to $1,200 billion. As in Problem 1, increase government spending by $50 billion starting from potential GDP. Calculate the paths of inflation, the price level, output, the interest rate, and the real and nominal exchange rates for 4 years. Describe the economy after prices have fully adjusted.

The technique for calculating π, P, and Y is described in Problem 2 of Chapter 9. Once Y is determined, R can be found from either the IS or LM curve. Knowing R, the real exchange rate can be calculated. The nominal exchange rate E (with $P_w = 1$) is equal to the real exchange rate divided by P.

Year	π	P	Y	R	EP/P_w	E
0	.000	1.00	$1,200	.080	1.15	1.15
1	.000	1.00	1,246	.098	1.24	1.24
2	.019	1.02	1,235	.102	1.26	1.24
3	.015	1.04	1,224	.103	1.27	1.23
4	.012	1.04	1,224	.105	1.28	1.23

Once prices adjust fully, output will return to its original level. Both the real interest rate and the real exchange rate will be higher. The nominal exchange rate will also appreciate but not as much as the real exchange rate.

Review Problems

3. Consider the following macroeconomic model:

Y	$= C + I + G + X$	(Income identity)
C	$= 300 + .75Y_d$	(Consumption)
I	$= 300 - 2{,}000R$	(Investment)
X	$= 500 - .2Y - 200(EP/P_w)$	(Net exports)
$EP/P_w = .5 + 5R$		(Real exchange rate)
M	$= (.5Y - 2{,}000R)P$	(Money demand)

with government spending $G = \$200$, the tax rate $t = .2$, and the money supply $M = \$550$. The U.S. price level P is predetermined at 1 and the ROW price level P_w is always equal to 1.

a. What are the IS curve, the LM curve, and values of Y, R, and E predicted by this model?

b. Derive the aggregate demand curve. Calculate the effect of an increase in the money supply of $100 on Y, R, and E.

4. Assume that prices in Problem 3 adjust according to the price adjustment equation

$$\pi = (Y_{-1} - Y^*)/Y^*,$$

where π is the rate of inflation and potential output Y^* is equal to $1,500 billion. As in Problem 3, increase the money supply by $100 starting from potential GDP. Calculate the paths of inflation, the price level, output, the interest rate, and the real and nominal exchange rates for 4 years. Describe the economy after prices have fully adjusted.

5. Consider the following macroeconomic model:

Y	$= C + I + G + X$	(Income identity)
C	$= 400 + .8Y_d$	(Consumption)
I	$= 400 - 3{,}000R$	(Investment)
X	$= 114 - .2Y - 40(EP/P_w)$	(Net exports)
$EP/P_w = .75 + 5R$		(Real exchange rate)
M	$= (.4Y - 1{,}000R)P$	(Money demand)

with government spending $G = \$100$, the tax rate $t = .5$, and the money supply $M = \$180$. The U.S. price level P is predetermined at 1 and the ROW price level P_w is always equal to 1.

a. What are the IS curve, the LM curve, and values of Y, R, and E predicted by this model?

b. Derive the aggregate demand curve and calculate the effect of increases in government spending and the money supply of $20 on Y, R, and E.

6. Assume that prices in Problem 5 adjust according to the price adjustment equation

$$\pi = (Y_{-1} - Y^*)/Y^*,$$

where π is the rate of inflation and potential output Y^* is equal to $750 billion. As in Problem 5, increase the money supply and government spending by $20 starting from potential GDP. Calculate the paths of inflation, the price level, output, the interest rate, and the real and nominal exchange rates for 4 years. Describe the economy after prices have fully adjusted.

7. Consider the following model:

Y	$= C + I + G + X$	(Income identity)
C	$= 200 + .85Y_d$	(Consumption)
I	$= 300 - 1,000R$	(Investment)
X	$= 160 - .08Y - 200(EP/P_w)$	(Net exports)
EP/P_w	$= .6 + 10R$	(Real exchange rate)
M	$= (.8Y - 2,000R)P$	(Money demand)

with government spending $G = \$300$, the tax rate $t = .2$, and the money supply $M = \$600$. The U.S. price level P is predetermined at 1 and the ROW price level P_w is always equal to 1.

a. What are the IS curve, the LM curve, and values of Y, R, and E predicted by this model?

b. Derive the aggregate demand curve. Calculate the effect of increase in government spending of $100 on Y, R, and E.

8. Assume that prices in Problem 7 adjust according to the price adjustment equation

$$\pi = (Y_{-1} - Y^*)/Y^*,$$

where π is the rate of inflation and potential output Y^* is equal to $1,087.5. As in Problem 7, increase government spending by $100 starting from potential GDP. Calculate the paths of inflation, the price level, output, the interest rate, and the real and nominal exchange rates for 4 years. Describe the economy after prices have fully adjusted.

GRAPH IT

1. Go back to Problem 1 and graph the IS-LM and aggregate demand curves in a stacked diagram. Label the equilibrium associated with $G = 200$ as a

and the equilibrium associated with $G = 250$ as b. Plot the price adjustment path from Problem 2 in both graphs. Label the new equilibrium c.

2. Go back to Problems 3 and 4 and graph the IS-LM and aggregate demand curves in a stacked diagram. Plot the initial equilibrium and label it a. Plot the short-run impact of the monetary policy change and label it b. Plot the long-run equilibrium from Problem 4 and label it c.

ANSWERS TO THE SELF-TEST

1. Terms of trade
2. Exports minus imports
3. Floating or flexible
4. Capital inflow
5. Real exchange rate
6. Purchasing power parity
7. Real income and the real exchange rate
8. Marginal propensity to import
9. Interest-rate differential
10. Leakage
11. Tariffs, quotas, and bans
12. Stabilize
13. True.   When the exchange rate rises, 1 dollar can buy more foreign currency.
14. False.   U.S. monetary and fiscal policies have powerful effects on the exchange rate.
15. False.   Long-run purchasing power parity says that the real exchange rate is constant, not that the nominal exchange rate is constant.
16. False.   Nominal and real exchange rates move closely together in the short run.
17. True.   Higher domestic income increases imports, causing net exports to fall.
18. True.   Real exchange-rate appreciation increases the relative price of domestic goods, causing net exports to fall.
19. False.   They move together, or are positively correlated.
20. False.   The closed- and open-economy LM curves are identical.
21. False.   It is the real, not the nominal, exchange rate that matters for the neutrality of money. Increases in the money supply do not change the long-run real exchange rate.
22. False.   Importers tend to keep the dollar price of their goods stable in the short run.
23. False.   In order to stabilize the exchange rate, the Fed holds interest rates constant.
24. True.   The money supply is determined by the need to intervene in order to fix the exchange rate.

25. False. With floating exchange rates, different countries can have different inflation rates, even in the long run.
26. We do not know which IS curve is steeper. The open-economy IS curve is steeper because the multiplier is smaller, but it is flatter because net exports depend negatively on the interest rate.
27. In the short run, a decrease in government spending lowers interest rates, depreciates the exchange rate, causes a trade surplus, and lowers output. In the long run, prices fall, output returns to potential, and the real exchange rate and interest rate are lower.
28. In the short run, a decrease in the money supply raises interest rates, appreciates the exchange rate, and lowers output. In the long run, prices fall, output returns to potential, the nominal interest rate appreciates by the amount that prices fall, and the real exchange rate is unchanged.
29. The government budget deficit is partially financed by borrowing abroad, causing a capital inflow.
30. When the interest rate rises, domestic assets become more attractive and the exchange rate appreciates.
31. Today's international monetary system is a floating or flexible exchange-rate system.
32. Exchange-rate changes immediately affect the price level for a small country by changing the price of imports. The United States is insulated from these price changes in the short run because importers keep the dollar price of their goods stable.
33. Protectionist measures help domestic producers by reducing foreign competition but hurt consumers by raising the prices of imports.
34. The Fed stabilizes the exchange rate by using monetary policy to keep the interest rate constant.
35. When the Fed stabilizes the exchange rate it keeps the interest rate constant. This makes the LM curve flat, increasing fluctuations of GDP when spending disturbances shift the IS curve.
36. Both price and exchange-rate stabilization require the Fed to set the money supply, and it can be set at only one level at a time.

SOLUTIONS TO REVIEW PROBLEMS

3. a. The IS curve is $Y = 2,000 - 5,000R$. The LM curve is $Y = 1,100 + 4,000R$. $Y = 1,500R$, $R = .10$, and $E = 1.0$.
    b. The aggregate demand curve is $Y = 1.11(M/P) + 741 + .74G$. If M increases by 100 to 650, $Y = \$1,611$, $R = .078$, and $E = .89$.

4. a.

Year	π	P	Y	R	EP/P_w	E
0	.000	1.00	$1,500	.100	1.00	1.00
1	.000	1.00	1,611	.078	.89	.89
2	.074	1.07	1,563	.087	.94	.88
3	.042	1.11	1,536	.091	.97	.86
4	.024	1.14	1,524	.096	.98	.86

Once prices adjust fully, output will return to its original level. The nominal exchange rate will depreciate by the same percentage that prices increase. Both the real interest rate and the real exchange rate will be unchanged.

5. a. The IS curve is $Y = 1,230 - 4,000R$. The LM curve is $Y = 450 + 2,500R$. $Y = 750R$, $R = .12$, and $E = 1.35$.
  b. The aggregate demand curve is $Y = 1.54(M/P) + 425 + .48G$. If M and G increase by $100 to $20, $Y = 791, $R = .116$, and $E = 1.33$.

6. a.

Year	π	P	Y	R	EP/P_w	E
0	.000	1.00	$750	.120	1.35	1.35
1	.000	1.00	791	.116	1.33	1.33
2	.054	1.05	775	.120	1.35	1.29
3	.034	1.09	767	.123	1.37	1.26
4	.022	1.11	759	.123	1.37	1.23

Once prices fully adjust, output will return to its original level. The real interest rate and the real exchange rate will both be slightly higher because of the increase in government spending. The nominal exchange rate will depreciate because it is more affected by the increase in the money supply than by the increase in government spending.

7. a. The IS curve is $Y = 2,100 - 7,500R$. The LM curve is $Y = 750 + 2,500R$. $Y = 1,087.5R$, $R = .135$, and $E = 1.95$.
  b. The aggregate demand curve is $Y = .94(M/P) + 337.5 + .62G$. If G increases by $100 to $400, $Y = $1,150$, $R = .16$, and $E = 2.2$.

8. a.

Year	π	P	Y	R	EP/P_w	E
0	.000	1.00	$1,087.5	.135	1.95	1.45
1	.000	1.00	1,150.0	.160	2.20	2.20
2	.057	1.06	1,119.3	.165	2.25	2.12
3	.029	1.09	1,102.9	.166	2.26	2.07
4	.014	1.11	1,096.2	.168	2.28	2.06

Once prices adjust fully, output will return to its original level. Both the real interest rate and the real exchange rate will be higher. The nominal exchange rate will also appreciate, but not as much as the real exchange rate.

ANSWERS TO GRAPH IT

1. The LM curve shifts left as the price level rises. The R that solves the new IS curve for $G = 250$ and $Y = 1,200$ is $R = .1133$ (or 11.33 percent). The P that solves the AD equation for $Y^* = 1,200$, $M = 800$, and $G = 250$ is $P = 1.09$. the real exchange rate is higher at $EP/P_w = 1.317$ and $E = 1.21$.

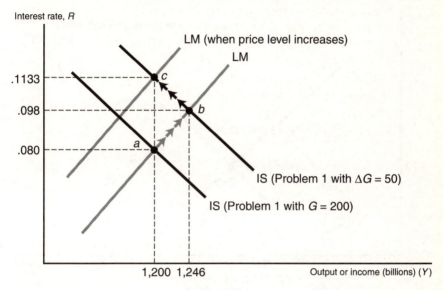

Figure 12–1

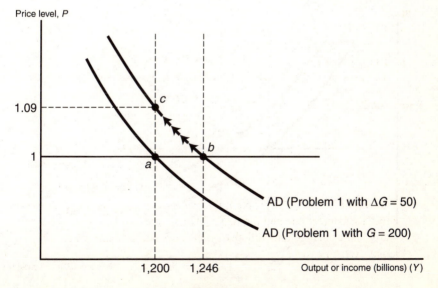

Figure 12–2

2. Expansionary monetary policy shifts the LM right but raising the price level pulls it back to the initial position. Real money balances M/P are the same ($550/1 = 650/1.18$). Solving the new AD curve for $Y = 1,500$, $G = 200$, and $M = 650$ yields $P = 1.18$. With $R = .10$ and $EP/P_w = 1$, solving for $E = .85$.

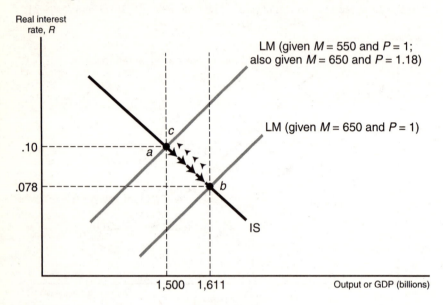

Figure 12–3

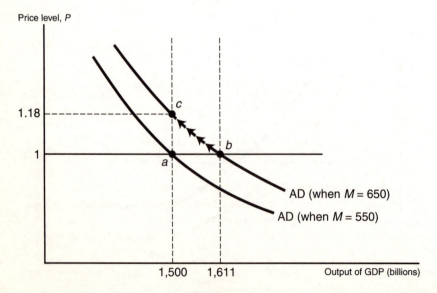

Figure 12–4

CHAPTER 13

Spending, Taxes, and the Budget Deficit

MAIN OBJECTIVES

The record-setting U.S. government budget deficits of the 1980s and early 1990s focused attention on the government's influence on the economy. We have already glimpsed the government's influence on aggregate demand: It purchases goods and services, it makes transfer payments such as social security and unemployment compensation, and it taxes personal and business income. Until now, we have treated the government as exogenous—not explained by our model. Chapter 13 looks closely at each of these influences and ties them into the model. You should learn how the government reacts to economic fluctuations and how these reactions influence economic policy. You should also understand the relation between deficits, consumption, and interest rates.

KEY TERMS AND CONCEPTS

The **government budget** is a summary of the government's yearly spending plans. It consists of both **outlays**, purchases of goods and services and transfer payments, and **receipts**, taxes and other revenue. The government budget includes both the federal budget and state and local government budgets.

Automatic stabilizers are government transfer programs that respond to the state of the economy. These include social security, unemployment insurance, food stamps, welfare, and Medicaid. In a recession, with low income and high unemployment, transfer payments from these programs automatically increase.

Discretionary stabilization measures are fiscal policies that the government uses to affect demand. These include temporary income tax changes, investment tax credits, home purchase credits, and public works projects.

Tax receipts also rise and fall with economic fluctuations. The **elasticity of real tax receipts** with respect to real GDP is greater than 1. For every 1 percent change in real GDP, tax receipts change by more than 1 percent. The most important reason the elasticity is greater than 1 is that the income tax system is progressive—tax rates rise and fall with income. Discretionary changes in tax rates during recessions, such as the tax cuts of the early 1960s, early 1980s, and early 2000s, also contribute to the high elasticity of real tax receipts.

The **budget deficit** is the difference between outlays and receipts. It is equal to government **purchases** plus **transfers** plus **interest on the government debt** minus **taxes**. The **structural** or **full-employment deficit** is the one that would occur, given the current fiscal policies, if the economy were at full employment. The **cyclical deficit** is the difference between the actual deficit and the structural deficit. It measures the impact of the current state of the economy on the deficit.

The relation between the deficit and real interest rates is one of the most important issues regarding the government's role in affecting aggregate demand. Over the past 40 years, the empirical evidence suggests that the relation between deficits and high real interest rates is relatively weak. Recent evidence is mixed. From 1982 to 1990, both real interest rates and the budget deficit were higher than normal, but in the early 1990s and early 2000s, real interest rates fell while the large deficits continued.

Government debt at the start of next year equals debt at the start of this year plus this year's deficit (or minus the surplus). This relationship is called the **intertemporal government budget constraint**:

$$D_{t+1} = D_t + G_t + F_t + RD_t - T_t, \tag{13-1}$$

where D is government debt, G is purchases, F is transfers, R is the interest rate (so RD is interest payments on the debt), ant T is taxes. The government budget is balanced when the stock of government debt is not growing.

With high federal budget deficits throughout the 1980s, the economic significance of the national debt became a topic of great concern. According to standard analysis, deficit spending raises consumption, causing interest rates to rise and investment to fall. Debt displaces productive capital in portfolios, creating a **burden of the national debt**.

An alternative analysis, however, combines the forward-looking theory of consumption with the intertemporal government budget constraint to argue that there is no burden of the debt. When the government lowers taxes in order to raise disposable income, it must borrow. Eventually, this borrowing must be paid back through tax increases. If families are rational and very forward looking, they anticipate these tax increases and do not change their consumption.

If consumption does not change, there is no reason for interest rates or investment to change. The proposition that government budget deficits do not affect consumption, and therefore do not affect interest rates, is called **Ricardian equivalence**, after the nineteenth-century British economist David Ricardo. Even if these tax increases will not occur until the next generation, it has been argued by Robert Barro of Harvard University that consumption will not increase because the family should be viewed as a dynasty in which future generations are as important as the current generation. While these ideas are by no means universally accepted, there is no strong consensus among macroeconomists regarding the magnitude of the burden of the debt.

Fiscal policy shifts the IS curve directly through government purchases and indirectly through the effect of taxes and transfers on consumption. The experience of the last 40 years is that government purchases rarely offset fluctuations in aggregate demand, leading to the conclusion that government purchases should be thought of as a disturbance rather than an instrument to control aggregate demand. The magnitude of the effect of tax cuts, both because of uncertainty about whether the cut is permanent or temporary and because of the possibility that people increase saving in anticipation of future tax increases, is highly uncertain.

Government reaction functions are descriptions of the systematic response of fiscal policy to economic fluctuations. They are examples of **policy rules**, discussed in Chapter 9. For instance, we have seen that transfer payments rise and fall in relation to the departures of output from potential GDP. An algebraic government reaction function for transfer payments might be

$$F = 350 - .25(Y - Y^*), \tag{13-2}$$

where F is transfer payments, Y is GDP, and Y^* is potential GDP. Transfer payments are automatic stabilizers because, when income rises above potential, transfer payments automatically fall. This reduces the multiplier and makes the IS curve steeper.

SELF-TEST

Fill in the Blank

1. Federal government purchases of goods and services and transfers are collectively referred to as _____.

2. While most federal government purchases of goods and services are for _____, the largest single purchase item for state and local governments is _____.

3. Expenditures rise and taxes fall during _____.

4. Government transfer programs that respond to the state of the economy are _____.

5. _____ stabilization measures, such as home purchase credit or a temporary income tax change, are another tool the government uses to affect demand.

6. The elasticity of changes in real tax receipts with respect to changes in real GDP is _____ 1.

7. The government budget deficit is the difference between government _____ and _____.

8. The _____ or _____ deficit is the deficit that would occur if the economy were at potential GDP.

9. The _____ deficit is the difference between the actual deficit and the structural deficit.

10. The relation between the deficit and the accumulation of debt is the _____.

11. The proposition that government budget deficits do not affect consumption is called _____.

12. _____ are descriptions of the systematic response of fiscal policy to economic fluctuations.

13. Automatic stabilizers, such as transfer payments, make the IS curve _____.

True-False

14. Most federal government outlays are purchases of goods and services.

15. The federal and state and local governments raise revenue from similar sources.

16. Like the federal government, state and local governments usually run deficits.

17. Discretionary programs to increase federal purchases of goods and services have been a major force toward ending recessions.

18. Automatic stabilizers help mitigate recessions.

19. Tax receipts fluctuate more than real GDP.

20. There has been a strong empirical relation between deficits and high real interest rates during the past 40 years.

21. Deficits and high real interest rates were more strongly related during the 1980s than in the 1960s and 1970s.

22. Deficits and high real interest rates have been closely related in the early 1990s.

23. The intertemporal budget constraint says that the government budget must be balanced each year.

24. Automatic stabilizers make the IS curve steeper.

25. If tax cuts do not affect consumption, they will not affect interest rates.

26. Ricardian equivalence is the only explanation for tax cuts not affecting consumption.

Review Questions

27. What are the government transfer programs which constitute automatic stabilizers?

28. Which government programs are discretionary stabilization measures?

29. How can deficit spending create a burden of the national debt?

30. Aside from automatic stabilizers, how are taxes lowered during recessions?

31. Why do deficits increase during recessions?

32. What is the structural deficit? What is the cyclical deficit? Is one or the other the actual deficit?

33. What is the intertemporal government budget constraint?

34. If families are very forward looking, why might a tax cut not affect consumption at all?

35. How can fiscal policy shift the IS curve?

36. Why are transfer payments automatic stabilizers?

37. How do automatic stabilizers affect the slope of the IS curve?

38. What is Ricardian equivalence?

39. Why should government purchases be thought of as disturbances to aggregate demand?

PROBLEM SET

Worked Problems

1. Suppose that federal government purchases G = \$500 billion, taxes $T = .4Y$, and transfers $F = .2Y$, with the price level $P = 1$. The federal debt D is \$1,000 billion with the interest rate $R = .1$ (10 percent).

   a. If real output $Y = \$2,000$ billion, what is the deficit?

   b. Calculate the structural deficit if potential output $Y^* + \$2,500$ billion.

   c. What is the cyclical deficit in Part b?

   a. *The deficit* = G + F + RD – T
   $$= G + .2Y + .1(1,000) - .4Y$$
   $$= 500 + 400 + 100 - 800$$
   $$= \$200 \text{ billion.}$$

b. *The structural deficit* $= G + .2Y + .1(1,000) - .4Y^*$
$$= 500 + 500 + 100 - 1,000$$
$$= \$100 \text{ billion.}$$

c. *The cyclical deficit* $=$ *Actual deficit – Structural deficit*
$$= 200 - 100 = \$100 \text{ billion.}$$

2. Suppose that transfer payments are given by

$$F = 180 - .2(Y - Y^*)$$

with potential output $Y^* = \$1,600$ billion. Add this reaction function to the IS-LM model given by Problem 1 of Chapter 8:

$$
\begin{aligned}
Y &= C + I + G + X &\text{(Income identity)} \\
C &= 100 + .9Y_d &\text{(Consumption)} \\
I &= 200 - 500R &\text{(Investment)} \\
X &= 100 - .12Y - 500R &\text{(Net exports)} \\
M &= (.8Y - 200R)P &\text{(Money demand)}
\end{aligned}
$$

with government spending $G = \$200$ billion, the tax rate $t = .2$, the nominal money supply $M = \$800$ billion, and the predetermined price level $P = 1$.

a. What is the IS curve? Compare it with the IS curve in Problem 1 of Chapter 8.

b. Derive the aggregate demand curve and calculate the effect of increases in government spending or real money on GDP. Compare your answer with Problem 2 of Chapter 8.

a. *As in Chapter 8, the IS curve is derived by substituting consumption, investment, net exports, and government spending into the income identity. It is important to remember that disposable income* Y_d = *income* Y + *transfers* F – *taxes* T.

$$Y = 100 - .9[Y + 180 - .2(Y - 1,600) - .2Y] + 200 - 500R + 200 + 100$$
$$- .12Y - 500R$$
$$= 1,050 + .42Y - 1,000R$$
$$= 1,810 - 1,724R.$$

It is steeper than the IS curve in Chapter 8 because the multiplier is smaller.

b. *The aggregate demand curve is calculated as in Chapter 8. From the LM curve,*

$$Y = 1.25(M/P) + 2,500R.$$

From the condition for spending balance,

$$2,500R = 2,125 - 1.45Y + 2.5G.$$

Substituting the spending balance condition into the LM curve, we
derive the aggregate demand curve,

$$Y = .51(M/P) + 867 + 1.02G.$$

Both monetary and fiscal policies are less effective than in Chapter 8
because the automatic stabilizers decrease the multiplier.

Review Problems

3. Suppose that federal government purchases $G = \$200$, taxes $T = .3Y$, and
transfers $F = .1Y$, with the price level $P = 1$. The federal debt D is $750
with the interest rate $R = .08$ (8 percent).

   a. If real output $Y = \$1,000$, what is the deficit?

   b. Calculate the structural deficit if potential output $Y^* + \$1,300$.

   c. What is the cyclical deficit in Part b?

4. Suppose that federal government purchases $G = \$400$, taxes $T = .4Y$, and
transfers $F = .1Y$, with the price level $P = 1$. The federal debt D is $1,000
with the interest rate $R = .12$ (12 percent).

   a. If real output $Y = \$1,500$ billion, what is the deficit?

   b. Calculate the structural deficit if potential output $Y^* + \$2,000$.

   c. What is the cyclical deficit in Part b?

5. Suppose that transfer payments are given by

$$F = 200 - .2(Y - Y^*)$$

with potential output $Y^* = \$1,000$. Add this reaction function to the IS-LM
model given by Problem 3 of Chapter 8:

$Y = C + I + G + X$	(Income identity)
$C = 300 + .8Y_d$	(Consumption)
$I = 200 - 1,500R$	(Investment)
$X = 100 - .04Y - 500R$	(Net exports)
$M = (.5Y - 2,000R)P$	(Money demand)

with government spending $G = \$200$, the tax rate $t = .2$, the nominal
money supply $M = \$550$ billion, and the predetermined price level $P = 1$.

   a. What is the IS curve? Compare it with the IS curve in Problem 3 of
   Chapter 8.

   b. Derive the aggregate demand curve and calculate the effect of increases
   in government spending or real money on GDP. Compare your answer
   with Problem 4 of Chapter 8.

6. Suppose that transfer payments are given by

$$F = 120 - .1(Y - Y^*)$$

with potential output $Y^* = \$800$ billion. Add this reaction function to the IS-LM model given by Problem 5 of Chapter 8:

$$\begin{aligned}
Y &= C + I + G + X &&\text{(Income identity)} \\
C &= 400 + .9Y_d &&\text{(Consumption)} \\
I &= 300 - 2{,}000R &&\text{(Investment)} \\
X &= 100 - .05Y - 1{,}000R &&\text{(Net exports)} \\
M &= (.4Y - 1{,}000R)P &&\text{(Money demand)}
\end{aligned}$$

with government spending $G = \$100$, the tax rate $t = .5$, the nominal money supply $M = \$180$, and the predetermined price level $P = 1$.

a. What is the IS curve? Compare it with the IS curve in Problem 5 of Chapter 8.

b. Derive the aggregate demand curve and calculate the effect of increases in government spending or real money on GDP. Compare your answer with Problem 6 of Chapter 8.

7. Suppose that transfer payments are given by

$$F = 300 - .3333(Y - Y^*)$$

with potential output $Y^* = \$2{,}100$. Add this reaction function to the IS-LM model given by Problem 7 of Chapter 8:

$$\begin{aligned}
Y &= C + I + G + X &&\text{(Income identity)} \\
C &= 400 + .9Y_d &&\text{(Consumption)} \\
I &= 200 - 1{,}800R &&\text{(Investment)} \\
X &= 200 - .1Y - 200R &&\text{(Net exports)} \\
M &= (.8Y - 3{,}000R)P &&\text{(Money demand)}
\end{aligned}$$

with government spending $G = \$200$, the tax rate $t = .3333$, the nominal money supply $M = \$1{,}104$, and the predetermined price level $P = 1$.

a. What is the IS curve? Compare it with the IS curve in Problem 7 of Chapter 8.

b. Derive the aggregate demand curve and calculate the effect of increases in government spending or real money on GDP. Compare your answer with Problem 8 of Chapter 8.

ANSWERS TO THE SELF-TEST

1. Outlays
2. National defense, education
3. Recessions

4. Automatic stabilizers
5. Discretionary
6. Greater than
7. Outlays and receipts
8. Structural or full-employment
9. Cyclical
10. Intertemporal budget constraint
11. Ricardian equivalence
12. Government reaction functions
13. Steeper
14. False. Transfer payments exceed government purchases.
15. False. The federal government raises almost all of its revenue from income and social security taxes. About 40 percent of state and local government receipts comes from property and sales taxes.
16. False. State and local governments usually run surpluses.
17. False. Because these spending programs have been small with long lags, they have not significantly contributed to ending recessions.
18. True. By quickly raising disposable income, automatic stabilizers increase aggregate demand and help mitigate recessions.
19. True. Tax receipts fluctuate more than real income because tax rates rise with income.
20. False. The empirical relation between deficits and real interest rates is weak.
21. True. Both real interest rates and the budget deficit were higher than normal during the 1982–1990 period.
22. False. Real interest rates fell in 1991 and 1992 while large deficits continued.
23. False. The intertemporal budget constraint describes the evolution of government debt over time. It does not require that the budget be balanced in any single year.
24. True. Automatic stabilizers lower the marginal propensity to consume, lower the multiplier, and make the IS curve steeper.
25. True. If consumption is unaffected, the IS curve does not shift and interest rates do not change.
26. False. Consumers may not react to tax cuts because of uncertainty regarding whether they are temporary or permanent.
27. Automatic stabilizers are social security, unemployment insurance, food stamps, welfare, and Medicaid.
28. Temporary income tax changes, investment tax credits, home purchase credits, and public works projects, are examples of discretionary stabilization measures.
29. If deficit spending lowers investment, debt replaces productive capital in portfolios, creating a burden of the national debt.
30. Discretionary changes in taxes, such as the 1964 and 1981 tax cuts, have lowered taxes during recessions.
31. Government outlays rise during recessions because of automatic stabilizers. Receipts fall during recessions because of the progressive tax system. Both cause budget deficits.

32. The structural deficit is the deficit that would occur at potential GDP. The cyclical deficit measures the impact of the current state of the economy on the deficit. The structural deficit and cyclical deficit sum to the actual deficit.
33. The intertemporal budget constraint says that the change in the government debt is equal to the deficit.
34. Very forward-looking families, using the government intertemporal budget constraint, anticipate future tax increases and do not change their consumption.
35. Government purchases shift the IS curve directly and policies on taxes and transfers shift the IS curve through the consumption function.
36. Transfer payments are automatic stabilizers because they fall when income rises above potential.
37. Automatic stabilizers operating through taxes and transfers reduce the marginal propensity to consume, reduce the multiplier, and make the IS curve steeper.
38. Ricardian equivalence is the proposition that government budget deficits do not affect consumption.
39. Government purchases should be thought of as disturbances to aggregate demand because, historically, they have rarely been timed to offset fluctuations in aggregate demand.

SOLUTIONS TO REVIEW PROBLEMS

3. a. The deficit $= G + F + RD - T = 200 + 100 + 60 - 300 = \$60$.
   b. The structural deficit $= 200 + 130 + 60 - 390 = 0$.
   c. The cyclical deficit $= \$60$.
4. a. The deficit $= \$70$.
   b. The structural deficit $= -\$80$ (surplus of \$80).
   c. The cyclical deficit $= \$150$.
5. a. The IS curve is $Y = 2,000 - 3,571R$. It is steeper than the IS curve in Chapter 8.
   b. The aggregate demand curve is $Y = 868 + .94G + .94(M/P)$. Both monetary and fiscal policies are less effective than in Chapter 8 because the multiplier is smaller.
6. a. The IS curve is $Y = 1,565 - 4,348R$. It is steeper than the IS curve in Chapter 8.
   b. The aggregate demand curve is $Y = 1.59(M/P) + 519 + .53G$. Both monetary and fiscal policies are less effective than in Chapter 8 because the multiplier is smaller.
7. a. The IS curve is $Y = 2,375 - 2,500R$. It is steeper than the IS curve in Chapter 8.
   b. The aggregate demand curve is $Y = .5(M/P) + 1,275 + .75G$. Both monetary and fiscal policies are less effective than in Chapter 8 because the multiplier is smaller.

CHAPTER 14 | The Monetary System

MAIN OBJECTIVES

In the basic model presented in Chapters 8 and 9, we saw how changes in the money supply and shocks to money demand play a central role in economic fluctuations. Now, in Chapter 14, we examine these factors more closely and focus on the Federal Reserve System, a powerful force in macroeconomic policy making. We look at how the Fed conducts monetary policy and how monetary policy influences GDP.

KEY TERMS AND CONCEPTS

The **monetary system** specifies how people pay each other when they conduct transactions (the **means of payment)** and the meaning of the prices put on goods (the **unit of account**). Although these are conceptually two separate functions, the dollar performs both in the United States.

The **money supply** consists of **currency**, the government's paper money and coins, plus **deposits** that individuals and firms hold at banks. The **monetary base** is currency plus **reserves** that banks hold at the Fed. The monetary base is also called **high-powered money**.

The Fed changes the money supply through **open-market operations**, purchases or sales of government bonds form the public with money. The money supply is increased by an open-market purchase and decreased by an open-market sale. The Fed directly controls the monetary base. The money supply is also influenced by the **reserve ratio** (r), the percentage of checking deposits that banks are required to hold on reserve at the Fed, and the **currency deposit ratio** (c), the amount of currency people hold as a ratio of their checking deposits.

The relation between the monetary base (M_B) and the money supply (M) is given by

$$M = mM_B, \qquad (14\text{--}1)$$

where $m = (1 + c)/(r + c)$ is the **money multiplier**. Because the reserve ratio r is less than 1, the money multiplier, which measures how much the money supply changes as a result of an open-market operation, is greater than 1.

Banks, in their **intermediation** role, receive deposits from and make loans to the private sector. **Required reserves** are the amount, currently 10 percent, of their deposits that banks have to hold. **Excess reserves** are banks' actual reserves minus required reserves. The Fed can lend reserves to banks, and this lending, by increasing the amount of reserves held by banks, increases the monetary base just as an open-market operation does. **Borrowed reserves** are the part of bank reserves borrowed from the Fed. The **discount rate** is the interest rate on these borrowings.

The **government budget identity** says that government spending (G) plus transfers (F) plus interest on the government debt (Q) minus taxes (T) equals the change in the monetary base (ΔM_B) plus the change in bonds (ΔB):

$$G + F + Q - T = \Delta M_B + \Delta B. \qquad (14\text{--}2)$$

We can use the government budget identity to be more precise in our definitions of monetary and fiscal policy. Fiscal policy is bond-financed changes in government spending, transfers, and taxes. Suppose government spending is increased. The monetary base and money supply remain unchanged ($\Delta M_B = 0$) while $\Delta G = \Delta B$. Monetary policy is an increase in the monetary base matched by a decrease in government bonds ($\Delta M_B = -\Delta B$). The government budget deficit, $G + F + Q - T$, remains unchanged.

One classification of the demand for money, originated by John Maynard Keynes, distinguishes among three motives: the **transactions motive**, or the desire to hold money to facilitate day-to-day transactions; the **precautionary motive**, or the desire to hold money in case of unexpected expense; and the **speculative motive**, or the desire to hold money because of an expected decrease in the future price of bonds.

The transactions demand for money can be analyzed by using inventory theory. The **square-root rule** says that the value of average money holdings M that minimizes the total costs of holding money is given by

$$M = \sqrt{kW/2R_o}, \qquad (14\text{--}3)$$

where k is the cost of making each transaction, W is income for the period, and R_o is the opportunity cost of holding money rather than another asset.

The demand for money as a store of wealth encompasses the precautionary and speculative demands. Money is riskless but pays relatively low interest, while bonds are risky but have a higher expected return. In general, people who are averse to risk hold a diversified portfolio and balance their wealth between money and bonds.

Combining all of the motives for holding money, the **demand for currency** depends negatively on the interest rate and positively on income and the price level. The **demand for checking deposits** depends negatively on the difference between the market interest rate and the rate on checking deposits and positively on income and the price level. The **demand for money**, the sum of the demand for currency and the demand for checking deposits, depends negatively on the interest rate, positively on the price level, and positively on real income.

The **Federal Open Market Committee** (**FOMC**) makes decisions about monetary policy in the United States. The FOMC consists of the 7 members of the Board of Governors of the Federal Reserve System plus 5 of the 12 presidents of the Federal Reserve District Banks. At different times, the FOMC has used one of two alternative procedures:

Set the growth rate of the money supply. Under this procedure, the FOMC sets the money-supply growth rate and the bond traders at the New York Fed make the appropriate open-market purchases or sales. For example, if the FOMC wants to increase the money supply growth rate, the traders make an open-market purchase (buy bonds), using the formula given n Equation 14–1 to determine how much of an increase in the monetary base is necessary to achieve the desired increase in the money supply. This procedure was used in the late 1970s and early 1980s.

Set the short-term interest rate. Under this procedure, the FOMC sets the federal funds rate, the 1-day interest rate on loans between banks, and the bond traders at the New York Fed make the appropriate open-market purchases or sales. For example, if the FOMC wants to increase the interest rate, the traders make an open-market sale (sell bonds), which lowers the money supply and raises the interest rate. This procedure has been used since the mid-1980s.

How does the FOMC choose between interest-rate setting and money-supply setting? Because there is uncertainty about money and the LM curve, interest-rate setting is a more appropriate Fed policy. Setting the short-term interest rate mitigates fluctuations in real GDP and inflation that otherwise would be caused by large shifts in the LM curve. On the other hand, if high and variable inflation causes the real interest rate and the IS curve to fluctuate, then money-supply setting is a more appropriate policy. This explains why the Fed moved from money-supply setting in the (high-inflation) late 1970s to interest-rate setting in the (lower-inflation) mid-1980s.

Lags in the effect of monetary policy greatly complicate the Fed's choices among various policies. These lags are the lag in the investment process and the lag in the response of net exports to dollar depreciation. At first, monetary expansion decreases interest rates without much effect on GDP. The peak effect on GDP takes about 1 to 2 years after investment and net exports respond to the lower interest rates. The effect on prices takes much longer.

SELF-TEST

Fill in the Blank

1. A monetary system specifies the _____ and the _____.

2. The money supply consists of _____ plus _____.

3. The monetary base equals _____ plus _____.

4. The Fed changes the money supply through _____.

5. The _____ describes the relation between the monetary base and the money supply.

6. Banks accept deposits and make loans in their _____ role.

7. The _____ says that government spending plus transfers plus interest on the government debt minus taxes equals the change in the monetary base plus the change in bonds.

8. According to Keynes, the three motives in people's demands for money are the _____, _____, and _____ motives.

9. The _____ is the sum of the demand for currency and the demand for checking deposits.

10. The _____ makes decisions about monetary policy in the United States.

11. Over the past 20 years inflation has been relatively _____.

12. The Fed has been using the_____ approach to monetary policy since the mid-1980s.

True-False

13. The Fed directly controls the money supply.

14. When the Fed increases the monetary base, the money supply rises by more than the change in the monetary base.

15. The money multiplier is constant.

16. Required reserves are a constant percentage of banks' deposits.

17. The government budget identity says that the federal budget is balanced each year.

18. The Fed changed its operating procedures in the mid-1980s.

19. If inflation is high, interest-rate setting is preferable to money-supply setting.

20. The Fed currently targets a money supply growth rate.

21. The federal funds rate was at 6.5 percent in the fall of 2000.

22. Countercyclical monetary policy loses its effectiveness once the nominal interest rate hits zero.

23. Policy lags are a problem only for fiscal policy.

Review Questions

24. What factors, apart from the Fed, influence the money supply?

25. According to the square-root rule, what are the determinants of people's average money balances?

26. What determines the demand for currency?

27. What determines the demand for checking deposits?

28. What is the government budget identity?

29. What two procedures are available to the Federal Open Market Committee (FOMC)?

30. Why did the Fed move from money-supply setting in the late 1970s to interest-rate setting in the mid-1980s?

PROBLEM SET

Worked Problems

1. a. According to the square-root rule, what is the average money balance M if income $W = \$1,000$ billion, the cost of making a transaction $k = 4$, and the opportunity cost of holding money $R_o = .05$ (5 percent)?

   b. What happens to the average money balance M if income increases to $\$2,000$ billion?

   a. *The square-root rule says that the average money balance*

   $$M = \sqrt{kW/2R_o}$$
   $$= \sqrt{4(1,000)/2(.05)}$$
   $$= \sqrt{40,000}$$
   $$= \$200 \text{ billion.}$$

   b. *The average money balance*

   $$= \sqrt{4(2,000)/2(.05)}$$
   $$= \sqrt{80,000}$$
   $$= \$283 \text{ billion.}$$

The average money balance is higher because the demand for money increases when income rises.

2. Suppose that the money supply is given by

$$M = 800 - .2(Y - Y^*)$$

with potential output $Y^* = \$1,250$ billion. Add this monetary policy rule to the equations in Problem 1 of Chapter 8:

$$
\begin{aligned}
Y &= C + I + G + X &&\text{(Income identity)}\\
C &= 100 + .9Y_d &&\text{(Consumption)}\\
I &= 200 - 500R &&\text{(Investment)}\\
X &= 100 - .12Y - 500R &&\text{(Net exports)}\\
M &= (.8Y - 2,000R)P &&\text{(Money demand)}
\end{aligned}
$$

with government spending $G = \$200$ billion, the tax rate $t = .2$, and the predetermined price level $P = 1$.

a. What is the LM curve? Compare it with the LM curve in Problem 1 of Chapter 8.

b. Derive the aggregate demand curve and calculate the effect of an increase in government spending on GDP. Compare your answer with Problem 2 of Chapter 8.

a. *The LM curve is derived by equating the supply of money with the demand for money:*

$$800 -.2(Y - 1,250) = .8Y - 2,000R$$
$$Y = 1,050 + 2,000R.$$

It is steeper than the LM curve of Chapter 8 because of the Fed's "leaning against the wind" policy of decreasing the money supply when output rises above potential.

b. *The LM curve is*

$$Y = 1,050 + 2,000R.$$

From the condition for spending balance,

$$2,000R = 800 - .8Y + 2G.$$

Substituting the spending balance condition into the LM curve, we derive the aggregate demand curve,

$$Y = 1,028 + 1.11G.$$

An increase in government spending has less effect on GDP than in Chapter 8 because the LM curve is steeper.

Review Problems

3. a. According to the square-root rule, what is the average money balance M if income $W = \$6,000$, the cost of making a transaction $k = 3$, and the opportunity cost of holding money $R_o = .1$ (10 percent)?

   b. What happens to the average money balance M if the opportunity cost of holding money R_o increases to .15?

4. a. According to the square-root rule, what is the average money balance M if income $W = \$2,000$ billion, the cost of making a transaction $k = 5$, and the opportunity cost of holding money $R_o = .08$ (8 percent)?

   b. What happens to the average money balance M if the cost of making a transaction k rises to 6?

5. Suppose that the money supply is given by

$$M = 550 - .3(Y - Y^*)$$

with potential output $Y^* = \$1,500$ billion. Add this monetary policy rule to the equations in Problem 3 of Chapter 8:

$Y = C + I + G + X$	(Income identity)
$C = 300 + .8Y_d$	(Consumption)
$I = 200 - 1,500R$	(Investment)
$X = 100 - .04Y - 500R$	(Net exports)
$M = (.5Y - 2,000R)P$	(Money demand)

with government spending $G = \$200$, the tax rate $t = .2$, and the predetermined price level $P = 1$.

   a. What is the LM curve? Compare it with the LM curve in Problem 3 of Chapter 8.

   b. Derive the aggregate demand curve and calculate the effect of an increase in government spending on GDP. Compare your answer with Problem 4 of Chapter 8.

6. Suppose that the money supply is given by

$$M = 180 - .6(Y - Y^*)$$

with potential output $Y^* = \$800$ billion. Add this monetary policy rule to the equations in Problem 5 of Chapter 8:

$Y = C + I + G + X$	(Income identity)
$C = 400 + .9Y_d$	(Consumption)
$I = 300 - 2,000R$	(Investment)
$X = 100 - .05Y - 1,000R$	(Net exports)
$M = (.4Y - 1,000R)P$	(Money demand)

with government spending $G = \$100$, the tax rate $t = .5$, and the predetermined price level $P = 1$.

a. What is the LM curve? Compare it with the LM curve in Problem 5 of Chapter 8.

b. Derive the aggregate demand curve and calculate the effect of an increase in government spending on GDP. Compare your answer with Problem 6 of Chapter 8.

7. Suppose that the money supply is given by

$$M = 1,104 - .2(Y - Y^*)$$

with potential output $Y^* = \$1,680$. Add this monetary policy rule to the equations in Problem 7 of Chapter 8:

$$
\begin{aligned}
Y &= C + I + G + X && \text{(Income identity)} \\
C &= 400 + .9Y_d && \text{(Consumption)} \\
I &= 200 - 1,800R && \text{(Investment)} \\
X &= 200 - .1Y - 200R && \text{(Net exports)} \\
M &= (.8Y - 3,000R)P && \text{(Money demand)}
\end{aligned}
$$

with government spending $G = \$200$, the tax rate $t = .3333$, and the predetermined price level $P = 1$.

a. What is the LM curve? Compare it with the LM curve in Problem 7 of Chapter 8.

b. Derive the aggregate demand curve and calculate the effect of an increase in government spending on GDP. Compare your answer with Problem 8 of Chapter 8.

ANSWERS TO THE SELF-TEST

1. Means of payment and unit of account
2. Currency plus deposits
3. Currency plus reserves
4. Open-market operations
5. Money multiplier
6. Intermediation
7. Government budget identity
8. Transactions, precautionary, and speculative
9. Demand for money
10. Federal Open Market Committee
11. Low
12. Short-term interest-rate setting

13. False.   The Fed directly controls the monetary base.
14. True.   The money multiplier is greater than 1.
15. False.   The money multiplier depends on the reserve ratio and the currency deposit ratio, neither of which is constant.
16. True.   Required reserves are 10 percent of each bank's deposits.
17. False.   The government budget identity says that the budget deficit equals the change in the money supply plus the change in bonds.
18. True.   The Fed moved from money-supply setting in the late 1970s to interest-rate setting in the mid-1980s.
19. False.   Money-supply setting is a more appropriate policy when inflation is high.
20. False.   The Fed currently targets the federal funds rate.
21. True.   It then fell to 1 percent in the summer and fall of 2003.
22. True.   The constraint of a zero bound on nominal interest rates limits the scope of the monetary policy.
23. False.   Monetary policy also encounters lags.
24. The money supply is influenced by the reserve ratio and the currency deposit ratio.
25. The average money balance depends positively on income and the cost of making transactions and negatively on the opportunity cost of holding money.
26. The demand for currency depends negatively on the interest rate and positively on income and the price level.
27. The demand for checking deposits depends negatively on the difference between the market interest rate and the rate on checking deposits and positively on income and the price level.
28. The government budget identity says that government spending plus transfers plus interest on the government debt minus taxes equals the change in the monetary base plus the change in bonds.
29. The FOMC can set the growth rate of the money supply or set the short-term interest rate.
30. Because inflation decreased and became less variable, shifts to the IS curve became relatively less important than shifts to the LM curve.

SOLUTIONS TO REVIEW PROBLEMS

3. a. The average money balance $M = \$300$.
   b. $M = \$245$. The demand for money falls when the opportunity cost of holding money rises.
4. a. The average money balance $M = \$250$.
   b. $M = \$274$. The demand for money falls when the cost of making a transaction rises.
5. a. The LM curve is $Y = 1{,}250 + 2{,}500R$. It is steeper than the LM curve in Chapter 8.

b. The aggregate demand curve is $Y = 1,333 + .83G$. Because the LM curve is steeper, increases in government spending have less effect on GDP than in Chapter 8.

6. a. The LM curve is $Y = 660 + 1,000R$. It is steeper than the LM curve in Chapter 8.

b. The aggregate demand curve is $Y = 733 + .28G$. Because the LM curve is steeper, increases in government spending have less effect on GDP than in Chapter 8.

7. a. The LM curve is $Y = 1,440 + 3,000R$. It is steeper than the LM curve in Chapter 8.

b. The aggregate demand curve is $Y = 1,509 + .86G$. Because the LM curve is steeper, increases in government spending have less effect on GDP than in Chapter 8.

CHAPTER 15

The Microeconomic Foundations of Price Rigidity

MAIN OBJECTIVES

Why is the short run different from the long run? In particular, why does an increase in the money supply raise real GDP in the short run but not in the long run? The answer comes from price rigidity. In the short run, the price level does not increase as much as the money supply. This chapter considers two micro-economic explanations for price rigidity: imperfect information, and sticky prices or nominal wage contracts. Both are necessary for a complete explanation of price rigidity. You should learn how the two models work and understand the similarities and differences between them.

KEY TERMS AND CONCEPTS

Price rigidity is the phenomenon that, in the short run, the price level does not increase as much as the money supply. Because of price rigidity, an increase in the money supply causes real money, the money supply divided by the price level, to rise, decreasing the interest rate and raising real GDP. While this chapter is about the short run, it is important to remember that, in the long run, the price level does increase by as much as the money supply, real money is unchanged, and real GDP is unaffected.

Theories of **imperfect information** start with the assumption that prices set by individual firms are perfectly flexible. When firms see that the demand for their products has shifted, they do not know whether the cause is a change in the money supply or some firm-specific factor. As we will see, this lack of information causes prices to change by less than they would if information were perfect.

Microeconomic theory tells us that a firm produces up to the point where the price of its good equals its marginal cost (the extra cost of producing one more unit of the good), which depends on the price of the firm's inputs to production. If the price of the firm's output rises relative to the price of other goods, including the price of its inputs, the firm produces more. If the general price level rises, so that all prices rise, the relative price of the firm's output is unchanged and it does not increase its production.

Firms do not have complete information on the general price level in the economy. The representative firm's supply curve when the firm has to estimate the general price level is given by

$$Y_i = h(P_i - P^e) + Y_i^*, \tag{15-1}$$

where Y_i is the firm's production, P_i is the firm's price, P^e is the estimate of the general price level, and Y_i^* is the firm's potential or normal production. The firm's output Y_i, is greater than normal, Y_i^*, by an amount equal to a constant h times the difference between the firm's price P_i and its estimate of the general price level P^e.

The firm's estimate of the general price level can be described by:

$$P^e = \hat{P} + b(P_i - \hat{P}), \tag{15-2}$$

where $\hat{P}$ is the forecast, made at the start of the year, of the general price level. The firm's estimate of the general price level, P^e, is greater than what was forecast at the start of the year, $\hat{P}$, by an amount equal to a constant b times the difference between the firm's own price P_i and the forecast of the general price $\hat{P}$. The coefficient b represents the influence of the firm's own price on its estimate of the general price level and is between zero and 1.

The **Lucas supply curve** is derived by substituting the firm's estimate of the general price level into the representative firm's supply curve, then adding up across the n firms in the economy. It is named for Robert Lucas of the University of Chicago, who did the original research on the information-based model:

$$Y = nh(1 - b)(P_i - \hat{P}) + Y^*. \tag{15-3}$$

The Lucas supply curve says that output Y is greater than potential GDP Y^* if the price level P is greater than what was forecast, $\hat{P}$. An unexpected general price rise causes firms, which cannot perfectly distinguish general and relative price changes, to raise their output above potential.

In order to show the relation between the Lucas supply curve and price rigidity, first rewrite the Lucas supply curve with the price level on the left-hand side,

$$P = \hat{P} + c(Y - Y^*), \tag{15-4}$$

where $c = 1/[nh(1 - b)]$. The Lucas supply curve is illustrated in Figure 15-1. It slopes upward because GDP is greater than potential GDP when the price level exceeds the forecasted price level. The aggregate demand (AD curve), as derived in Chapter 8, is given by

$$Y = k_0 + k_1(M - P), \tag{15-5}$$

where M is the money supply. The AD curve is also shown in Figure 15-1.

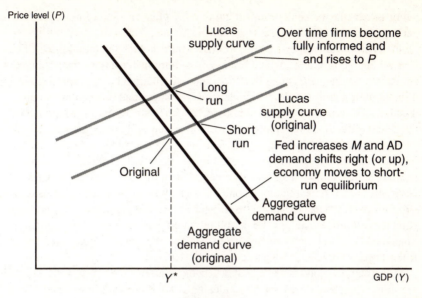

Price level (*P*)

Lucas supply curve

Over time firms become fully informed and and rises to *P*

Long run

Lucas supply curve (original)

Short run

Fed increases *M* and AD demand shifts right (or up), economy moves to short-run equilibrium

Original

Aggregate demand curve

Aggregate demand curve (original)

Y*

GDP (*Y*)

Figure 15–1

What happens when the Fed increases the money supply? The aggregate demand curve shifts to the right, raising both output and the price level in the short run. Price rigidity occurs because, while the price level increases, it does not increase as much as the money supply. Imperfect information is necessary for this result because, if firms were fully informed, $b = 1$ and real GDP would always equal potential GDP in Equation 15–3.

What happens in the long run? Over time, firms become fully informed about what is happening in other markets and the forecasted price level $\hat{P}$ rises by as much as the actual price level P. The Lucas supply curve in Figure 15–1 shifts up by as much as the money supply increase, and there is no impact on real GDP.

The **policy ineffectiveness theorem** is that *anticipated monetary policy is ineffective* in increasing real GDP. Suppose the Fed announced that, starting at potential GDP, it was increasing the money supply. If people have rational expectations about the future, they make the most of the information available when making forecasts, including the equations describing the economy. From the aggregate demand curve (Equation 15–5), people know that either output *Y* or the price level *P* must rise. If their expectations are rational, they forecast the price increase. From the Lucas supply curve (Equation 15–3), price increases that are forecast have no effect on output. Returning to the aggregate demand curve, since output does not change, the price level must rise by as much as the money supply. This can be seen in Figure 15–1 as an immediate shift in the Lucas supply curve when the aggregate demand curve shifts. The price level increases by as much as the money supply and real GDP is unchanged.

Sticky prices occur when nominal prices are insensitive to shifts in demand. For the United States, nominal prices are set in dollars. In high-inflation countries, where prices may be set in terms of commodity units or even a foreign country's currency, nominal prices are not sticky.

Sticky nominal wages are an important cause of sticky nominal prices. For either a competitive firm, where price equals marginal cost, or a firm with market power, where prices are a fixed markup over marginal cost, the price moves directly with marginal cost, which depends on wages and other inputs to production. If wages are sticky in nominal terms, then so are prices. **Menu costs**, the actual costs of changing prices, are another cause of sticky prices.

Wage determination in the United States is not **synchronized**. At any one time, only a small fraction of workers are signing contracts. The others either have recently signed contracts or will sign contracts in the near future. **Adjustment costs**, the cost of renegotiating a contract, make long-term wage contracts desirable. Wage contracts are said to be **staggered** because the period in which one contract is in force overlaps the period in which other contracts are in force. Staggered wage setting is advantageous because it provides information to firms and workers about wages and prices elsewhere.

Indexing provisions in wage contracts could insure workers against unexpected inflation. The primary reason why indexing is not more widespread and why it is not 100 percent when it occurs, is that indexing to the cost of living can be harmful if there are import price or technology shocks. With such disturbances, the real wage must eventually decline so that it equals the marginal product of labor. With 100 percent indexation, the real wage cannot adjust. This can be harmful to both workers and firms because, if the real wage cannot decrease to equal the marginal product of labor, firms reduce employment. If prices rise because of expansionary monetary policy, these problems do not occur. It is not possible, however, to tell in advance what might cause prices to rise. Indexing also adds complexity to wage negotiations and uncertainty about the wage that the workers will actually receive, both of which may be considered undesirable.

Three major factors influence the outcome of wage bargaining. The first factor is the state of the labor market. If unemployment is high, labor is in a relatively weak bargaining position and wage settlements ought to be low. Conversely, wage settlements ought to be high if unemployment is low. The second factor is the wage paid to comparable workers in other industries. Because of the staggering of wage contracts, this includes both the wage settlements of workers who have recently signed contracts and the expected wage settlements of workers who will be signing their contracts in the near future. The third factor is the expected rate of inflation. If inflation is expected to be high, workers ask for larger wage increases. Firms are willing to pay them because their own prices are expected to rise.

A simple algebraic model of staggered wage setting and price determination can be used to express these ideas. Suppose all wage contracts last 2 years, all wage adjustment occurs at the beginning of the contract, and there is no indexation. Let the subscript –1 represent the previous period and +1 represent expectations of the next period. The average wage is given by

$$W = \frac{1}{2}(X + X_{-1}), \tag{15-6}$$

where this period's wage W is the simple average of last period's contract wage X_{-1} and this period's contract wage X. The contract wage X is set each period according to

$$X = \frac{1}{2}(W + W_{+1}) - \frac{d}{2}[(U - U^*) + (U_{+1} - U^*)], \tag{15-7}$$

where U is the unemployment rate, U^* is the natural rate of unemployment, and d is a coefficient describing the response of wages to unemployment. The contract wage depends on the expected average wage and expected labor market conditions over the life of the contract. Using Equations 15–6 and 15–7, we can solve for the contract wage X to get

$$X = \frac{1}{2}(X_{-1} + X_{+1}) - d[(U - U^*) + (U_{+1} - U^*)]. \tag{15-8}$$

The contract wage depends o the past and expected future contract wages as well as on labor market conditions. Wage determination has a backward-looking component X_{-1} and a forward-looking component X_{+1}.

The long-run trade-off between inflation and unemployment is the same in the model of staggered wage setting and price determination as in the model of imperfect information. There is no trade-off between inflation and unemployment in the long run. Regardless of the rate of inflation, as long as it is steady and anticipated the unemployment rate is always equal to the natural rate.

The **theory of price adjustment** indicates that inflation rises when demand conditions are tight, when expectations of inflation rise, or when there are price shocks. Algebraically,

$$\pi = f(Y_{-1} - Y^*)/Y^* + \pi^e + Z, \tag{15-9}$$

where π is inflation, π^e is expected inflation, Y^* is potential GDP, Y_{-1} is last year's GDP, Z is a price shock, and f is a positive coefficient.

One of the most important features of Equation 15–9 is that there is no long-run trade-off between inflation and unemployment. This proposition is sometimes called the *natural rate property*, because unemployment moves to its natural rate in the long run, and the *accelerationist property*, because attempts to get output above normal result in accelerating inflation rates.

Equation 15–9 is an approximation that explains basic facts about inflation and is consistent with the theories of imperfect information and staggered contracts. The coefficient (f), which describes the sensitivity of inflation to recent market conditions, can change when the economic environment changes.

One example of an economic environment change is the degree to which indexing exists. Wage indexing means that wages are affected by current as well as lagged inflation. This can create a **wage-price spiral**, as higher prices and wages reinforce each other driving each other higher. Indexing makes nominal wages more responsive to market conditions, raising the value of f, and to price shocks, raising the value of Z. Another economic environment change is the length and severity of business cycles. If the average length of the business cycle decreases, inflation is less responsive to departures of output from potential and f is smaller.

Modeling **expected inflation** is one of the most difficult issues in under-standing the price adjustment process. One factor to consider is forward-looking forecasts. Wage negotiations are influenced by people's expectations of future wage setting. Another factor is staggered contracts and backward-looking wage behavior. Wage negotiations are influenced by contracts signed in the recent past because they have an effect on future inflation. Both factors need to be included in any realistic model of expected inflation.

It is also important to consider whether or not people believe the changes in the policy rules. For example, when the Fed announces a change in monetary policy that puts more weight on controlling inflation, the model of expected inflation changes if people believe the announcement. If the announcement is not believed, the model does not change until an actual change in inflation convinces people that the new policy is real.

We can summarize the preceding discussion with an important concept: **No mechanical model of expected inflation is universally applicable**. The sim-plest algebraic model of expected inflation, which we used in Chapter 9, says that expected inflation equals last year's inflation:

$$\pi^e = \pi_{-1}. \tag{15-10}$$

This is not a bad model to describe inflation in the United States since the mid-1990s. Inflation has been low, around 2 to 3 percent, and expecting more of the same seems reasonable. But suppose the Fed conducted monetary policy to try to keep GDP above potential GDP over several years. Inflation would increase each year and Equation 15–9, which predicts constant inflation, would be systematically wrong. Eventually, people would realize what the Fed was doing and incorporate that knowledge into their expectations of inflation. While you can create more elaborate mechanical models of expected inflation, they would be subject to the same problems.

SELF-TEST

Fill in the Blank

1. _____ is the phenomenon that, in the short run, the price level does not increase as much as the money supply.

2. Theories of _____ allow for price rigidity even though the prices set by individual firms are perfectly flexible.

3. According to the Lucas supply curve, GDP can exceed potential GDP only if the price level is greater than the _____ price level.

4. According to the _____, anticipated monetary policy cannot affect output.

5. _____ is the insensitivity of prices to shifts in demand.

6. Sticky _____ are an important cause of sticky prices.

7. _____ are the actual costs of changing prices.

8. Wages would be _____ if all contracts were signed at the same time.

9. Wages are set for long period of time because of _____.

10. Wage contracts are said to be _____ because the period in which one contract is in force overlaps the period in which other contracts are in force.

11. The coefficient (f), which describes the sensitivity of _____ to recent market conditions, can change when the economic environment changes.

12. A _____ occurs when higher prices and wages reinforce each other.

13. If inflation is approximately constant form year to year, it is reasonable to assume that expected inflation equals _____.

True-False

14. Price rigidity describe the relation between the price level and the money supply in the long run

15. According to theories of imperfect information, price rigidity occurs because individual firms' prices are sticky.

16. The firm's estimate of the general price level depends on the forecast of the general price level and the firm's own price.

17. The Lucas supply curve slopes upward.

18. According to the model with imperfect information, an unanticipated increase in the money supply increases real GDP in the short run.

19. According to the model with imperfect information, an anticipated increase in the money supply increases real GDP in the short run.

20. The policy ineffectiveness theorem is that unanticipated monetary policy is ineffective in increasing real GDP.

21. Sticky prices occur in all countries.

22. Menu costs are the costs of renegotiating contracts.

23. Wage determination in the United States is not synchronized.

24. Most contracts do not insure workers against unexpected inflation.

25. Wage determination is solely forward looking.

26. In the long run, the unemployment rate is equal to the natural rate regardless of the rate of inflation.

Review Questions

27. What is price rigidity?

28. What does price rigidity imply about the behavior of real money when the money supply increases?

29. According to the Lucas supply curve, what is the relation between GDP and the price level?

30. In the model with imperfect information, what happens in the short run when the Fed increases the money supply?

31. In the model with imperfect information, what happens in the long run when the Fed increases the money supply?

32. What is the policy ineffectiveness theorem?

33. Why do prices depend on wages for both competitive firms and firms with market power?

34. Why is staggered wage setting advantageous to firms and workers?

35. Why is indexing not more widespread?

36. What three major factors influence the outcome of wage bargaining?

37. According to the model of staggered wage setting and price determination, what determines the contract wage?

38. What is the long-run trade-off between inflation and unemployment in the model of imperfect information and the model of staggered wage setting and price determination?

39. How does indexing change the coefficients of the price adjustment model?

40. Why are expectations of inflation both forward and backward looking?

PROBLEM SET

Worked Problems

1. Suppose that the Lucas supply curve is

    $$Y = 475(P - P^e) + Y*$$

    and the aggregate demand curve is

    $$Y = 750 + .625(M/P)$$

    With the money supply $M = \$800$ billion and potential output $Y* = \$1,250$ billion.

    a. What is the price level P if output Y is equal to potential output $Y*$ with no expected changes in policy?

    b. Suppose that the Fed announces that it will increase the money supply to $880 billion, then enacts that policy. What are the new levels of output and the price level?

    c. Suppose that the increase in the money supply is unanticipated. What are the new levels of output and the price level?

    a. *From the aggregate demand curve with output equal to potential output,*

    $$1,250 = 750 + .625(800)/P$$
    $$P = 1.$$

    Also note that, when $Y = Y*$, $P = P^e$ *in the Lucas supply curve.*

    b. *Since the increase in the money supply is anticipated, people expect the new higher price level. With no price surprises,* $Y = Y* = \$1,250$ *billion. The price level can be calculated from the aggregate demand curve:*

    $$1,250 = 750 + .625(800)/P$$
    $$P = 1.1.$$

    The price level rises in proportion to the anticipated increase in the money supply. Output is unchanged.

    c. *Because the increase in the money supply is unanticipated, the expected price does not adjust, so* $P^e = 1$. *From the Lucas supply curve,*

    $$Y = 475(P - 1) + 1,250.$$

    From the aggregate demand curve,

    $$Y = 750 + .625(880)/P.$$

Solving for P,

$$475(P - 1) + 1,250 = 750 + 550/P$$
$$475P^2 + 25P - 550 = 0.$$

Using the quadratic formula,

$$P = \frac{(-25) \pm \sqrt{(25)2 - 4(475)(-550)}}{2(475)}.$$

The only economically sensible solution is for the price level to be positive:

$$P = 1.05.$$

Solving for Y *using the Lucas supply curve,*

$$Y = 475(1.05 - 1) + 1,250$$
$$= \$1,273.75 \text{ billion.}$$

The unanticipated increase in the money supply increases prices less than proportionately and raises output above potential.

2. Suppose that the contract wage is given by

$$X = \frac{1}{2}(X_{-1} + X_{+1}) - 2[(U - .06) + (U_{+1} - .06)],$$

where last period's contract wage $X_{-1} = 1$ and the unemployment rate $U = .06$ (6 percent).

a. If neither the contract wage nor the unemployment rate is expected to change next period, what is the contract wage X?

b. What is the effect on X if next period's unemployment rate is expected to be .08 (8 percent)?

a. *The contract wage* $X = \frac{1}{2}(1 + 1) = 1.$

b. *The contract wage* $X = \frac{1}{2}(1 + 1) - 2(.08 - .06) = .96.$ *It decreases because the expected unemployment rate increases.*

Review Problems

3. Suppose that the Lucas supply curve is

$$Y = 430(P - P^e) + Y^*$$

and the aggregate demand curve is

$$Y = 700 + 1.5(M/P)$$

With the money supply $M = \$400$ and potential output $Y^* = \$1,000$.

   a. What is the price level P if output Y is equal to potential output Y^* with no expected changes in policy?

   b. Suppose that the Fed announces that it will increase the money supply to $480, then enacts that policy. What are the new levels of output and the price level?

   c. Suppose that the increase in the money supply is unanticipated. What are the new levels of output and the price level?

4. Suppose that the Lucas supply curve is

$$Y = 560(P - P^e) + Y^*$$

and the aggregate demand curve is

$$Y = 1{,}000 + 1.25(M/P)$$

With the money supply $M = \$400$ and potential output $Y^* = \$1{,}500$.

   a. What is the price level P if output Y is equal to potential output Y^* with no expected changes in policy?

   b. Suppose that the Fed announces that it will decrease the money supply to $320, then enacts that policy. What are the new levels of output and the price level?

   c. Suppose that the decrease in the money supply is unanticipated. What are the new levels of output and the price level?

5. Suppose that the Lucas supply curve is

$$Y = 556(P - P^e) + Y^*$$

and the aggregate demand curve is

$$Y = 1{,}582 + 90(M/P)$$

With the money supply $M = \$1{,}275$ and potential output $Y^* = \$2{,}500$.

   a. What is the price level P if output Y is equal to potential output Y^* with no expected changes in policy?

   b. Suppose that the Fed announces that it will increase the money supply to $1,020, then enacts that policy. What are the new levels of output and the price level?

   c. Suppose that the decrease in the money supply is unanticipated. What are the new levels of output and the price level?

6. Suppose that the contract wage is given by

$$X = \frac{1}{2}(X_{-1} + X_{+1}) - 2[(U - .06) + (U_{+1} - .06)],$$

where last period's contract wage $X_{-1} = 1$ and the unemployment rate $U = .09$ (9 percent).

   a. If neither the contract wage nor the unemployment rate is expected to change next period, what is the contract wage X?

   b. What is the effect on X if next period's contract wage is expected to be .9?

7. Suppose that the contract wage is given by

$$X = \frac{1}{2}(X_{-1} + X_{+1}) - 1.5[(U - .06) + (U_{+1} - .06)],$$

where last period's contract wage $X_{-1} = 1$ and the unemployment rate $U = .04$ (4 percent).

   a. If neither the contract wage nor the unemployment rate is expected to change next period, what is the contract wage X?

   b. What is the effect on X if next period's unemployment rate is expected to be .6 and next period's contract wage is expected to be 1.06?

GRAPH IT

1. Go back to Problem 1 and graph the general relation of the Lucas supply curve and the aggregate demand curve. Denote the value output and price level in on their respective axes at long-run equilibrium. Show the shift in the aggregate demand curve in Part b and label the new equilibrium *b* that reflects an *anticipated* monetary policy change. Label the new short-run equilibrium *c* that reflects the *unanticipated* monetary policy change described in Part c.

2. Go back to Problem 5 and graph the general relation of the Lucas supply curve and the aggregate demand curve. Denote the value output and price level in on their respective axes at long-run equilibrium. Show the shift in the aggregate demand curve in Part b and label the new equilibrium *b* that reflects an *anticipated* monetary policy change. Label the new short-run equilibrium *c* that reflects the *unanticipated* monetary policy change described in Part c.

ANSWERS TO THE SELF-TEST

1. Price rigidity
2. Imperfect information
3. Forecasted

4. Policy ineffectiveness theorem
5. Sticky prices
6. Nominal wages
7. Menu costs
8. Synchronized
9. Adjustment costs
10. Staggered
11. Inflation
12. Wage-price spiral
13. Actual inflation
14. False. Price rigidity is a short-run phenomenon.
15. False. Theories of imperfect information start with the assumption that prices set by individual firms are perfectly flexible.
16. True. These two factors determine the firm's estimate of the general price level.
17. True. It slopes upward because GDP is greater than potential GDP when the price level exceeds the forecasted price level.
18. True. The aggregate demand curve shifts to the right along the upward-sloping Lucas supply curve, raising both output and the price level in the short run.
19. False. The Lucas supply curve shifts when the aggregate demand curve shifts. The price level increases by as much as the money supply, and real GDP is unchanged.
20. False. The policy ineffectiveness theorem is that anticipated monetary policy is ineffective in increasing real GDP.
21. False. Nominal prices in high-inflation countries are not sticky.
22. False. Menu costs are the actual costs of changing prices. Adjustment costs are the costs of renegotiating contracts.
23. True. At any one time, only a small fraction of workers are signing contracts.
24. True. Most contracts are not indexed.
25. False. Wage determination has both a backward-looking and a forward-looking component.
26. True. There is no long-run trade-off between inflation and unemployment.
27. Price rigidity is the phenomenon that, in the short run, the price level does not increase as much as the money supply.
28. An increase in the money supply causes real money, the money supply divided by the price level, to rise.
29. The Lucas supply curve says that output is greater than potential GDP if the price level exceeds the forecasted price level.
30. In the short run, the aggregate demand curve shifts to the right, raising both output and the price level.
31. In the long run, the Lucas supply curve shifts up by as much as the money supply increases, and there is no impact on real GDP.

32. The policy ineffectiveness theorem is that anticipated monetary policy is ineffective in increasing real GDP.
33. For either type of firm, prices move directly with marginal cost, which depends on wages and other inputs to production.
34. Staggered wage setting is advantageous because it provides information to firms and workers about wages and prices elsewhere.
35. Indexing is not more widespread because it can be harmful if prices rise because of import price or technology shocks.
36. Wage bargaining is influenced by the state of the labor market, the wage paid to comparable workers in other industries, and the expected rate of inflation.
37. The contract wage is determined by past and expected future contract wages as well as by labor market conditions.
38. There is no long-run trade-off between inflation and unemployment in either model.
39. Indexing makes nominal wages more responsive both to market conditions and price shocks, raising the value of f and Z.
40. Expectations of inflation are forward looking because they are influenced by people's expectations of future wage setting. They are backward looking because they are influenced by contracts signed in the recent past.

SOLUTIONS TO REVIEW PROBLEMS

3. a. The price level $P = 2$.
   b. The price level $P = 2.4$. Output is unchanged.
   c. The price level $P = 2.1$. Output $Y = \$1,043$.
4. a. The price level $P = 1$.
   b. The price level $P = .8$. Output is unchanged.
   c. The price level $P = .9$. Output Y is $\$1,444$.
5. a. The price level $P = 1.25$.
   b. The price level $P = 1$. Output is unchanged.
   c. The price level $P = 1.1$. Output $Y = \$2,417$.
6. a. The contract wage $X = .88$.
   b. The contract wage X decreases to .83 because the expected contract wage falls.
7. a. The contract wage $X = 1.06$.
   b. The contract wage is unchanged. It increases because the expected unemployment rate rises.

ANSWERS TO GRAPH IT

1.

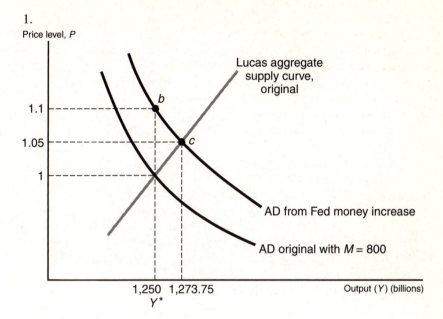

Figure 15–2

2.

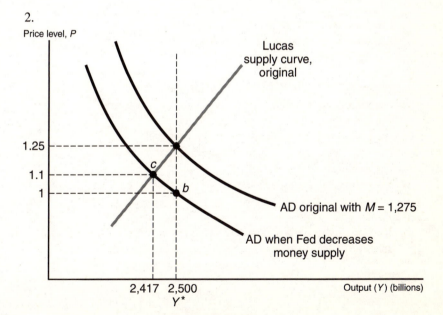

Figure 15–3

Part V

Macroeconomic Policy

CHAPTER 16

The Macroeconomic Policy Model

MAIN OBJECTIVES

When we derived the economic fluctuations model, we assumed that the money supply was an exogenous variable. While this is useful for understanding the short- and long-run effects on one-time changes in government purchases and money supply, it does not help describe the workings of macroeconomic policy. When central banks make monetary policy decisions, it is in response to various shocks and economic events.

This chapter goes further to understand the workings of macroeconomic policy. We recognize the extent to which policy responses to shocks and disturbances in the economy are systematic responses. We focus in particular on a policy rule that accurately describes the behavior of the Fed since the mid-1980s.

We construct the macroeconomic policy model by combining this policy rule with the IS curve and the price adjustment line, then examine macroeconomic policy and events in the United States.

KEY TERMS AND CONCEPTS

The **target inflation rate** is the central banks' goal for the average level of inflation. While the Fed is not explicit about its inflation target, it currently appears to be about 2 percent. The European central bank (ECB) has an explicit inflation target, also of 2 percent. Central banks are also concerned with fluctuations in real GDP and unemployment.

A **monetary policy rule**, or reaction function, describes how the Fed and other central banks react to events in the economy. The **Taylor rule** is a specific example of a monetary policy rule that works well for the United States. It states that the Fed changes the nominal interest when the real GDP deviates

239

from the potential GDP and when the inflation rate deviates from the target inflation rate:

$$r = \pi + \beta \hat{Y} + \delta(\pi - \pi^*) + R^* \qquad (16\text{–}1)$$

where r is the short-term nominal (federal funds) interest rate set by the Fed, $\hat{Y}$ is the percentage deviation of real GDP from potential GDP, π is inflation, π^* is the target inflation rate, R^* is the long-run **equilibrium real interest rate**, and β and δ are positive coefficients. The coefficients indicate the extent to which the Fed changes its setting for the interest rate r when real GDP or inflation changes. If both coefficients are set at .5 then the Taylor rule is given by

$$r = \pi + .5\,\hat{Y} + .5(\pi - .02) + .02 \qquad (16\text{–}2)$$
$$r = 1.5\pi + .5\hat{Y} + .01$$

when the target inflation rate $\pi^* = .02$ and the equilibrium real interest rate $R^* = .02$. We use this example to show that the Taylor rule is *stabilizing*. When real GDP exceeds potential GDP by 1 percent, the Fed raises short-term nominal interest rates r by .5 percent. Since the expectation has not changed, this also raises the real interest rate (r – expected π), lowering investment and net exports and causing real GDP to fall toward potential GDP.

In general, if the Fed systematically raises real interest rates in response to inflation rate increases, then it is employing a stabilizing monetary policy rule, and we say that the rule obeys the **Taylor principle**. Our example illustrates the Taylor principle. If the inflation rate rises by 1 percent, then the Fed raises short term nominal interest rates by more than the inflation rate increase, in this

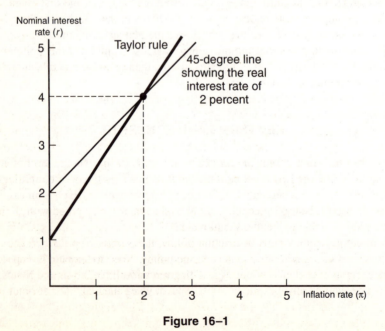

Figure 16–1

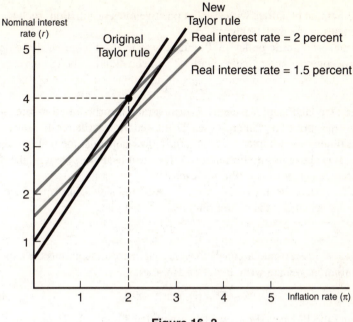

Figure 16–2

case 1.5 percent. This raises the real interest rate, decreasing investment and net exports. This lowers real GDP and causes the inflation rate to fall.

The Taylor rule from Equation 16–1 is graphed in Figure 16–1 for the situation where real GDP equals potential $\hat{Y} = 0$). The nominal interest rate is on the vertical axis and the inflation rate is on the horizontal axis. The 45-degree line depicts a constant real interest rate of 2 percent. The Taylor rule is a steeper line, showing that, when inflation rises, the Fed increases the nominal interest rate by more than the increase in inflation. An equilibrium occurs where the two lines intersect.

The Taylor rule can be used to study the interaction between monetary and fiscal policy. Suppose that, because of a change in fiscal policy that reduces the deficit, the equilibrium real interest rate R^* falls by half a percentage point. As shown in Figure 16–2, if the Fed did not shift its Taylor rule line, inflation would fall below the target. Following the policy rule in Equation 16–2, the Fed shifts the policy rule line, raising the nominal interest rate to maintain the inflation target.

In Chapters 8 and 9, we conducted policy analysis using a diagram with the price level P on the vertical axis and real GDP Y on the horizontal axis. While this model provides a good description of how the economy operates, it does not allow us to understand macroeconomic policy. Now, we expand the framework for policy analysis and through a diagram with the inflation rate π on the vertical axis and the **GDP gap** $\hat{Y} = (Y - Y^*)/Y^*$, the percentage deviation of real GDP from potential GDP, on the horizontal axis. This diagram is useful for looking both at countries with moderate inflation, such as the United States in the 1970s, and at countries with low but positive rates of inflation, such as the United States in the mid-1990s.

The **macroeconomic policy (MP) curve** is shown in Figure 16–1. To derive the macroeconomic policy curve, start with an equation for the IS curve:

$$R - R^* = -\sigma\hat{Y}, \tag{16–3}$$

where $\hat{Y}$ is the GDP gap, R is the real interest rate, π is the inflation rate, and R^* is the equilibrium real interest rate. This IS curve is written differently from the IS curve in Chapter 8. If output is below potential, the real interest rate $(r - \pi)$ is above its equilibrium level. If output is above potential, the real interest rate is below its equilibrium level.

Next, we restate the Taylor rule with the left-hand side as the difference between the actual and the equilibrium real interest rate:

$$r - \pi - R^* = \beta\hat{Y} + \delta(\pi - \pi^*). \tag{16–4}$$

Since the real interest rate R equals the nominal interest rate minus the expected rate of inflation, we can write Equation 16–4 as

$$R - R^* = \beta\hat{Y} + \delta(\pi - \pi^*). \tag{16–5}$$

Combining the IS curve, Equation 16–3, with the Taylor rule, Equation 16–5, we get

$$-\sigma\hat{Y} = \beta\hat{Y} + \delta(\pi - \pi^*). \tag{16–6}$$

or

$$\hat{Y} = [-\delta/(\beta + \sigma)](\pi - \pi^*). \tag{16–7}$$

The macroeconomic policy curve is derived from Equation 16–7. It shows a negative relationship between inflation and the GDP gap. The slope of the MP curve is determined by the IS curve's slope (σ) and the Fed's determination of the nominal interest rate in reaction to output gaps (β) and inflation (δ) in the Taylor rule. The macroeconomic policy curve is graphed in Figure 16–3. The graph shows the Fed changing its target inflation rate π^* in the policy rule from 2 percent to 3 percent, thereby shifting the MP curve right. When the inflation rate π equals the target rate, the GDP gap is zero.

The **macroeconomic policy model** combines the IS curve, Taylor rule, and price adjustment. Figure 16–3 illustrates the macroeconomic policy model as the combination of the macroeconomic policy curve and the price adjustment (PA) line from Chapter 9. The PA line horizontal at the current inflation rate because prices are sticky. Algebraically,

$$\pi = \pi_{-1} + f\hat{Y}_{-1} + Z. \tag{16–8}$$

the PA line shows that *lagged* GDP gap $(\hat{Y}_{-1} = (Y_{-1} - Y^*)/Y^*)$ and note that the current GDP gap is on the right-hand side of Equation 16–8. The PA line shifts up if last year's real GDP was above potential GDP, if the expected rate of

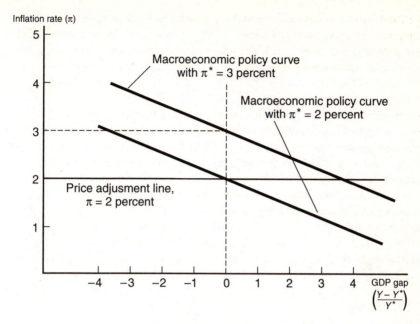

Figure 16–3

inflation rises (measured here by lagged inflation π_{-1}), and if there is a positive price shock Z.

The model simultaneously determines inflation and output. The macroeconomic policy model allows us to analyze a wide range of macroeconomic policies:

1. A **boom** is set off by the MP curve shifting right. This could be caused by a higher inflation target. In the short run, GDP expands above potential GDP at unchanged inflation. Over time, inflation rises and GDP returns to potential.

2. **Disinflation** is the opposite of a boom. A decrease in the Fed's target rate of inflation causes GDP to fall below potential GDP at unchanged inflation in the short run. Over time, inflation falls to its new target and GDP returns to potential.

3. A **boom-bust cycle** is a combination of the first two scenarios. This is the result of the Fed reversing its target for π^* from the higher rate in scenario 1 back to a lower rate in scenario 2.

4. An **oil price shock** is an upward shift of the price adjustment line. While there are other examples of price shocks, oil price shocks are the most important, particularly in the 1970s and in 1990. This initially results in **stagflation**, higher inflation that causes the Fed to raise interest rates, decreasing GDP below potential GDP. Over time, the economy returns to potential GDP at the original rate of inflation.

These four scenarios display **counterclockwise loops**. Following a disturbance, the economy returns toward potential GDP in a counterclockwise fashion. While the paths of inflation and the GDP gap in real-world economies are never as smooth as in the figures, the pattern of counterclockwise loops appears to characterize the experience of the United States over the last 30 years.

The macroeconomic performance for the United States has improved greatly since the 1970s. The **Great Inflation** of the late 1960s to the early 1980s is flanked by two periods of relative price stability. Lower inflation since the early 1980s is our first indication of improved macroeconomic performance. Changes in the conduct of monetary policy toward a greater emphasis on inflation are the most probable cause of the improvement in macroeconomic performance. Since the mid-1980s, the Fed increased the nominal interest rate by enough to raise the real interest rate when inflation rose. This was not true in the 1970s. By keeping inflation low since the mid-1980s, the Fed has also avoided the boom-bust cycle. Therefore, smaller fluctuations in GDP since 1984 are the second indication of improved macroeconomic performance. The third piece of evidence is the **Long Boom**. The back-to-back prolonged expansions in the 1980s and 1990s, were the longest expansions in peacetime history for the United States.

SELF-TEST

Fill in the Blank

1. The _____ makes decisions about monetary policy in the United States.

2. The _____ is the central banks' goal for the average level of inflation.

3. A _____ describes how the Fed or other central banks react to events in the economy.

4. The _____ states that the Fed raises the nominal interest rate when real GDP is greater than potential GDP and when inflation is greater than the target inflation rate.

5. If inflation is approximately constant from year to year, it is reasonable to assume that expected inflation equals _____.

6. The _____ is the percentage deviation of real GDP from potential GDP.

7. The _____ exists if a monetary policy rule raises the *real* interest rate when inflation rises.

8. The macroeconomic policy curve is derived from the _____ and the _____.

9. A _____ can be set off by the Fed targeting a higher inflation rate.

10. _____ is a decrease in the inflation rate.

11. An _____ is an important example of a shift in the price adjustment line.

12. The combination of higher inflation and GDP below potential GDP is called _____.

13. The _____ was the period of high inflation of the late 1960s to early 1980s.

True-False

14. According to the model of price adjustment, inflation responds immediately to a GDP gap.

15. The Fed changed its operating procedures in the mid-1980s.

16. The Fed currently attempts to keep the inflation rate at 0 percent.

17. Central banks are concerned only with inflation.

18. The GDP gap is negative if unemployment is above the natural rate.

19. The IS curve is a negative relation between the nominal interest rate and real GDP.

20. The macroeconomic policy curve shifts to the right when the Fed changes its policy rule to a lower target inflation rate π^*.

21. In the short run, a boom causes GDP to expand above potential GDP at unchanged inflation.

22. In the short run, stagflation causes GDP to expand above potential GDP at unchanged inflation.

23. An oil price shock shifts the aggregate demand–inflation curve.

24. Stagflation describes a situation of both high inflation and high unemployment.

25. Counterclockwise loops describe short-run movements in inflation and the GDP gap.

26. Monetary policy rules (such as the Taylor rule) can lower macroeconomic performance.

Review Questions

27. What is the target inflation rate for the Fed and the European Central Bank?

28. Describe the Fed's monetary policy rule.

29. Why is the Taylor rule line steeper than the 45-degree line?

30. How is the macroeconomic policy derived?

31. Why does the MP curve slope downward?

32. What causes the MP curve to shift?

33. Why is the PA line horizontal?

34. What causes the PA line to shift up?

35. What are several movements in inflation and the output gap that are described by counterclockwise loops?

PROBLEM SET

Worked Problems

1. Suppose that the IS curve is given by

$$-.75\hat{Y} = (R - R^*),$$

and the Fed's monetary policy rule is

$$r = \pi + .5\hat{Y} + .5(\pi - \pi^*) + R^*,$$

where $\hat{Y}$ is the GDP gap, r is the short-term nominal interest rate, π is the inflation rate, π^* is the target inflation rate, and R^* is the equilibrium real interest rate.

   a. What is the macroeconomic policy (MP) curve?

   b. If the inflation rate π is equal to the target inflation rate π^*, what is the GDP gap $\hat{Y}$?

   c. If the inflation rate π is 4 percent, the target inflation rate π^* is 2 percent, and the equilibrium real interest rate R^* is 2 percent, what is the GDP gap $\hat{Y}$?

   a. *Rearrange the IS curve:*

$$r - \pi - R^* = .5\hat{Y} + .5(\pi - \pi^*).$$

   The MP curve is obtained by substituting the Fed's monetary policy rule into the IS curve.

$$-.75\hat{Y} = .5\hat{Y} + .5(\pi - \pi^*).$$

   Solving for $\hat{Y}$,

$$-.5\hat{Y} - .75\hat{Y} = .5(\pi - \pi^*)$$
$$-1.25\hat{Y} = .5(\pi - \pi^*)$$
$$\hat{Y} = \frac{.5(\pi - \pi^*)}{-1.25}$$
$$\hat{Y} = -.4(\pi - \pi^*).$$

b. *From the MP curve in Part a, we see that, if $\pi = \pi^*$, the GDP gap $\hat{Y} = 0$. GDP equals potential GDP.*

c. *If $\pi = 4$, $\pi^* = 2$, and $R^* = 2$,*

$$\hat{Y} = -.4(.04 - .02) = -.4(.02) = -.008.$$

The GDP gap $\hat{Y} = -.8$ percent.

2. Suppose the macroeconomic policy (MP) curve is

$$\hat{Y} = -\frac{\delta}{\beta + \sigma}(\pi - \pi^*)$$

and the price adjustment (PA) line is

$$\pi = f\hat{Y}_{-1} + \pi_{-1} + Z,$$

with $\delta = .5$, $\beta = .5$, $\sigma = .75$, and $f = .25$.

a. Starting in Year 0 from potential GDP with $\pi = \pi^* = 2$ percent, the Fed increases the target π^* to 4 percent in Year 1. No further shocks occur ($\pi^* = 4$ percent for all subsequent years). What are the effects on inflation and the GDP gap for 4 years?

b. Starting in Year 0 from potential GDP with $\pi = \pi^* = 2$ percent, a price shock Z of 2 percent occurs in Year 1. No further shocks occur ($Z = 0$ for all subsequent years). What are the effects on inflation and the GDP gap for 4 years?

a. *In Year 0, the GDP gap is 0 with 2 percent inflation. Since the change in the target inflation rate in Year 1 does not affect inflation in Year 1, $\pi_1 = \pi_0 = 2$. To calculate the GDP gap, first substitute the values for the coefficients δ, β, and σ into the MP curve:*

$$\hat{Y}_1 = -.4(\pi - \pi^*).$$

Using the values for π, π^*, and R^*,

$$\hat{Y}_1 = -.4(.02 - .04) = .008, \text{ or } .8 \text{ percent.}$$

Inflation in Year 2 depends on the GDP gap in Year 1 and inflation in Year 1,

$$\pi_2 = .25\hat{Y} + \pi_1 = .25(.008) + .02 = .002 + .02 = .022, \text{ or } 2.2 \text{ percent.}$$

The GDP gap in Year 2 depends on the difference between inflation in Year 2 and the target inflation rate,

$$\hat{Y} = -.4(.022 - .04) = -.4(-.018) = .0072, \text{ or .72 percent.}$$

For the subsequent years, inflation depends on the lagged GDP gap and lagged inflation, and the GDP gap depends on the difference between π and π^*. The results for 4 years follow:

Year	π	$\hat{Y}$
0	.02	.00
1	.02	.008
2	.022	.0072
3	.0238	.00648
4	.0254	.00583

b. *In the Year 0, the GDP gap is 0 with 2 percent inflation. The price shock in Year 1 raises inflation by 2 percent, so that $\pi_1 = .04$:*

$$\pi_1 = .25\hat{Y}_0 + \pi_0 + Z_1 = 0 + .02 + .02 = .04, \text{ or 4 percent.}$$

The GDP gap in Year 1 becomes:

$$\hat{Y}_1 = -.4(.04 - .02) = -.04(.02) = -.008, \text{ or } -.8 \text{ percent.}$$

Inflation in Year 2 depends on the GDP gap in Year 1 and inflation in Year 1:

$$.25\hat{Y}_1 + \pi_1 + Z_2 = .25(-.008) + .04 + 0$$
$$\pi_2 = -.002 + .04 = .038, \text{ or 3.8 percent.}$$

The GDP gap in Year 2 depends on inflation in Year 2:

$$\hat{Y}_2 = -.4(.038 - .02) = -.0072, \text{ or } -.072 \text{ percent.}$$

For the subsequent years, inflation depends on the lagged GDP gap and lagged inflation, and the GDP gaps depend on the difference between π and π^*. The results for 4 years follow:

Year	π	$\hat{Y}$
0	.02	.00
1	.04	−.0080
2	.038	−.0072
3	.0362	−.00648
4	.0346	−.00583

REVIEW PROBLEMS

3. Suppose that the IS curve is given by

$$-.6\hat{Y} = (R - R^*),$$

and the Fed's Taylor rule is

$$r = \pi + .4\hat{Y} + .5(\pi - \pi^*) + R^*,$$

where $\hat{Y}$ is the GDP gap, r is the nominal interest rate, π is the inflation rate, π^* is the target inflation rate, and R^* is the equilibrium real interest rate.

a. What is the macroeconomic policy (MP) curve?

b. If the inflation rate π is 2 percent and the target inflation rate π^* is 4 percent, what is the GDP gap $\hat{Y}$?

4. Suppose that the IS curve is given by

$$-1.2\hat{Y} = (R - R^*),$$

and the Fed's Taylor rule is

$$r = \pi + .8\hat{Y} + .5(\pi - \pi^*) + R^*,$$

where $\hat{Y}$ is the GDP gap, r is the nominal interest rate, π is the inflation rate, π^* is the target inflation rate, and R^* is the equilibrium real interest rate.

a. What is the macroeconomic policy (MP) curve?

b. If the inflation rate π equals the target inflation rate π^*, what is the GDP gap $\hat{Y}$?

c. What is the GDP gap if π increases by 3 percentage points? If the inflation rate π is 6 percent and the target inflation rate π^* is 2 percent, what is the GDP gap $\hat{Y}$?

5. Suppose the macroeconomic policy (MP) curve is

$$\hat{Y} = -\frac{\delta}{\beta + \sigma}(\pi - \pi^*)$$

and the price adjustment (PA) line is

$$\pi = f\hat{Y}_{-1} + \pi_{-1} + Z,$$

with $\delta = .5$, $\beta = .4$, $\sigma = .6$, and $f = .25$.

Starting in Year 0 from potential GDP with $\pi = \pi^* = 4$ percent, a price shock Z of 2 percent occurs in Year 1. No further shocks occur ($Z = 0$ for all subsequent years). What are the effects on inflation and the GDP gap for 5 years?

6. Suppose the macroeconomic policy (MP) curve is

$$\hat{Y} = -\frac{\delta}{\beta + \sigma}(\pi - \pi^*)$$

and the price adjustment (PA) line is

$$\pi = f\hat{Y}_{-1} + \pi_{-1} + Z,$$

with $\delta = .5$, $\beta = .8$, $\sigma = 1.2$, and $f = .4$.

Starting in Year 0 from potential GDP with $\pi = \pi^* = 2$ percent, the Fed increases π^* in Year 1 to 5 percent. No further policy changes occur ($\pi^* = 5$ percent for all subsequent years). What are the effects on inflation and the GDP gap for 4 years?

a. Starting in Year 0 from potential GDP with $\pi = \pi^* = 2$ percent, a price shock Z of 2 percent occurs in Year 1. No further shocks occur ($Z = 0$ for all subsequent years). What are the effects on inflation and the GDP gap for 4 years?

GRAPH IT

1. Go back to Problem 2a and graph the original MP curve and PA line. Show the original π inflation rate as 2 percent. Label original or initial equilibrium as 0. Show what happens when π^* increases to 4 percent. Label Year 1 equilibrium as 1. Do your results for Years 2, 3, and 4 agree with your graph? Label those equilibrium points on your graph. Don't worry if your results from Problem 1 are not to scale.

2. Go back to Problem 5 and graph the price shock. Show the original inflation rate as 4 percent. Label Year 0 equilibrium as 0 and Year 1 equilibrium as 1. Do your results for Years 2, 3, and 4 agree with your graph? Label those points on your graph. Do not worry if your results from Problem 5 are not to scale.

ANSWERS TO THE SELF-TEST

1. Federal Open Market Committee
2. Target inflation rate

3. Monetary policy rule
4. Taylor rule
5. Last year's inflation
6. GDP gap
7. Taylor principle
8. IS curve and the Taylor rule
9. Boom
10. Disinflation
11. Oil price shock
12. Stagflation
13. Great inflation
14. False. Inflation responds to a GDP gap with a lag.
15. True. The Fed moved from money-supply setting in the late 1970s to nominal interest-rate targeting in the mid-1980s.
16. False. The Fed currently appears to target inflation at 2 percent.
17. False. Central banks are also concerned with fluctuations in real GDP and unemployment.
18. True. If unemployment is above the natural rate, GDP is below potential GDP, creating a negative GDP gap.
19. False. The IS curve shows the negative relation between the real interest rate and real GDP.
20. False. This would shift the MP curve left.
21. True. In the short run, GDP expands above potential GDP at unchanged inflation.
22. False. In the short run, GDP falls below potential GDP at unchanged inflation.
23. False. An oil price shock shifts the price adjustment line.
24. True. Stagflation occurs with both high inflation and real GDP below potential GDP.
25. False. Counterclockwise loops describe how the economy returns toward potential GDP following a disturbance.
26. False. In the United States, the lower inflation rates and decreased volatility of GDP since the early 1980s is evidence that the Taylor rule is stabilizing.
27. The target for inflation is 2 percent.
28. The Fed's monetary policy rule says that the short-term interest rate is determined by inflation, the target inflation rate, the percentage deviation of real GDP from potential GDP, and the equilibrium real interest rate.
29. The Taylor rule is steeper than the 45-degree line because, when inflation rises, the Fed increases the nominal interest rate by more than the increase in inflation. This raises the real interest rate, which follows the Taylor principle.

30. The MP curve is derived by substituting the Fed's monetary policy rule into the IS curve and solving for the GDP gap.
31. The MP curve slopes downward because, when inflation rises, the Fed increases the real interest rate, causing real GDP to fall.
32. The MP curve shifts when the Fed changes its inflation target.
33. The PA line is horizontal because prices are sticky; they do not respond immediately to changes in market conditions.
34. The PA line shifts up if last year's real GDP was above potential GDP, if the expected rate of inflation rises, and if there is a positive price shock.
35. A boom, disinflation, boom-bust cycle, and an oil price shock all create counterclockwise loops.

SOLUTIONS TO REVIEW PROBLEMS

3. a. The MP curve is $\hat{Y} = -.5(\pi - \pi^*)$.
    b. $\hat{Y} = -.5(.02 - .04) = -.5(-.02) = .01$.
        The GDP gap $\hat{Y} = 1$ percent.
4. a. The MP curve is $\hat{Y} = -.25(\pi - \pi^*)$.
    b. $\hat{Y} = -.25(.03) + -.0075$, or $-.75$ percent.
    c. $\hat{Y} = -.25(.06 - .02) = -.25(.04) = -.01$.
        The GDP gap is -1 percent.
5. The price shock in Year 1 causes 6 percent inflation and a GDP of -1 percent in Year 1. The results for 5 years follow:

Year	π	$\hat{Y}$
0	.04	.00
1	.06	−.01
2	.0575	−.0088
3	.0553	−.0077
4	.0534	−.0067
5	.0517	−.0059

6. The inflation target change in Year 1 causes a GDP gap of -1 percent in Year 1, but does not affect inflation until Year 2. The results for 4 years follow:

Year	π	$\hat{Y}$
0	.02	.00
1	.02	.0075
2	.023	.00675
3	.0257	.00607
4	.0281	.00547

ANSWERS TO GRAPH IT

1.

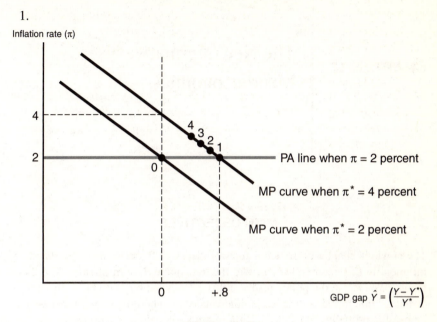

Figure 16–4

2. The price shock in Year 1 shifts the PA line to $\pi = 6$ percent. The adjustment back ultimately moves to the original equilibrium where $\hat{Y} = 0$ and $\pi = 4$ percent.

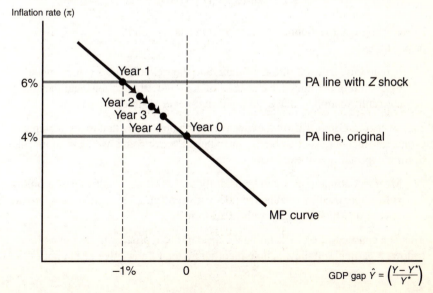

Figure 16–5

CHAPTER 17

The New Normative
Macroeconomics

MAIN OBJECTIVES

The previous chapter presented a positive theory of fluctuations in GDP and inflation. In this chapter, we consider the **new normative implications** of this theory. We look at the policy research that asks "what ought to be" rather than "what is" that has already been outlined and think about how the two views can be mixed optimally. You should learn the trade-offs along the policy frontier between inflation and unemployment stability and consider how the frontier can be improved.

KEY TERMS AND CONCEPTS

In analyzing macroeconomic policy, economists rely on the following five propositions.

1. People look forward into the future, and their expectations can be modeled by assuming that they have a sense of economic fluctuations and they use their information to make unbiased (but not error-free) forecasts.

This is the premise of **rational expectations**. People know that many features of economic fluctuations characterize each business cycle and use their knowledge to form expectations of the future.

2. Macroeconomic policy can be usefully described and evaluated as a **policy rule**, rather than by treating the policy instruments as exogenous and looking only at one-time changes in these instruments.

This is a consequence of the rational expectations approach. If the government follows a particular policy, people incorporate their knowledge of the policy into their expectations. Thus the policy instruments become an integral part of the model. For policy evaluation, we can stipulate policy as a rule. These rules can be **activist**, and thus incorporate feedback from the state of the economy to the policy instruments, or **passive**, as, for instance, the fixed growth rate rule for the money supply.

3. In order for a particular policy rule to work well, it is necessary to establish a commitment to that rule.

This follows from the problem of **time inconsistency**. When people are forward looking, there is incentive for policy makers to deviate from an announced policy rule—they can make things better by being inconsistent. However, once people realize that policy is inconsistent, the policy makers lose credibility and the outcome becomes inferior to the original plan. Research on time inconsistency suggests that the scope for discretionary policy should be limited.

4. The economy is basically stable; after a shock, the economy eventually returns to its normal trend paths of output and employment. However, because of rigidities in the economy, the return could be slow.

Demand and price shocks move output and employment away from their long-run, or potential, growth paths. Because wage and price setting have both forward- and backward-looking components, there are **wage-price rigidities**. These rigidities prevent the economy from quickly returning to equilibrium following a shock.

5. The objective of macroeconomic policy is to reduce the size (or the duration) of the fluctuations from normal levels of output, employment, and inflation after shocks hit the economy.

Macroeconomic policy rules that respond to shocks in a systematic manner exert considerable influence on the size and duration of he fluctuations caused by the shocks How these rules should be constructed is the main concern of this chapter.

The **targets** of macro policy are the variables, such as inflation and unemployment, that we care about, while the **instruments** are the variables, such as the monetary base and tax rate, that are used to carry out the policy. The **social welfare function** summarizes the costs of having the target variables deviate from their desired levels. It reflects value judgments regarding the relative importance of the targets.

Whenever the number of instruments is less than the number of targets there is a trade-off between the different target variables. Equality of instruments and targets is not sufficient to avoid a trade-off unless the instruments affect the targets independently. For example, since both monetary and fiscal policy affect the aggregate demand curve, the two are not sufficient to avoid a trade-off between inflation and unemployment variability.

The **policy frontier** describes the set of different combinations of employment and price stability that can be achieved. The **squared error** is a simple measure of the loss from having a variable not equal its target value. One example is the **inflation loss**—the average of the squared deviation of the inflation rate from its target, near zero. (If inflation is 3 percent and target inflation is zero, the inflation loss is 9.) Another example is the **output loss**—the average squared departure of unemployment from the natural rate. (If unemployment is 10 percent and the natural rate of unemployment is 6 percent, the output loss is 16.)

The costs of inflation are hard to quantify. They include "shoe-leather" costs of conserving money holdings, distortions because much of the tax system is not indexed, capricious gains and losses by debtors and creditors, and problems caused by the failure of private pension plans to be indexed. Other, probably more important, reasons why people dislike inflation are that they see inflation as a breakdown of the basic government responsibility to provide a stable unit of purchasing power and some people view inflation as a decrease in their wages relative to prices, rather than as a general increase in both.

The costs of unemployment are clearer. The direct costs of lost GDP, as measured by Okun's law, are very high in a typical recession. In addition, there are indirect costs such as the loss of training when a young worker becomes unemployed and the social costs from the experience of unemployment itself. The costs of periods when GDP is above potential and unemployment is below the natural rate are less intuitive. If the marginal value of time in other uses rises and falls with employment, workers may prefer, during booms, to work less and have more time available for other activities.

The **policy trade-off** between inflation and output fluctuations can be analyzed by using the model from Chapter 16. As we saw there, aggregate demand shocks can be offset through a policy that moves aggregate demand back to its original level. Countering price shocks is more complicated. The price adjustment line with expected inflation equal to last year's inflation is

$$\pi = f(Y_{-1} - Y^*)/Y^* + \pi_{-1} + Z. \tag{17–1}$$

A simple form of the macroeconomic policy (MP) curve is

$$(Y - Y^*)/Y^* = -g(\pi - \pi^*), \tag{17–2}$$

where g depends on the Fed's monetary policy rule.

The slope of the MP curve depends on the Fed's monetary policy rule and the slope of the IS curve. If the Fed raises interest rates sharply when inflation rises above target, g is larger and the MP curve is flatter. If the Fed raises interest rates more slowly, g is smaller and the MP curve is steeper. If g is zero, the monetary policy rule keeps the output gap at zero and fully accommodates inflation. If g is positive, the output gap is negative if inflation is above the target inflation rate.

The effects of different values of g on inflation can be seen by lagging Equation 17–2 by 1 year,

$$(Y_{-1} - Y^*)/Y^* = -g(\pi_{-1} - \pi^*), \tag{17-3}$$

and substituting Equation 17–3 into Equation 17–1,

$$\pi = (1 - fg)\pi_{-1} + fg\pi^* + Z. \tag{17-4}$$

For simplicity, we define $k = (1 - fg)$. If g is zero so that $k = (1 - 0) = 1$, then the price shock Z permanently raises the inflation rate by Z. If k is zero, the effect of the price shock disappears after only 1 year. If k is between zero and 1, the effect of the price shock gradually disappears.

A policy of **strict price stability** ($k = 0$) involves a large amount of unemployment loss. A policy of **strict unemployment stability** ($k = 1$) involves a large amount of inflation loss. The best policy achieves a compromise between the two types of losses and has k between zero and 1.

The optimal policy for responding to price shocks is illustrated in Figure 17–1. The policy frontier shows the alternative combinations of inflation and unemployment loss that can be achieved using different policies. The social indifference curves illustrate combinations of inflation and unemployment loss, which improve as the curves get closer to the origin. The optimal policy is when the policy frontier is tangent to the indifference curve. The Taylor rule produces a point on the policy frontier between strict price stability and strict output stability. Although that does not imply a tangency between the policy frontier and the social indifference curves, it does mean that the Taylor rule is consistent with an optimal policy.

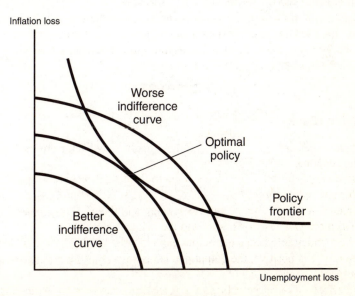

Figure 17–1

Nominal GDP targeting is an example of a compromise policy that is easy to express (when $\delta = \beta + \sigma$, the Taylor rule is equivalent to nominal GDP targeting). Since aggregate demand disturbances do not initially affect the price level, nominal GDP targeting correctly offsets them. For price shocks, nominal GDP targeting, which sets $g = 1$, favors unemployment stability over price stability. Since a reasonable value for f is .2, $k = .8$. This means that 80 percent of a price shock is tolerated as a continued increase in inflation the year after it occurs.

We have focused on how to conduct macroeconomic policy in order to choose the best point on the policy frontier. These choices always involve a trade-off between output and price stability. If we could move the frontier toward the origin, we could improve the trade-off. Comparing the 1970s with the 1990s by implementing a stabilizing monetary rule along the lines of the Taylor rule, the Fed moved the policy frontier closer to the origin.

Streamlining the labor market, or making wages more responsive to price shocks, also would move the policy frontier closer to the origin. Some proposals to increase the speed of adjustment of wages include better job matching, eliminating government price and wage fixing, and reforming unemployment compensation. It is not clear that any of these proposals would be effective or that their benefits would outweigh their costs.

Other proposals to move the frontier toward the origin include improving indexation so that price increases arising from imports and other materials costs would be excluded, avoiding government price shocks, and using controls and incentives that reward businesses and workers who follow government guidelines for price and wage increases. As with the proposals to streamline the labor market, it is not clear how effective these would be.

Protectionist trade measures, such as tariffs and quotas, raise inflation when they are imposed and lower inflation when they are removed. Avoiding these price shocks keeps the policy frontier as close to the origin as possible.

SELF-TEST

Fill in the Blank

1. Policy rules are _____ if they involve feedback from the state of the economy.

2. _____ policy is formulated on a case-by-case basis.

3. There is a _____ between output and inflation fluctuations.

4. The _____ of macro policy are the variables that we care about.

5. The _____ of macro policy are the variables used to carry out the policy.

6. The _____ summarizes the costs of having the target variable deviate from their desired levels.

7. The _____ describes the set of different combinations of employment and price stability that can be achieved.

8. The _____ is the average of the squared deviation of the inflation rate from its target.

9. The unemployment loss is the _____ of unemployment from the natural rate.

10. Two extreme policies are _____ and _____ stability.

11. An example of a compromise policy is _____ targeting.

12. Optimal policy is when the policy frontier is _____ to the social indifference curve.

13. The trade-off between output and price fluctuations would be improved if the policy frontier could be moved _____ the origin.

True-False

14. According to the rational expectations hypothesis, people use the information available to them to make unbiased forecasts.

15. A fixed growth rate rule for the money supply is an activist policy rule.

16. The economy returns quickly to equilibrium following a shock.

17. Equality of instruments and targets is not sufficient to avoid a trade-off between the different target variables.

18. The target level of unemployment should be zero.

19. The costs of unemployment are not very large.

20. Aggregate demand shifts can be offset through a policy that moves the aggregate demand curve back to its original level.

21. The slope of the MP curve depends only on the slope of the IS curve.

22. If policy is fully accommodative, a price shock permanently raises the inflation rate.

23. The best policy is normally one of either strict price stability or strict unemployment stability.

24. Nominal GDP targeting is not optimal if there are demand shocks.

25. Moving the policy frontier toward the origin could improve both output and price stability.

26. Tariffs and quotas are examples of demand disturbances.

Review Questions

27. What is the premise of rational expectations?

28. Why does the rational expectations model lead to consideration of policy rules?

29. What is the difference between activist and passive policy rules?

30. What does research on time inconsistency indicate about the conduct of economic policy.

31. Why can monetary and fiscal policy not be used to avoid a trade-off between inflation and unemployment variability?

32. Why is it difficult to compare the costs of inflation with the costs of unemployment?

33. How does the slope of the MP curve depend on the Fed's monetary policy rule?

34. What is the relation between the degree that policy is accommodative and the persistence of price shocks?

35. Why does the best policy normally involve a compromise between inflation and unemployment losses?

36. What are the implications of nominal GDP targeting for the response to price shocks?

37. What is the relation between nominal GDP targeting and recent monetary policy in the United States?

38. What types of policies could potentially improve the trade-off between output and price stability?

39. Why do protectionist measures worsen the policy frontier?

PROBLEM SET

Worked Problems

1. Suppose that price adjustment is given by

$$\pi = .2[(Y_{-1} - Y^*)/Y^*] + \pi_{-1} + Z$$

and the macroeconomic policy (MP) curve is

$$(Y_{-1} - Y^*)/Y^* = -1(\pi_{-1} - \pi^*).$$

a. What equation describes inflation?

b. What type of policy rule is depicted by this MP curve? Does it favor unemployment or price stability?

c. Suppose that the MP curve is instead

$$(Y_{-1} - Y^*)/Y^* = -4(\pi_{-1} - \pi^*).$$

What equation describes inflation? How is the balance between unemployment and price stability affected?

a. *Substituting the MP curve into the price adjustment equation,*

$$\pi = 2(-1)(\pi_{-1} - \pi^*) + \pi_{-1} + Z$$
$$= (1 - .2)\pi_{-1} + .2\pi^* + Z$$
$$= .8\pi_{-1} + .2\pi^* + Z.$$

. *Since g = 1, the policy rule targets nominal GDP. It favors unemployment stability since k = .8.*

c. *The equation that describes inflation is*

$$\pi = .2\pi_{-1} + .8\pi^* + Z.$$

This less accommodative policy favors inflation stability since k = .2.

2. Suppose that price adjustment is given by

$$\pi = .25(Y_{-1} - Y^*)/Y^* + \pi_{-1} + Z,$$

and the MP curve is

$$(Y_{-1} - Y^*)/Y^* = -1(\pi_{-1} - \pi^*),$$

with potential output $Y^* = \$1,500$ billion and the target inflation rate $\pi^* = .04$ (4 percent).

a. Suppose the economy starts out at potential output with the inflation rate equal to the target inflation rate. Describe the path of the economy for 5 years following a price shock Z of 6 percent.

b. Suppose that the MP curve is instead

$$(Y_{-1} - Y^*)/Y^* = -2(\pi_{-1} - \pi^*).$$

Describe the path of the economy following the same shock and compare it with the path in Part a.

a. *Inflation is determined by substituting the MP curve into the price adjustment equation,*

$$\pi = .75\pi_{-1} + .25\pi^* + Z.$$

Inflation is 10 percent, $(.75 \times .04) + (.25 \times .04) + .06$, in the first year and 8.5 percent, $(.75 \times .10) + (.25 \times .04)$, in the second. Output, which is calculated from the MP curve, is $1,410 billion in the first year

($1,500 billion minus the output gap of $90 billion) and $1,433 billion ($1,500 billion minus the output gap of $67 billion) in the second. Results of the first 5 years follow:

Year	π	$\hat{Y}$	Y
1	.100 (10 percent)	−.060	$1,410
2	.085 (8.5 percent)	−.045	1,433
3	.074 (7.4 percent)	−.034	1,449
4	.066 (6.6 percent)	−.026	1,461
5	.060 (6.0 percent)	−.019	1,471

b. *The inflation equation for the less accommodative MP curve is*

$$\pi = .5\pi_{-1} + .5\pi^* + Z.$$

Inflation is brought down more quickly but the initial decrease in output is larger:

Year	π	$\hat{Y}$	Y
1	.100 (10 percent)	−.12	$1,320
2	.070 (7.0 percent)	−.06	1,410
3	.055 (5.5 percent)	−.03	1,455
4	.048 (4.8 percent)	−.015	1,478
5	.044 (4.4 percent)	−.007	1,489

Review Problems

3. Suppose that price adjustment is given by

$$\pi = .25[(Y_{-1} - Y^*)/Y^*] + \pi_{-1} + Z$$

and the MP curve is

$$(Y_{-1} - Y^*)/Y^* = -2(\pi_{-1} - \pi^*).$$

a. What equation describes inflation?

b. What type of policy rule is depicted by this MP curve? Does it favor unemployment or price stability?

c. Suppose that the policy MP curve is instead

$$(Y_{-1} - Y^*)/Y^* = -4(\pi_{-1} - \pi^*).$$

What equation describes inflation? How is the balance between unemployment and price stability affected?

4. Suppose that price adjustment is given by

$$\pi = .2[(Y_{-1} - Y^*)/Y^*] + \pi_{-1} + Z$$

and the MP curve is

$$(Y_{-1} - Y^*)/Y^* = -3(\pi_{-1} - \pi^*).$$

a. What equation describes inflation?

b. What type of policy rule is depicted by this MP curve? Does it favor unemployment or price stability?

c. Suppose the MP curve is instead

$$(Y_{-1} - Y^*)/Y^* = 0.$$

What equation describes inflation? How is the balance between unemployment and price stability affected?

5. Suppose that price adjustment is given by

$$\pi = .2(Y_{-1} - Y^*)/Y^* + \pi_{-1} + Z,$$

and the MP curve is

$$(Y_{-1} - Y^*)/Y^* = -2(\pi_{-1} - \pi^*),$$

with potential output $Y^* = \$1,500$ billion and the target inflation rate $\pi^* = .02$ (2 percent).

a. Suppose the economy starts out at potential output with the inflation rate equal to the target inflation rate. Describe the path of the economy for 5 years following a price shock Z of 4 percent.

b. Suppose that the MP curve is

$$(Y_{-1} - Y^*)/Y^* = -5(\pi_{-1} - \pi^*).$$

Describe the path of the economy following the same shock and compare it with the path in Part a.

6. Suppose that price adjustment is given by

$$\pi = .2(Y_{-1} - Y^*)/Y^* + \pi_{-1} + Z,$$

and the MP curve is

$$(Y_{-1} - Y^*)/Y^* = -1.5(\pi_{-1} - \pi^*),$$

with potential output $Y^* = \$1,500$ billion and the target inflation rate $\pi^* = .06$ (6 percent).

a. Suppose the economy starts out at potential output with the inflation rate equal to the target inflation rate. Describe the path of the economy for 5 years following a price shock Z of 4 percent.

b. Suppose the MP curve is instead

$$(Y_{-1} - Y^*)/Y^* = 0.$$

Describe the path of the economy following the same shock and compare it with the path in Part a.

ANSWERS TO THE SELF-TEST

1. Activist
2. Discretionary
3. Policy trade-off
4. Targets
5. Instruments
6. Social welfare function
7. Policy frontier
8. Inflation loss
9. Average squared departure
10. Strict price and strict unemployment
11. Nominal GDP
12. Tangent
13. Toward
14. True.   This is an implication of the rational expectations assumption.
15. False.   It is a passive rule.
16. False.   Because of rigidities, the economy returns slowly to equilibrium.
17. True.   The instruments must have independent effects on the target variables.
18. False.   It should be the natural rate.
19. False.   The costs of lost GDP are very high in a typical recession.
20. True.   Aggregate demand shifts can be completely offset.
21. False.   The slope of the MP curve also depends on the Fed's monetary policy rule.
22. True.   Fully accommodative policy never lowers output to stabilize inflation.
23. False.   The best policy is normally a compromise between price and unemployment stability.
24. False.   Nominal GDP targeting completely offsets demand shocks.
25. True.   Moving the policy frontier toward the origin improves the trade-off between output and price stability.
26. False.   Tariffs and quotas are price shocks.
27. The premise of rational expectations is that people, in making forecasts, use their knowledge of economic fluctuations.
28. Rational expectations lead to consideration of policy rules because people use their knowledge of these rules to form their expectations of future events.
29. Activist policy rules involve feedback from the state of the economy to the policy instruments, while passive rules do not.
30. Research on time inconsistency indicates that in order for a particular policy rule to work well, it is necessary to establish a commitment to that rule.
31. Since both monetary and fiscal policy affect the aggregate demand curve, they cannot be used independently to avoid a trade-off.

32. The direct costs of lost GDP from high unemployment can be measured by Okun's law. The costs of inflation, such as the cost of conserving money holdings, are harder to quantify.
33. If the Fed raises interest rates sharply when inflation rises above target, the MP curve is flatter. If the Fed raises interest rates more slowly, the MP curve is steeper.
34. The higher is the degree of accommodation, the more persistent are price shocks.
35. Policies of strict price or strict output stability normally involve such large unemployment or inflation losses that compromise policies are better.
36. Nominal GDP targeting favors unemployment stability over price stability in response to price shocks.
37. Monetary policy in the United States has followed a path that is reasonably close to nominal GDP targeting during the 1980s and 1990s.
38. Policies to streamline the labor market, improve indexation, and avoid government price shocks, as well as the use of controls and incentives, could potentially improve the trade-off.
39. Protectionist measures impose price shocks, worsening the trade-off between output and price stability.

SOLUTIONS TO REVIEW PROBLEMS

3. a. Inflation $\pi = .5\pi_{-1} + .5\pi^* + Z$.
   b. The policy rule is moderately accommodative. It favors neither employment nor price stability.
   c. Inflation $\pi = \pi^* + Z$. The policy rule is completely nonaccommodative. The effects of the price shock on inflation disappear after 1 year.
4. a. Inflation $\pi = .4\pi_{-1} + .6\pi^* + Z$.
   b. The policy rule is moderately accommodative. It slightly favors price stability since $k = .4$.
   c. Inflation $\pi = \pi_{-1} + Z$. The policy rule is fully accommodative. The price shock permanently raises inflation by Z.
5. a. The inflation equation for is $\pi = .6\pi_{-1} + .4\pi^* + Z$. Inflation and output for 5 years are

Year	π	Y
1	.060 (6.0 percent)	$1,380
2	.044 (4.4 percent)	1,428
3	.034 (3.4 percent)	1,457
4	.029 (2.9 percent)	1,474
5	.025 (2.5 percent)	1,484

   c. Inflation $\pi = \pi^* + Z$. The MP curve is completely nonaccommodative. The effect of the price shock on inflation disappears after 1 year but the initial decrease in output is much greater:

Year	π	Y
1	.060 (6.0 percent)	$1,200
2	.020 (2.0 percent)	1,500

6. a. The inflation equation for is $\pi = .7\pi_{-1} + .3\pi^* + Z$. Inflation and output for 5 years are

Year	π	Y
1	.100 (10 percent)	$1,410
2	.088 (8.8 percent)	1,437
3	.080 (8.0 percent)	1,456
4	.074 (7.4 percent)	1,469
5	.070 (7.0 percent)	1,478

Inflation $\pi = \pi_{-1} + Z$. The MP curve is fully accommodative. The price shock permanently raises inflation by 4 percent but has not effect on output.

Year	π	Y
1	.100 (10 percent)	$1,500
2	.100 (10 percent)	1,500

CHAPTER 18

Macroeconomic Policy in the World Economy

MAIN OBJECTIVES

Macroeconomic policy in the United States is conducted under a regime of floating exchange rates, free movement of capital, an implicit inflation target of about 2 percent, and a Taylor rule for monetary policy, where the real interest rate is increased when inflation rises. In this chapter, we examine macroeconomic policy in the world economy and discuss, from both an international and historical perspective, why countries are moving away from fixed exchange rates. You should be able to compare and contrast the macroeconomic performance of the United States with other countries, including the United Kingdom, the countries of the Eurozone, China, and Japan. We consider the role of the exchange rate in the Taylor rule and see how the adoption of Taylor rules has improved macroeconomic performance in the world economy.

KEY TERMS AND CONCEPTS

The **international financial and monetary system** determines how trade and financial transactions are conducted among different countries. Full integration in the world market requires that countries impose few if any restrictions on currency transactions, capital movement, and movement of goods. Over time, the world economy is becoming more integrated.

The system is dominated by four large governments: the United States, Japan, Great Britain, and the Eurozone. These governments, along with Canada and a few others, have **floating exchange rates**, determined in free markets. Central banks **intervene** in the **foreign exchange market** when they conduct purchases (or sales) of foreign securities with domestic securities. Other countries maintain some degree of insulation from the world system, usually through **capital**

and exchange controls. Some currencies are **inconvertible**. They cannot be bought or sold on open markets.

Under **fixed exchange rates**, the central bank of a small country, which cannot affect the world interest rate, does not have control of its own money supply. The central bank of an open economy can hold domestic securities, called **domestic credit**, or foreign securities, called **foreign reserves**. The balance sheet of the central bank requires that the monetary base equal the domestic credit plus foreign reserves. If the central bank tries to increase the money supply by raising domestic credit through an open-market operation, it puts pressure on the interest rate to fall. With high capital mobility, investors demand foreign exchange so that they can receive the higher foreign return. This puts pressure on the currency to depreciate, which the central bank resists by intervention, selling its foreign reserves for domestic currency at the fixed exchange rate. The net result is that the monetary base is unchanged.

Sterilized intervention occurs when a central bank sells foreign reserves and buys domestic credit (or vice versa) at the same time in the same amount. This eliminates the effect of intervention on the money supply. With high capital mobility, sterilized intervention does not have much effect on the exchange rate. Many small countries impose capital controls, such as restrictions on the amount of currency that domestic residents can purchase, in an attempt to gain some control over their money supplies.

Until World War I, countries generally defined their monetary units in terms of gold or silver. Under the **gold standard**, exchange rates were determined by the agreement of each country to freely buy and sell gold at a set price. The **Bretton Woods System** was the international monetary system from the end of World War II until 1971. Each of the participating countries agreed to intervene in currency markets to keep the value of its currency against the dollar within a narrow range, called the **intervention band**, around its fixed exchange rate, called the **par value**. A **reserve inflow** occurred when a central bank prevented an appreciation of its currency by purchasing dollar securities. When a country defended its currency by selling dollar securities, there was a **reserve outflow**.

According to purchasing power parity, if inflation is higher in one country than in another, the exchange rate should appreciate by the difference between the foreign inflation rate and the domestic inflation rate. The Bretton Woods System allowed for the par values of exchange rates to be lowered, called a **devaluation**, or raised, a **revaluation**, but such changes did not occur very frequently. One problem with the Bretton Woods System was that, when traders expected a devaluation, as with the British pound in 1967, they pushed down the market rate, casing an exchange-rate crisis. Another problem was its vulnerability to mistakes in U.S. monetary policy. The Bretton Woods System was abandoned in 1971 after inflation worsened for several years in the United States.

Since 1973, the dollar has floated in relation to other currencies. While there have been occasional interventions when the dollar reached an extreme high, such as in 1985, or low, such as in 1978, the United States has not had a systematic exchange-rate policy. Today, the dollar floats freely; United States policy does little to control its movement.

The **macroeconomic policy trilemma** is that, among the macroeconomic policy objectives of *fixed exchange rates, free movement of capital,* and *an independent monetary policy,* only two of the three objectives can be obtained simultaneously. With the dollar floating against other currencies, the United States in turn allows for free capital mobility and an independent monetary policy (such as a Taylor rule). Australia, Canada, and the United Kingdom have pursued similar policy objectives.

An important development of the 1990s and 2000s is that, over time, more countries have chosen to abandon fixed exchange rates. Instead, they have either adopted a monetary policy based on flexible exchange rates or permanently connected their monetary policy to another country's monetary policy through monetary union, dollarization, or a currency board.

Monetary union is the situation where countries abandon their national currencies in favor of a single currency. In the European Union, the foremost example, 12 countries located in the **Eurozone** have permanently fixed their exchange rates by combining their national currencies into one single currency, the euro. The second macroeconomic policy objective Eurozone countries have pursued is free capital mobility; therefore, their national central banks have given up the ability to conduct independent monetary policy, the third policy objective of the trilemma.

Dollarization occurs when a country adopts another country's currency, usually the U.S. dollar, as its national money. A **currency board** is a fixed exchange rate where new issues of domestic currency are backed one-to-one by additional holdings of the key foreign currency. These developments were precipitated, in part by several currency crises during the 1990s and 2000s.

Exchange-rate policy affects growth and stability. Countries that do not impose controls on currency transactions and capital flows have to choose between a fixed exchange rate and an independent monetary policy. With fixed exchange rates, we learned in Chapter 12 that a country commits to conduct monetary policy so as to keep its interest rate equal to the world interest rate. Monetary policy is therefore precluded from raising real interest rates for other reasons, such as the Taylor rule in Equation 18–1:

$$r = \pi + \beta\hat{Y} + \delta(\pi - \pi^*) + R^* \qquad (18\text{–}1)$$

Here, positive coefficients b and d imply that the central bank raises real interest rates R ($= r + \pi$) whenever inflation π rises above its target level π^* or when the GDP gap $\hat{Y}$ increases. Recall that r is the short-term nominal (federal funds) interest rate set by the central bank and R^* is the long-run equilibrium real interest rate.

We define **stress** to be

$$\text{Stress} = r - r^T, \qquad (18\text{–}2)$$

the difference between the actual interest rate r and the interest rate implied by following a Taylor rule, r^T. If stress increases, then so too does the tension between pursuing the external goal of a fixed exchange rate and domestic goals of price stability and sustainable output growth. By adopting flexible exchange rates central banks can pursue an independent monetary policy rule. To summarize, unless a country permanently fixes its exchange rate through a currency board, a common currency, or dollarization, the only monetary policy that can work well in the long run is one based on the trinity of (1) a flexible exchange rate, (2) an inflation target, and (3) a monetary policy rule.

Although the exchange rate does not appear in the Taylor rule (Equation 18–1), there is an important indirect reaction of the interest rate to the exchange rate. If the nominal exchange rate rises, the real exchange rate will rise given sticky prices. A higher real exchange rate decreases net exports, lowering GDP in the short run and decreasing the GDP gap. A higher nominal exchange rate also, particularly in smaller countries, lowers inflation. According to the Taylor rule, the central bank responds in both cases by lowering the interest rate. The Taylor rule can be modified to account for a direct effect of the exchange rate on the interest rate set by the central bank. One specification is

$$r = \pi - \beta\hat{Y} + \delta(\pi - \pi^*) + R^* - \alpha(EP/P_w), \qquad (18\text{–}3)$$

where EP/P_w is the real exchange rate and α is a positive coefficient. When the real exchange rate rises, net exports and GDP fall. With the coefficient a positive, the central bank lowers real interest rates, mitigating the contraction.

In contrast to the 1980s, macroeconomic performance in Japan has been much worse than macroeconomic performance in the United States in the 1990s and 2000s. Japan experienced an **asset price bubble**, an enormous but unsustainable increase in land and stock prices, throughout the 1980s, which collapsed beginning in 1989. Japanese monetary policy was overly restrictive in the early 1990s, and as a result, Japan has experienced sustained **near-negative inflation** (inflation close to zero) and even periods of **deflation** (negative inflation). While low inflation, as in the case of Japan in the late 1970s and 1980s and the United States in the late 1980s and 1990s, is good for macroeconomic performance, near-negative inflation and deflation is not good for macroeconomic performance.

Once Japan found itself in the situation of near-negative inflation, monetary policy making became very difficult. Nominal interest rates were already low, so the central bank had very little scope to lower them further to stimulate the economy. A zero bound on the nominal interest rate makes it impossible for the central bank to stimulate the economy along the lines suggested by the Taylor rule.

Deflation makes this situation worse still. Deflation raises real interest rates, discourages investments, and encourages people to postpone consumption. Reversing deflation requires sustained increase in the growth rate of the money supply, which in turn depends on the willingness of the banking system to create new loans. However, Japanese banks have massive amounts of bad, or **nonperforming, loans**. As long as these loans remain on their balance sheets, banks have no incentive to issue new loans. Japan's deterioration is large enough to be called a depression. Restoring economic growth in Japan will require changes in both monetary and banking policy. Some improvements in Japan's macroeconomic performance occurred in 2003.

SELF-TEST

Fill in the Blank

1. The _____ determines how trade and financial transactions are conducted among different countries.

2. The _____ was the international monetary system until World War I

3. The _____ was the international monetary system from the end of World War II until 1971.

4. Since 1973, major industrialized countries have had _____ exchange rates against the dollar.

5. _____ is the situation where countries abandon their national currencies in favor of a single currency.

6. A country imposes _____ if it wants to maintain some degree of insulation from the world system.

7. With fixed exchange rates, countries _____ to keep currencies close to their par values.

8. _____ is when the central bank offsets the effects on the money supply of keeping the exchange rate fixed.

9. The narrow range around the par value within which, under fixed exchange rates, countries keep their exchange rates is called the _____.

10. Changes in par values of exchange rates are _____ or _____.

11. With an _____, central banks are free to target monetary policy toward objectives they really care about, such as limiting fluctuations in inflation and GDP.

12. If a country adopts another country's currency we call this _____.

True-False

13. Today's international monetary system is called the Bretton Woods System.

14. Under the Bretton Woods System, devaluations and revaluations occurred frequently.

15. In the last few years, a number of countries have chosen to abandon flexible exchange rates.

16. The monetary base equals domestic credit – foreign reserves.

17. Sterilized intervention does not affect the money supply.

18. Under the gold standard, exchange rates were automatically determined.

19. Stabilizing the exchange rate has been the most important determinant of U.S. monetary policy since 1973.

20. The euro was abandoned in 1973.

21. A fixed exchange rate is compatible with the Taylor rule.

22. China, Hong Kong, and Singapore have abandoned fixed exchange rates.

23. Japan has experienced sustained near-negative inflation and periods of deflation in the 1990s and 2000s.

24. European countries created a monetary union with a single currency, the euro.

Review Questions

25. What must a country do to be fully integrated in the world market?

26. Why does a small country lose control of its money supply under fixed exchange rates and high capital mobility?

27. What two problems caused the downfall of the Bretton Woods System?

28. How does the concept of stress explain the downfall of the European Monetary System (EMS)?

29. If a country adopts a flexible exchange rate system, what else must it do to perform well in the long run?

30. How can the real exchange rate have an indirect effect on the Taylor rule?

31. Describe the macroeconomic performance of the United Kingdom, Canada, and Australia since the 1990s.

32. What is an asset price bubble?

33. What is the difference between near-negative inflation and deflation?

34. Why has Japan's economic performance been so poor in the 1990s and 2000s?

35. Why is a monetary union a stronger commitment than fixed exchange rates?

PROBLEM SET

Worked Problems

1. Suppose this is the balance sheet of the central bank (billions of dollars):

Assets		Liabilities	
Domestic credit	300	Currency	280
Foreign reserves	50	Bank reserves	70

What would be the effect on domestic credit, foreign reserves, currency, and bank reserves of

a. An open market purchase of $20 billion?

b. A foreign exchange market intervention to prevent depreciation of $20 billion?

c. A sterilized foreign exchange intervention of $20 billion?

a. *The Fed purchase of $20 increases domestic credit by $20. This is financed by creating $20 more in bank reserves:*

Assets		Liabilities	
Domestic credit	*320*	*Currency*	*280*
Foreign reserves	*50*	*Bank reserves*	*90*

The monetary base has increased by $20 to $370. The money supply also increases so interest rates fall. Capital flows out of the country when interest rates fall below world rates. The currency depreciates.

b. *Working from Part a, the central bank sells $20 in foreign reserves, so they fall by that amount. The central bank collects currency as payment, so $20 in currency is no longer part of the liabilities of the central bank:*

Assets		Liabilities	
Domestic credit	*320*	*Currency*	*260*
Foreign reserves	*30*	*Bank reserves*	*90*

c. *Sterilized intervention is the combined and offsetting effects of Part a and Part b. Note that the monetary base, after foreign reserves are sold to counteract the depreciation in Part a, returns to the original amount of $350 billion.*

2. Suppose that the Taylor rule is given by

$$r = \pi + \beta \hat{Y} + \delta(\pi - \pi^*) + R^*,$$

where $\beta = .5$, $\delta = .5$, $\pi^* = .02$, and $R^* = .02$

a. Suppose that the inflation rate $\pi = 0$. According to the Taylor rule, what would the nominal interest rate be if the output gap $\hat{Y} = 0$?

b. Now suppose that the inflation rate $\pi = -1$ percent. Can monetary policy be conducted according to the Taylor rule?

c. What has happened to real rates?

a. Nominal rates $r = 0 + .5(0) + .5(0 - .02) + .02 = .01$, *or 1 percent.*

b. Nominal rates $r = -.01 + .5(0) + (-.01 - .02) + .02 = -.005$, *or* $-.5$ *percent. No, nominal rates reach a zero bound and cannot go below 0 percent.*

c. $r - \pi = R$.
Part a, $1 - 0 = 1$ *percent.*
Part b, $0 - (-1) = 1$ *percent.*
Real rates have not decreased despite the decrease in nominal rates to zero.

Review Problems

3. Suppose this is the balance sheet of the central bank (billions of dollars):

Assets		Liabilities	
Domestic credit	400	Currency	75
Foreign reserves	50	Bank reserves	375

What would be the effect on domestic credit, foreign reserves, currency, and bank reserves of

a. An open market purchase of $15 billion?

b. A foreign exchange market intervention to prevent appreciation of $15 billion?

c. A sterilized foreign exchange intervention of $15 billion?

4. Suppose that the Taylor rule is given by

$$r = \pi + \beta \hat{Y} + \delta(\pi - \pi^*) + R^*,$$

where $\beta = .5$, $\delta = .5$, $\pi^* = .01$, and $R^* = .02$

a. Suppose that the inflation rate $\pi = .01$. According to the Taylor rule, what would the nominal interest rate be if the output gap $\hat{Y} = -.02$?

b. Now suppose that inflation is zero. Can monetary policy be conducted according to the Taylor rule?

c. Suppose further that inflation is -1 percent and the output gap $\hat{Y} = -.03$. Can monetary policy still be conducted?

ANSWERS TO THE SELF-TEST

1. International financial and monetary system
2. Gold standard
3. Bretton Woods System
4. Floating
5. Monetary union
6. Capital and exchange controls
7. Intervene
8. Sterilized intervention
9. Intervention band
10. Devaluations or revaluations
11. Independent monetary policy
12. Dollarization
13. False. The Bretton Woods System was the international monetary system from the end of Word War II until 1971.
14. False. Changes in par values occurred infrequently.
15. False. They abandoned fixed exchange rates.
16. False. Monetary base = domestic credit plus foreign reserves.
17. True. Sterilization involves offsetting open-market operations to keep the money supply constant.
18. True. They were determined by the agreement of each country to freely buy and sell gold at a set price.
19. False. The United States has not had a systematic exchange-rate policy since 1973.
20. False. The euro was adopted in 1999.
21. False. With a fixed exchange rate, monetary policy is dedicated to keeping the country's interest rate equal to the world interest rate.
22. False. These Asian countries have fixed their national currencies to the U.S. dollar.
23. True. Overly restrictive monetary policy in the early 1990s was a major cause of poor Japanese macroeconomic performance.
24. True. The European Union is currently a group of 12 European countries.
25. Full integration requires that countries impose few if any restrictions on currency transactions, capital movement, and movement of goods.
26. Because high capital mobility requires that the domestic and foreign interest rates be equal, the commitment to fix the exchange rate determines the level of the money supply.
27. The Bretton Woods System was vulnerable to exchange-rate crises and mistakes in U.S. monetary policy.

28. EMS was the exchange-rate system within Europe from 1979 until the establishment of the euro in 1999. All member countries were required to fix their national currencies to the German mark, while the Bundesbank assumed the responsibility for maintaining low inflation. This worked fine until German interest rates began to rise after German reunification in 1991. Stress is the difference between the actual interest rate (which had to rise to keep pace with Germany's interest rate) and a Taylor rule interest rate. Stress measures the extent to which other central banks have to raise their interest rates above the interest rates implied by the Taylor rule to maintain the fixed exchange rate. Increasing stress means increasing tension between maintaining fixed exchange rates and pursuing domestic goals. Measures of stress peaked, predictably, for the United Kingdom, France, and Italy when these national currencies left the EMS.

29. Unless a country permanently fixes its exchange rate through a currency board, a common currency, or dollarization, the only monetary policy that can work well in the long run is one based on (1) flexible exchange rates, (2) an inflation target, and (3) a monetary policy rule.

30. If the nominal exchange rate rises, the real exchange rate will rise given sticky prices. A higher real exchange rate decreases net exports, lowering GDP in the short run and decreasing the GDP gap. A higher nominal exchange rate also, particularly in smaller countries, lowers inflation. According to the Taylor rule, the central bank responds in both cases by lowering the nominal interest rate r.

31. All countries adopted all three parts of the trinity (flexible exchange rates, an inflation target, and an independent Taylor rule) mentioned in Question 29. Like the United States, all three countries had inflation fall in the early 1980s, pick up again in the late 1980s, and fall again in the 1990s. Also, fluctuations in real GDP have decreased since the mid-1980s.

32. The word *bubble* evokes a picture of something growing steadily until it finally pops. In this case, we can think of asset price bubbles as an upward price movement over an extended time period that eventually bursts. The key is that the value is unsustainable; at some point, the asset price falls.

33. Near-negative inflation is inflation rates close to zero; deflation is negative inflation rates.

34. Japan suffered from a bubble in stock and land prices imploding in the late 1980s. Rather than adopting expansionary monetary policy afterward, the Japanese monetary policy was restrictive in the early 1990s. Japan soon found itself in near-negative inflation, or deflation, and monetary policy became very difficult, since nominal interest rates fell to virtually zero. Nonmonetary factors, such as a need to restructure businesses, also contributed to poor economic performance. Japan also needs to address the significant amount of nonperforming loans on banks' balance sheets.

35. A monetary union is a stronger commitment than fixed exchange rates because it eliminates the possibility of devaluation.

SOLUTIONS TO REVIEW PROBLEMS

3. a. Domestic credit would fall to $385 billion and bank reserves would fall to $360 billion.
   b. Foreign reserves would increase to $35 billion and currency would increase to $90 billion.
   c. The combination of Part a and Part c, leaving the monetary base unchanged at $450 billion.
4. a. $r = .01 + .5(-.02) + .5(.01 - .01) + .02 = .02$, or 2 percent.
   b. $r = .0 + .5(-.02) + .5(.0 - .01) + .02 = .005$, or .5 percent. Yes, monetary policy is still effective.
   c. $r = -.01 + .5(-.03) + .5(.0\ 1- .01) + .02 = -.015$, or -1.5 percent. No, monetary policy is not effective because nominal interest rates cannot fall below zero.